The A to Z of Soft Animals

OTHER BOOKS BY THE AUTHOR

Stitched and Stuffed Art
I Love Popcorn
I Love Ice Cream
The Sewing Machine Craft Book
Soft Sculpture
The Teddy Bear Craft Book

The A to Z of SOFT ANIMALS

CAROLYN VOSBURG HALL

Prentice Hall Press · New York

Acknowledgments

Thanks to my pattern testers, LOIS GOODRICH and JEANETTE STANFORD, two women who sew well and enjoy a challenge. They tried out the animal patterns and offered comments that helped me to write clear, complete directions.

Consultant Lois Goodrich (also my sister) teaches home economics at Great Valley High School in Malvern, Pennsylvania. We enjoy chatting by phone about these projects, often recalling toys we shared in childhood and others we made later for our own children. Jeanette Stanford consults by mail from Dayton, Ohio. Her sharp eye is an invaluable aid for me.

Thanks also to the Detroit Zoological Park for having a wonderful collection of real animals from near and far for me to study and enjoy. I looked at animals everywhere to be sure my patterns were true to the originals, including television nature shows, and the following books and magazines: *National Geographic Magazine, Smithsonian Magazine,* Time/Life Nature Library, *World Book Encyclopedia, The Cat* (Grosset & Dunlap), *Young Animals* (Paul Hamlin), *Zoo in Colour* (Grosset & Dunlap), *Insects In Their World* (Doubleday & Co.), *Animals in Motion* (Dover), *Frogs* (Van Nostrand Reinhold), and many others.

Published by Prentice Hall Press
A Division of Simon & Schuster, Inc.
Gulf + Western Building
One Gulf + Western Plaza
New York, NY 10023

PRENTICE HALL PRESS is a trademark of Simon & Schuster, Inc.

Library of Congress Cataloging-in-Publication Data

Hall, Carolyn Vosburg, 1927–
The A to Z of soft animals.

1. Soft toy making. 2. Decorating and ornament—Animal forms. I. Title.
TT174.3.H3 1986 745.592′4 86-12233
ISBN 0-671-61397-9

Designed by Irving Perkins Associates

Manufactured in the United States of America

10 9 8 7 6 5 4 3 2 1

First Edition

Contents

Introduction

Why this book? Because ever since childhood I have loved animals—those close at hand, including our various cats, dogs, mice, salamanders (even a pony we won in a contest), and all those exotic animals from far-off places. Working on this book provided a chance for me to share my fondness for the animal world. And here is the result . . . patterns for making more than twenty-six soft animals—one for each letter of the alphabet, and then some.

Animals aren't furry humans. Each animal has its own remarkable qualities that makes it uniquely endearing. To create these patterns, I studied real animals at home and at the zoo, as well as photographs and skeletal diagrams. My cat is tired of being palpated to see how her back legs bend when she's sitting. But I do thank her for unknowingly posing for the lion pattern. My goal was to make each animal as realistic as possible.

During the process of researching, I learned curious new facts. For example, koala's pouches open downward, sea scallops have thirty-two (more or less) blue eyes, and armadillos leap three feet straight up when alarmed. Bits of similar information appear at the beginning of each animal pattern.

In addition to authenticity, I tried to design patterns that would assemble as easily as possible. Some do have narrow legs, long necks, or unusual tails, however. Directions for making these animals describe the easiest way to assemble these small parts. Note that some techniques do vary from standard procedure.

Each animal pattern in this book includes:

- Full-size pattern pieces
- Notes about the pattern, and variations for other animals
- A listing of materials needed
- The name and number of pattern pieces
- Written instructions for making the animal
- Directions by diagram for construction
- Data about each animal's size, type, and lifestyle

Materials I used came from local shops, collected over several years. Some of these may no longer be available, but you can be sure that new and better ones may be found in your neighborhood fabric stores. Most were selected to simulate the color and scaled-down fur length of the animal. Occasionally I chose a playful print or an easy-to-sew felt for variety. Toys you make, with their magical realism, may become tomorrow's folk art (if they survive the loving), so it pays to choose good fabrics. Since each pattern takes very little fabric, you can risk an elegant choice, or you may find just the right piece in the remnant piles.

People think I'm crazy when I proudly show them my "eye collection": three compartmented plastic boxes full of various colors and sizes of animal eyes. Even so, I didn't find the right red eyes until *after* I'd made the penguin. To spare you this trauma, a list of places to find eyes and noses is included. Another section tells how to select fabrics and how to sew fur fabrics, and another tells how to make appealing faces. You do not necessarily have to make these animals the same size as I did. Instructions are given for scaling patterns up or down to the size you want.

Toy animals like these can have a lasting effect on their young owners, teaching them about the world they live in by presenting animals realistically. But stuffed animals, especially the "serious" ones made from good fabrics that look real and have character, are not just children's toys; they appear in college dorms and living rooms as well.

Designers must have a basic premise in mind when setting out to create. Mine was my great affection for animals and my respect for their special characteristics. I had a wonderful time creating my A to Z stuffed zoo for this book. I hope you have as much pleasure making these animals as I did.

Important Tips

The Patterns

IMPORTANT! READ THIS SECTION, ESPECIALLY IF YOU ARE THE KIND OF PERSON WHO NEVER READS DIRECTIONS UNTIL ALL ELSE HAS FAILED. The following are tips I learned from problems encountered by my pattern testers. I want to pass them along to you.

- Follow directions because instructions for making the animals often vary from the expected. Small pattern pieces require atypical methods of construction. Fingers and sewing machines simply won't fit into tiny shapes. For example, the zebra's leg measures only 2 inches in circumference. With skilled fingers and persistence, it is possible to sew around the leg by machine to join it to the body in the usual manner, but an easier method in which most of the seams are sewn flat is given. Follow the written instructions or study the diagrams for these methods.
- Patterns are designed full size ready for use. The resulting animals are small, just right for hugging, but you might prefer to make them larger. Instructions are given for scaling up, tracing, photocopying, projecting, and photostating.
- Some pattern pieces come in two or more sections since they would not fit on one page. These pieces are designated as A and B, and, in one case, C and D. Trace, then pin or tape the pattern pieces together before cutting them out of fabric. Store pattern pieces for future use.
- All fabrics are different. Pile or fur fabric makes a fatter animal. Stretchy fabrics may distort the animal's shape. Loosely woven or fraying fabrics are unsuitable for these small, firmly stuffed patterns. Read the section on choosing fabrics.
- All directions refer to fabrics right sides facing during construction of the animal, unless otherwise stated in the pattern instructions.
- "Cut 2, 4, or 8" marked on the pattern means that half of the pieces are to be cut in reverse for opposite sides.
- Seam allowances are all narrow as shown, to provide a well-defined seam line. Knitted-back fur fabrics do not fray and are easier to sew with narrow seam allowances. If you add wider seam allowances for fraying fabric, mark the seam line as a stitching guide.
- Stay-Stitch the edges of openings to turn and stuff if you use a woven fabric. The edges can fray, distorting the animal. The stay-stitching provides a guide and anchor for the closing hand-stitching after stuffing. (Stay-stitch the entire edge of every pattern piece if a loosely woven fabric is used.)
- Some copy machines distort, so be sure to check the photocopied pattern against the one in the book for accuracy.
- Trace patterns and cut fur on the back side to avoid cutting off the fur pile. See the section on sewing fur fabrics for more details.
- "Clip seam allowances" means to make short snips across it almost to the seam line. This leaves enough fabric to hold the seam, but releases wrinkle-causing pulls on the seam allowance.
- "Trim seam allowances" means to cut away extra fabric inside ears, tails, paws, or horns.
- Stuff all animals very firmly so they can stand by themselves.

Scaling Patterns Up and Down

All patterns in this book are given full size. (Keep in mind, however, that by scaling up or down you can make any pattern in any size.) Trace or photocopy the patterns for your use to avoid cutting up the book and losing the back of each page in the process. Compare the photocopy with the original to see if the pattern has been distorted. Make two copies if pattern pieces overlap, and tape A and B pattern sections together.

Three of the animals are shown in varying sizes in the photographs. I made the large hog 2 times larger than the pattern; the larger dog about 1½ times larger, and the frog 4 times larger. Larger animals are easier to make.

To scale up, begin by drawing a 1-inch grid overlay over the pattern. If you wish, for example, to make an animal twice as large as the pattern, make a second grid overlay with 2-inch squares, and transfer all the pattern lines within each square of the smaller grid to the corresponding square of the larger grid. (Remember that for an animal twice as large you will need to use 4 times as much fabric and 8 times as much stuffing.) You can, of course, draw a grid with any size squares you want.

The most accurate way to scale up or down is by photostating the pattern to the exact size you want. Another option, if you have access to an opaque projector, is to project the pattern on a surface and trace it. To do this, tape large sheets of paper to the wall and draw a scale up one side and across the width as a check. This will also help with accurate line-up if you must move the page in the projector to copy the entire pattern.

Enlarged animals may need to be modified with lighter stuffing, and/or armatures in the legs, neck, or tail. Use bamboo plant stakes, wires, or round wooden dowel rods in various sizes for supports. If a child might ride on the animal, build a wooden framework and hand-sew the leg seams around the wooden legs as you would upholster.

Large-size animals may need "touch-up" details such as combinations of fabrics, sewn or appliquéd areas, or textile paint for accent. The largest hog looked boringly pink until I softly brushed acrylic color around his eyes, on his nose and feet.

Animal Faces

Eyes, nostrils, ears, and other parts have been carefully placed on the patterns, since animals have distinctive "faces" or head shapes adapted to the way they live. Noses, for example, vary tremendously in shape, from the bird's beak to the elephant's trunk.

The more you try to make an animal look human, the less it will look like the actual animal. (The only case in which I have knowingly applied human characteristics to an animal was the frog. I tipped his head forward as if he had a flexible neck, and angled the eyes to suggest a human's binocular vision.) I'd like to encourage you to use the size, type, and color of eyes specified in the directions, as well as the placement indicated for eyes, nostrils, ears, horns, and tails to achieve the best effect.

Finding the Right Fabrics

I tried three stores before finding the right striped fabric for the zebra, but happened to have a scrap of material on hand for the giraffe. Both, chosen for their designs, were fraying fabrics difficult to stitch. If you use flimsy fabric, or a fabric that pills, such as velveteen, try this: Stay-stitch all edges before cutting out the pattern, or double-stitch all seams during construction. Use removable paper backing to stabilize the fabric, or to help begin a seam.

With good luck, you'll find a firmly woven fabric or a just-right fake fur for your animal. It is more likely, however, that the right color will be a wrong fabric. For stretchy or loosely woven fabrics, line the entire animal (except for tails and ears) with a firmly woven fabric. For a fabric that's too heavy-weight, make the animal larger. As a final solution, compromise. Use tan instead of gray, for example.

Finding fur fabrics can also be a problem. They are carried by fabric stores that specialize in crafts. The best assortment of fur and novelty fabrics is available in the fall for holiday gift making. No one can ever tell what they will have. Fur fabrics are often purchased from the wholesalers in groups of short lots, with little or no choice. It's possible to order specific fur fabrics from a wholesaler, but you may need to order as much as 25 yards. For this reason I often buy half yards of appealing fur fabrics when I see them.

Sewing Fur Fabrics

Most fur fabrics consist of a "face" pile on a doubleknit backing. This means that they stretch some, but will not fray. Fur jacket fabrics have been spray-coated on the back to stabilize the fabric, but the lighter-weight soft fur fabrics for robes and toys have not. Both can be sewn on home portable sewing machines.

Always work from the reverse side on fur fabrics. Make additional paper pattern pieces so none need to be cut out folded. For best results, make templates of the patterns. Trace the pattern on heavy-weight paper or cardboard and cut out along the seam line. Trace around the stiff template on the fur backing, leave space to add and cut out seam allowances, then stitch on the traced seam line for accuracy.

To cut fur fabrics, use sharp scissors from the back side and make short snips, or slide the blade under the pile to avoid cutting off the pile. Furriers use a single-edge razor blade or Exacto knife to slice the backing and pull the cut apart. You get less fuzz up your nose this way. Wear a pollen mask (available at the drug store) if the flying fur bothers you. Save the large fur scraps for later use and use the small ones for stuffing.

If you have difficulty stitching fur fabrics, try these ideas:

1. When you stitch, be sure to tuck the pile out of the seam line with your fingers or with strokes of a long strong needle. This neatens and diminishes the thickness of the seam, and lessens the amount of pile that needs to be pried out of the seam later.
2. Pin the seam at intervals to hold placement in case of stretching. Control the seam with your fingers while you stitch. Stitch slowly, although you may need a moving start to sew over some seams. For thick seams, trim away all possible seam allowances and pile, and offset the seam joining slightly.
3. Try a new needle. The old one may have a spur on the point. A ball-point needle for synthetics, a smaller gauge needle, or a blade-shaped leather needle may be what you need. Keep a good supply of sewing-machine needles on hand.
4. If completed fabric seams are visible, brush tucked-in fur pile from the seams with a dog-grooming brush, or run the tip of a needle parallel with the seam to loosen the pile. Once you've learned to sew fur fabrics, you'll discover that they are more forgiving and easier to sew than other fabrics.

Turning Tips

To turn narrow parts use a long, narrow tool, such as a ¼-inch dowel, a wooden chopstick, a paintbrush handle, a knitting needle, or the eraser end of a pencil. Turn the narrow parts before turning the whole animal. Begin as close to the tip as possible and work the piece onto the turning tool slowly and carefully. Don't let too much fabric bunch up on the turning tool.

For a really narrow part, lay a string inside the part and sew over the knotted end. Pull on the string to turn the piece, not allowing the fabric to bunch up too much, and clip off the string.

If the fabric just won't turn, settle for exposed seams on the narrow parts, and trim close to the seam line.

Types of Stuffing

Polyester fiberfill ranks as the number one stuffing for toys. It is lightweight, safe, washable, easy to use, readily available, doesn't mat, shift, or decompose. But sometimes you need other qualities. For a shifting stuffing use styrene pellets, dried beans, lentils, or popcorn. For resilient stuffing use solid or shredded polyurethane foam. For very solid stuffing use sawdust or excelsior.

These animals will look best if stuffed very firmly. Add stuffing in small wads to heads, horns, and hoofs first. Keep building the shape bit by bit. Be sure to add firm wads at the tops of legs for support. Keep on stuffing until all shapes are filled out. This stuffing compresses much more than you can imagine, and will continue to compress a bit more with use.

ARMADILLOS wear a tough coating that resembles medieval armor for protection since they can neither run fast nor fight. This nine-banded armadillo can't roll himself into an invulnerable ball with his feet, head, and tail tucked in as fabled, but the South American three-banded armadillo can. The giant armadillo has larger legs and plating only on his back, which makes him look more prehistoric than his cousins.

Armadillos doze in their burrows during the heat of the day and come out at dusk to dig in anthills, licking ants up with a long sticky tongue. One armadillo was discovered to have eaten ten tarantulas, a scorpion, a small snake, and a toad.

Researchers have discovered that armadillos are the only mammal to bear identical quadruplets consistently, a useful aspect for studying heredity. The armadillo is unique, too, in the way it reacts when startled, vaulting 3 feet straight up like a jack-in-the-box. Sadly this accounts for many accidents with cars.

NOTE: The completed armadillo measures 18 inches long, 7 inches high, and 4 inches wide. The designer upholstery fabric used simulates the scales, but any other fabric could be used or even embellished by machine embroidery, marking pen, or textile paint. Since heavy velveteens bulk at the seams and fray readily, lighter-weight, firmly woven fabrics will be easier to use for small pattern pieces such as these. All pattern pieces appear full size except the banded section. The only parts of this pattern that require special care are making and

PATTERN

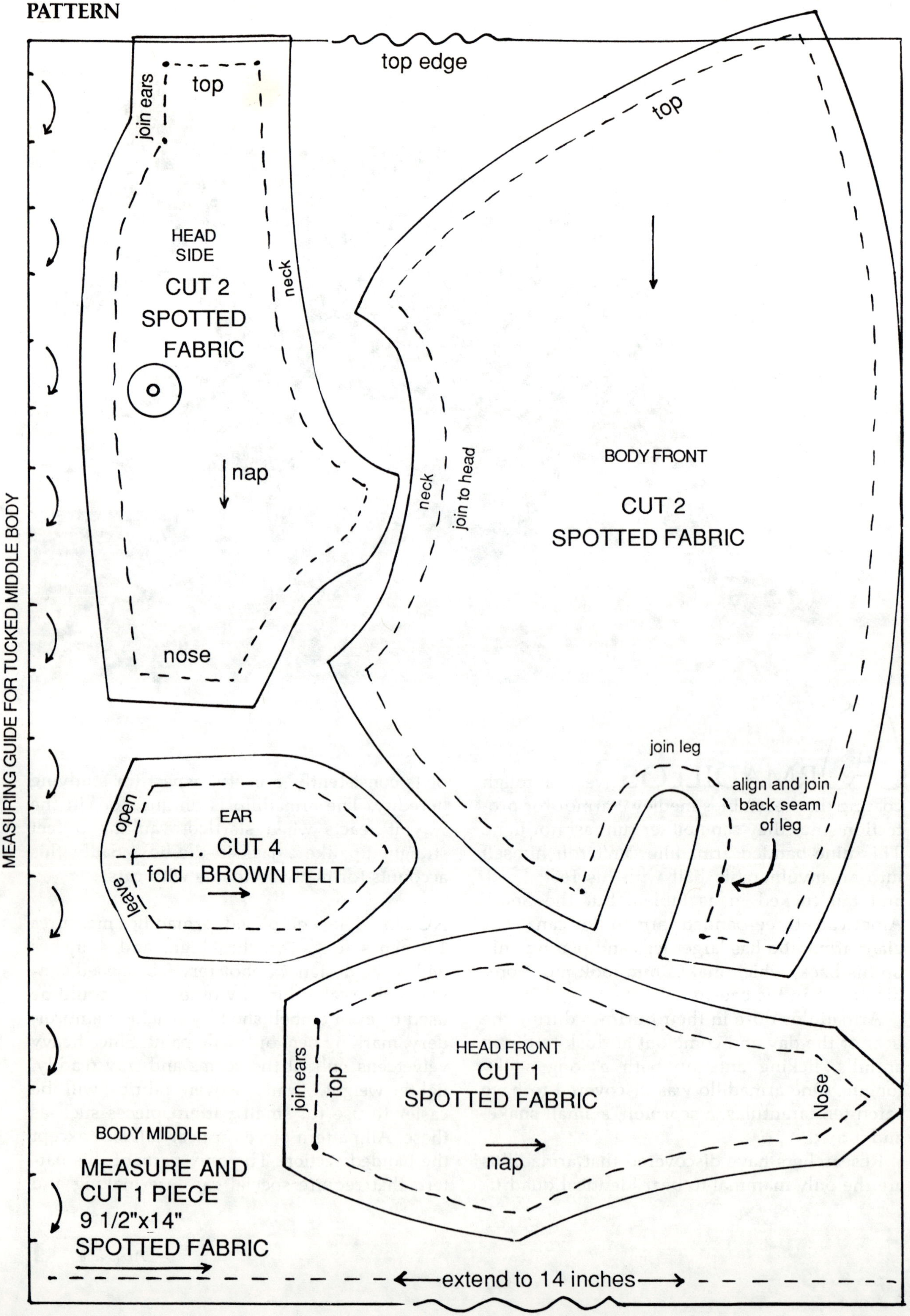
MEASURING GUIDE FOR TUCKED MIDDLE BODY
top edge
join ears
top
HEAD
SIDE
CUT 2
SPOTTED
FABRIC
neck
nap
nose
top
BODY FRONT
CUT 2
SPOTTED FABRIC
neck
join to head
join leg
align and join
back seam
of leg
open
EAR
CUT 4
fold
BROWN FELT
leave
HEAD FRONT
CUT 1
SPOTTED FABRIC
join ears
top
Nose
nap
BODY MIDDLE
MEASURE AND
CUT 1 PIECE
9 1/2"x14"
SPOTTED FABRIC
extend to 14 inches

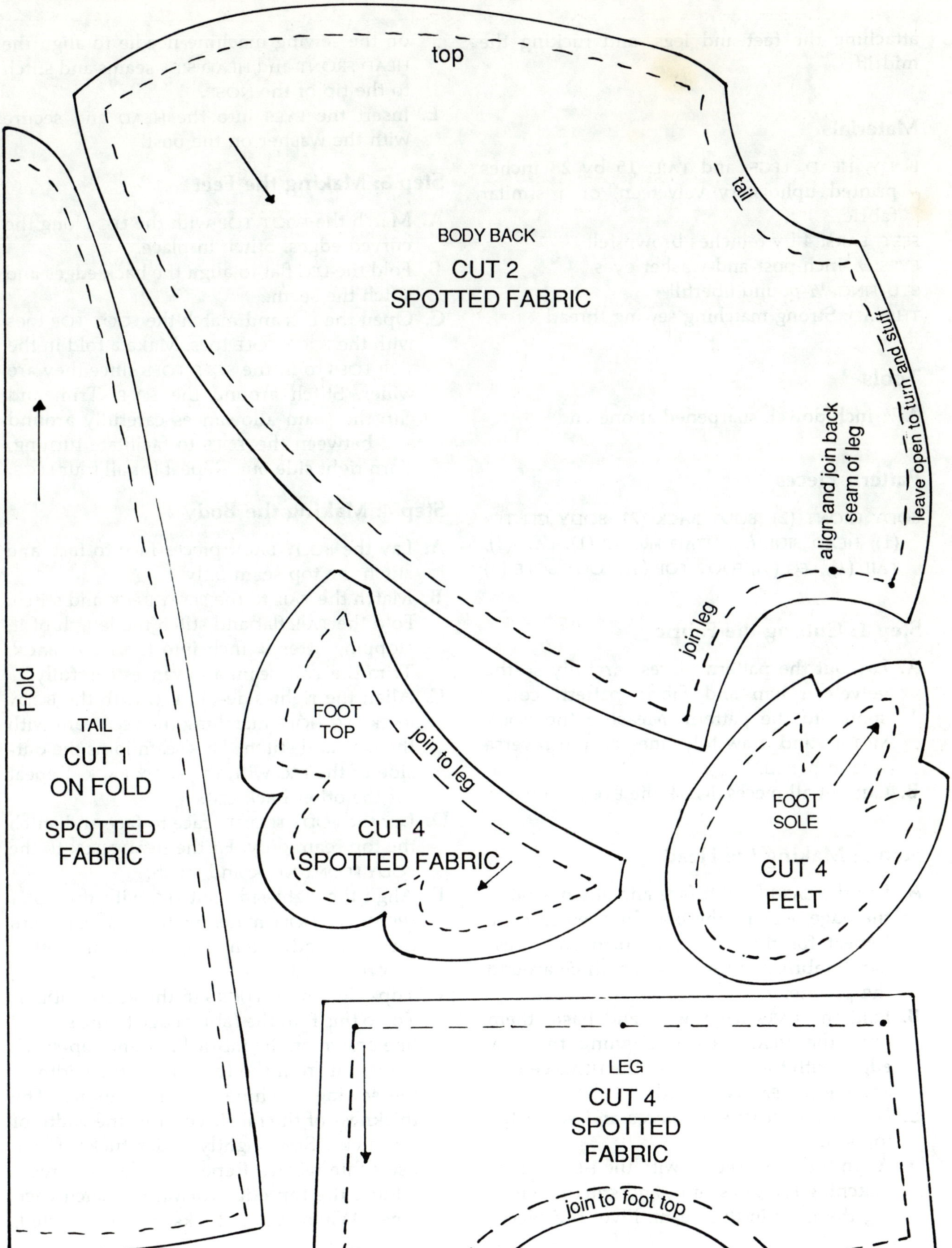
top
tail
BODY BACK
CUT 2
SPOTTED FABRIC
leave open to turn and stuff
align and join back seam of leg
join leg
Fold
TAIL
CUT 1
ON FOLD
SPOTTED FABRIC
join to body
FOOT TOP
join to leg
CUT 4
SPOTTED FABRIC
FOOT SOLE
CUT 4
FELT
LEG
CUT 4
SPOTTED FABRIC
join to foot top

attaching the feet and legs, and tucking the midriff.

Materials

BODY, HEAD, LEGS, and TAIL: 15 by 28 inches printed upholstery velveteen, or a similar fabric
FEET, EARS: 4 by 6 inches brown felt
EYES: ⅜-inch post-and-washer eyes
STUFFING: ½-pound fiberfill
THREAD: Strong matching sewing thread

Tools

A ¼-inch dowel, sharpened at one end

Pattern Pieces

BODY FRONT (2), BODY BACK (2), BODY CENTER (1), HEAD SIDE (2), HEAD FRONT (1), EAR (4), TAIL (1), LEG (4), FOOT TOP (4), FOOT SOLE (4)

Step 1: Cutting the Fabric

A. Lay out the pattern pieces carefully so the velveteen nap and fabric pattern correspond to the pattern. Measure the BODY MIDDLE and draw fold lines on the reverse side in pencil.
B. Cut out all pieces. Mark the EYE placement.

Step 2: Making the Head

A. Lay the EARS face to face and stitch around the edge, leaving the bottom open to turn. Repeat for the other EAR, turn and press flat. If fabric EARS puff up, top-stitch around the perimeter.
B. Fold the EARS lengthwise and baste them onto the HEAD FRONT, aligning the raw edges with the fold toward the HEAD center, angling the EARS outward.
C. Match the HEAD SIDE pieces and stitch the top seam.
D. Align the HEAD FRONT with the HEAD SIDES, matching the top seams, and stitch, including the EARS in this seam. Pivot the pieces on the sewing machine needle to align the HEAD FRONT and HEAD SIDE seams and stitch to the tip of the NOSE.
E. Insert the EYES into the HEAD and secure with the washer on the post.

Step 3: Making the Feet

A. Match the FOOT TOP with the LEG along the curved edges. Stitch in place.
B. Fold the LEG flat to align the back edges and stitch the seam.
C. Open the LEG and match the FOOT TOP toes with the FOOT SOLE toes. Make a fold in the TOP TOES to fit the SOLE TOES since they are wider. Stitch around the SOLE. Trim and clip the seam allowances carefully around and between the TOES to facilitate turning. Turn right side out. Repeat for all four LEGS.

Step 4: Making the Body

A. Lay the BODY BACK pieces face to face and stitch the top seam only.
B. Match the TAIL to the BODY BACK and stitch. Fold the TAIL flat and stitch the length of it, stopping after ¼ inch into the BODY BACK. Trim the TAIL seam allowances carefully.
C. Align the right-side-out LEG with the BODY BACK LEG HOLE matching the LEG seam with the DOT and stitch. This seam joins the outside of the LEG with the BODY BACK. Repeat for the other back LEG.
D. Lay the BODY FRONTS face to face and stitch the top seam only. Fit the HEAD NECK to the BODY FRONT NECK and stitch.
E. Align the right-side-out LEG with the BODY FRONT LEG HOLE matching the LEG seam with the DOT and stitch. Repeat for the other FRONT LEG.
F. Top-stitch nine TUCKS in the BODY MIDDLE. To do this fold the fabric edge to the second line drawn on the fabric back and top-stitch ¼ inch in from the fold, using the width of the sewing machine foot as a guide. (The thickness of the fabric controls the width of the tucks. Sew slightly wider tucks if you use a thin fabric.) Repeat this for each tuck, folding the top edge forward an inch each time. When all 9 tucks are completed,

DIRECTIONS

Align ear, stitch and turn.

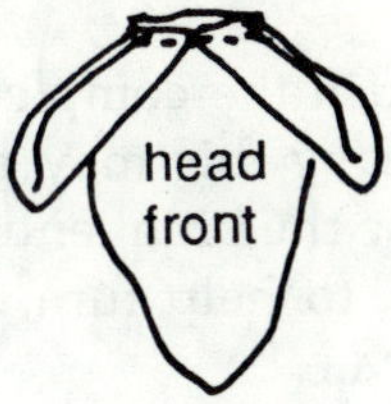

Fold ears, pin and stitch to head.

Sew top seam of head sides.
Sew head front to head sides.

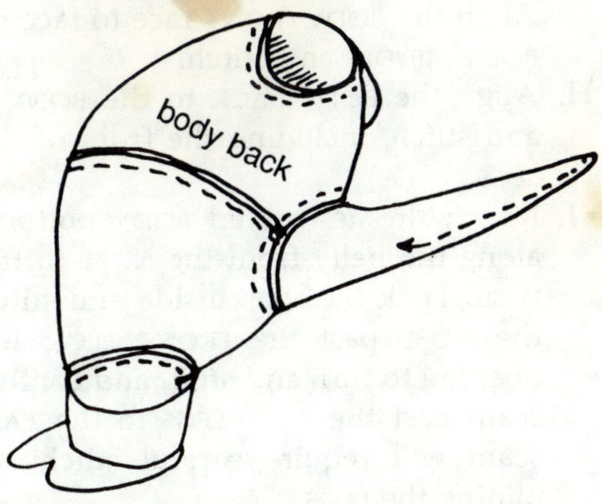

Sew top seam of body back; join tail. Insert legs (right side out) and stitch to body.

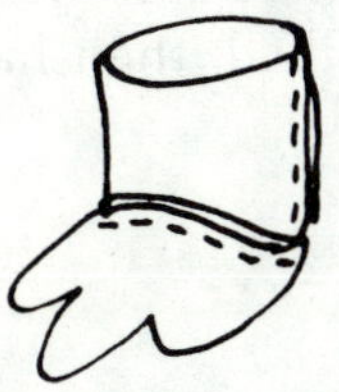

Sew foot top to leg; sew leg seam.

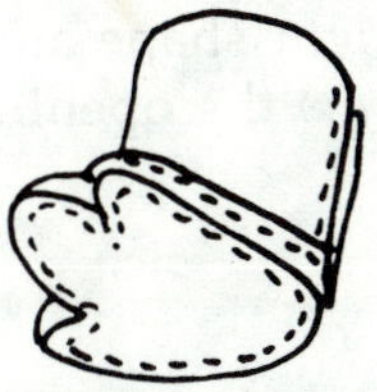

Sew foot top to foot sole (all four), turn legs.

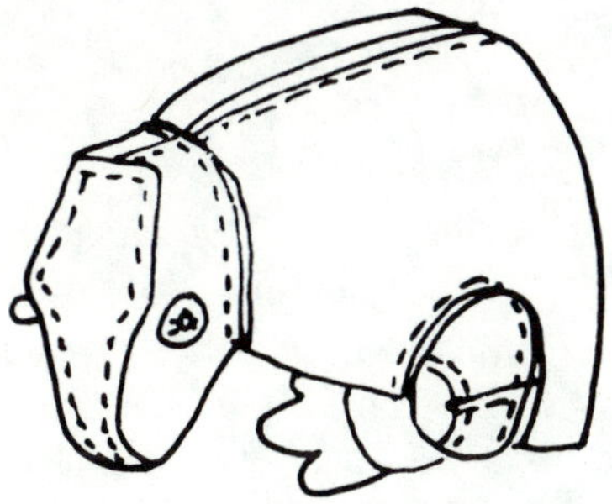

Sew top seam of body fronts.
Attach head, insert eyes.
Sew leg in body front hole.

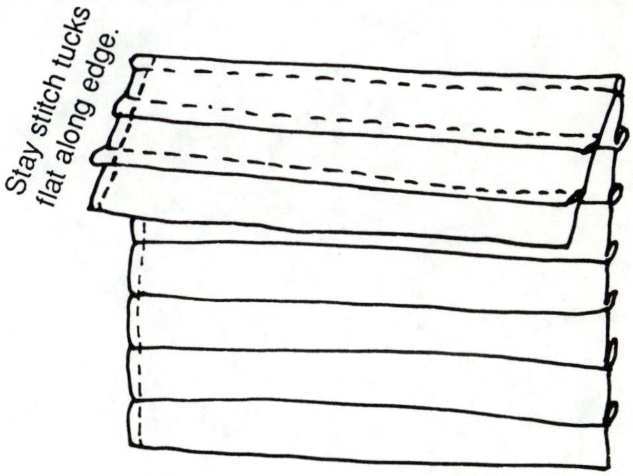

Measure, fold and stitch nine 1/4-inch tucks in the body middle and stay-stitch.

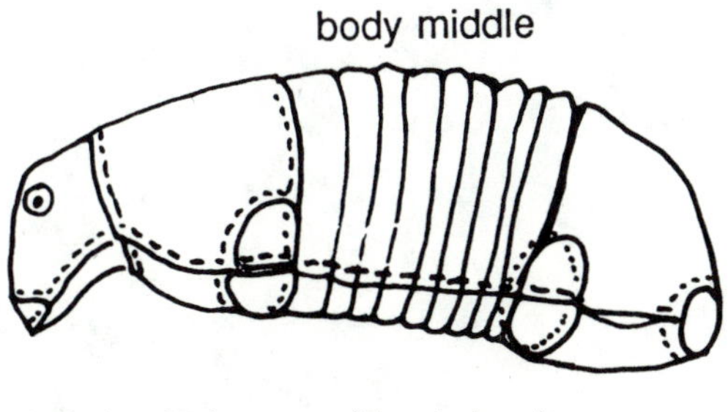

Join body front and body back to body middle, turn tail.

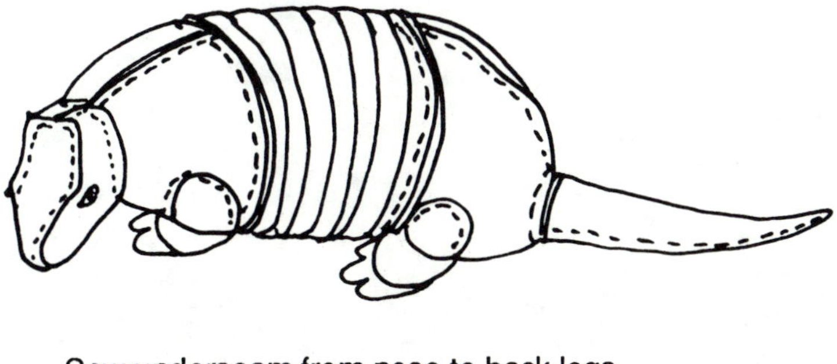

Sew underseam from nose to back legs opening. Trim, turn, stuff, and sew opening closed.

brush them in place facing the rear and stay-stitch them flat along the fabric edge.

G. Align the BODY FRONT face to face with the BODY MIDDLE and stitch.

H. Align the BODY BACK to the BODY MIDDLE and stitch, including the front of the BACK LEGS.

I. Match the assembled BODY bottom edges along the belly from the NOSE to the BACK LEGS. Tuck the LEGS inside and stitch from the NOSE past the FRONT LEGS, leave an opening to turn and stuff, and continue this seam past the BACK LEGS to the TAIL. This seam will require careful stitching when joining the LEGS.

Step 5: Finishing the Armadillo

A. Carefully turn the completed animal. If the fabric is heavy this may prove to be quite difficult. Use the blunt end of the sharpened dowel stick to help turn, beginning at the HEAD and TAIL.

B. Stuff firmly. Use the sharp end of the dowel to push small wads of stuffing into the HEAD and TAIL. If the TAIL appears lumpy, roll it between your hands to smooth. Stuff the legs, beginning with the toes.

C. Fill and pat until the armadillo assumes the right shape and is firmly filled, then hand-sew the opening closed.

BUTTERFLIES, like flowers, have an exquisite transient beauty. The common Viceroy butterfly shown has black stained-glass patterns on orange wings touched with white spots. This light-as-a-thistle creature is often confused with the Monarch butterfly, which lacks the half circle on the lower wing. Monarchs are noted for their lengthy migrations. Anybody inspecting a butterfly collection of some size can't help but be impressed with the enormous variety and range of color. Some are simple white butterflies with a dusting of black markings, and some shimmer in iridescent colors. The color results from the scales on the wings, as fine as pollen as they brush off on fingers.

Butterflies fly during the day, while their cousins the moths fly at night. Moths emerge transformed from cocoons spun by caterpillars. A different transformation takes place with the butterfly. The caterpillar forms a shell called a chrysalis from which the compressed butterfly emerges to spread his wings.

PATTERN

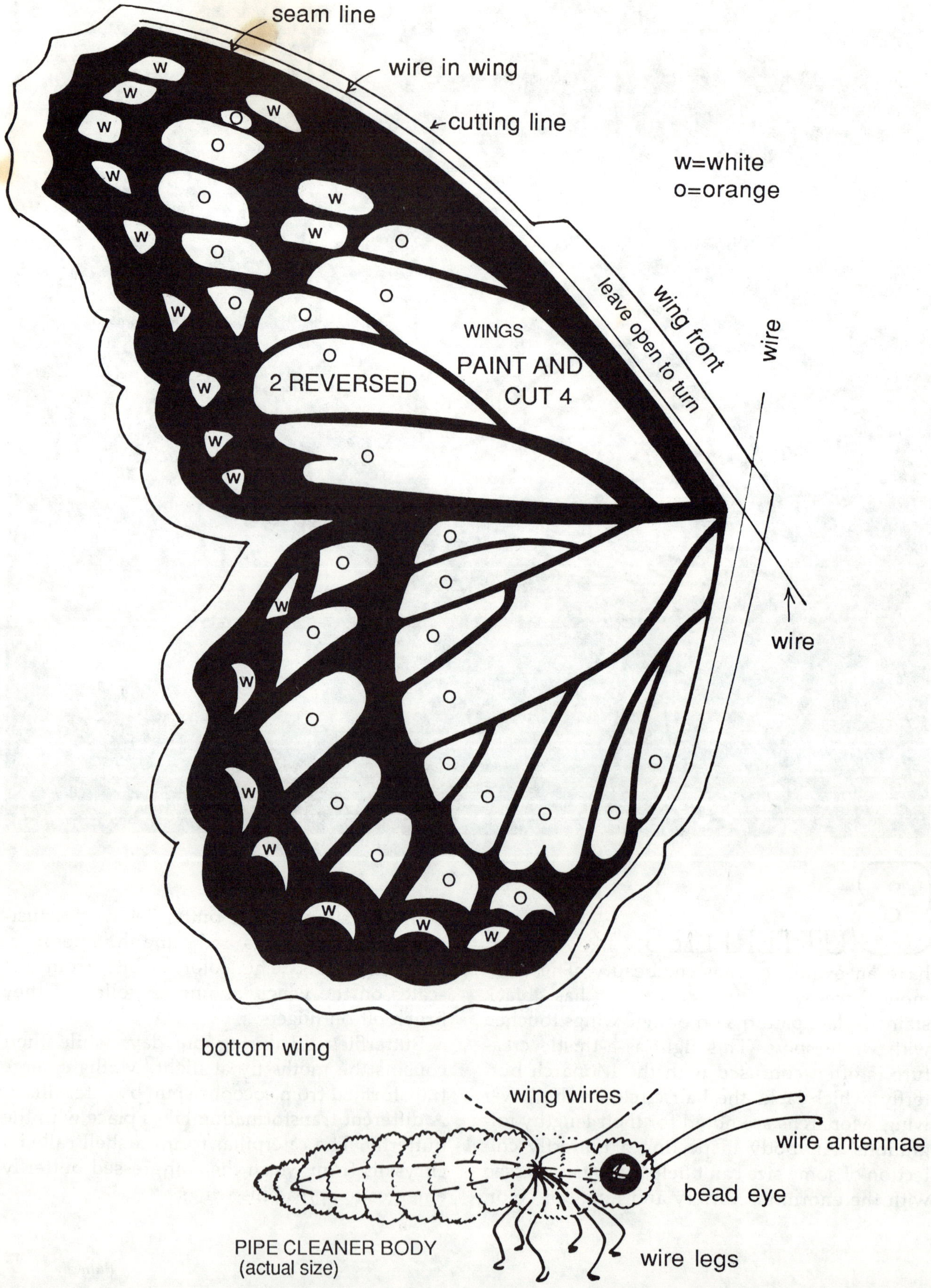
seam line
wire in wing
cutting line
w=white
o=orange
wing front
leave open to turn
wire
WINGS
PAINT AND
CUT 4
2 REVERSED
wire
bottom wing
wing wires
wire antennae
bead eye
PIPE CLEANER BODY
(actual size)
wire legs

NOTE: The pattern given makes a butterfly 3 times normal size, with each wing measuring 5 by 7 inches. Designs are painted on unstuffed wings, but if you sew much better than you paint, machine-embroider the wings instead. To make other butterflies consult a butterfly field guide for accurate markings, or make up your own designs. It's even possible to make the wings of paper.

Materials

WINGS: 14 by 16 inches orange silk, rayon, or nylon fabric
BODY: Spool of florist's wire, three or more "jumbo" black pipe cleaners,
EYES: Two ¼-inch black post eyes or black beads.

Tools

¼-inch dowel with one end sharpened, wire cutters, needle-nose pliers, craft glue, black and white acrylic artist's paint, fine brush

Pattern Pieces

UPPER WING (2), UNDER WING (2), WING INTERFACING (4)

Step 1: Transferring the Pattern

A. Do not cut out pattern pieces.
B. Trace or photocopy the WING pattern on paper. This copy placed over a light source will be used as a painting guide. For a light source, tape it to a window or a glass table

DIRECTIONS

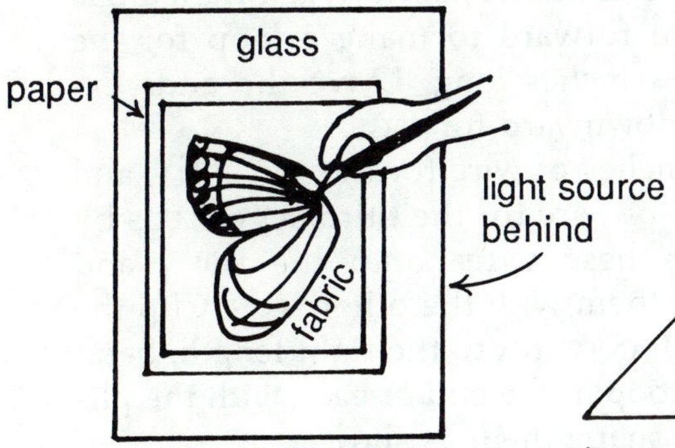

Lay fabric over paper pattern and paint.

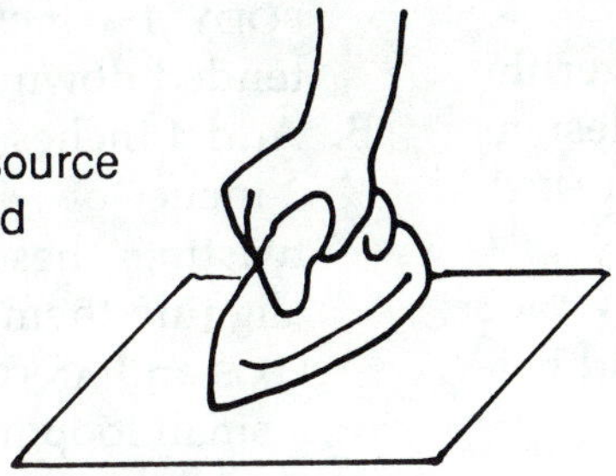
Iron on reverse side to set color.

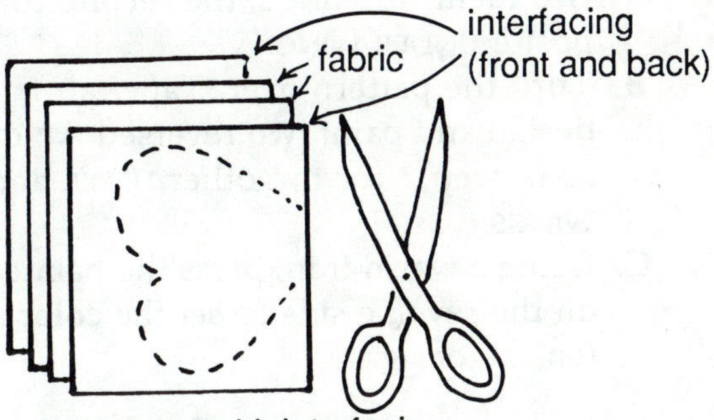

Line fabrics with interfacing. Sew seam line, trim, turn.

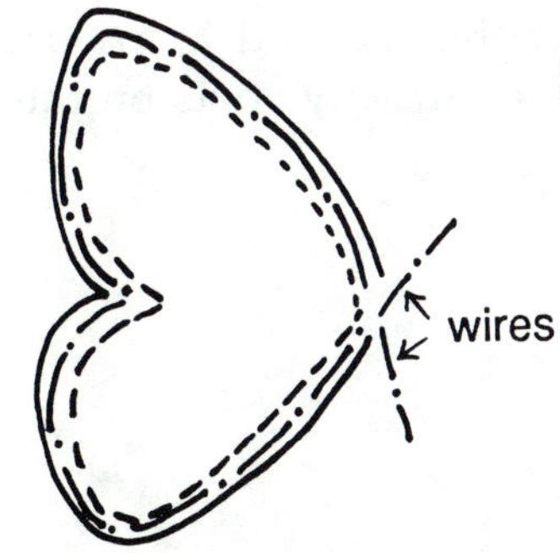

Top-stitch over inserted wires.

Twist wires into a body loop; add 2 legs and antennae.

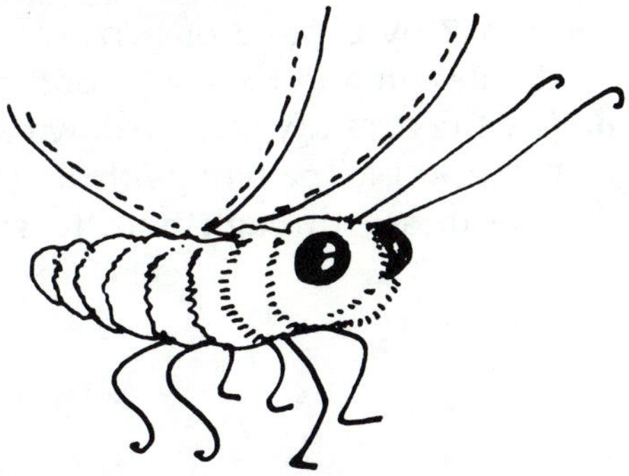
Wrap body and head with pipe cleaners. Glue in eyes, paint wire legs.

with a light underneath, or use an artist's light box (translucent top with fluorescent lights inside).

Optional: To make machine-embroidered wings, choose heavier fabric. Make 4 copies of the paper pattern, 2 in reverse. Pin the paper pattern to the face side of the fabric, pin these to INTERFACING (which helps to keep the fabric from puckering during stitching), satin-stitch the designs through the paper, tear off the needle perforated paper, and continue from Step 3C.

Step 2: Painting the Wings:

A. Tape a 7- by 8-inch piece of orange fabric over the design. Paint over the black lines carefully. Mistakes are not removable. When painting the edges, extend the black paint beyond the cutting line. When the black has dried add the white spots. Make two identical WINGS, the second for the opposite UNDER WING.

B. Turn the pattern over. Tape fabric over the design and paint two reversed WING designs as in step 2 for the other UPPER and UNDER WINGS.

C. Using a warm iron, press the painted WINGS on the reverse side to set the color and flatten the design.

Step 3: Sewing the Wings

A. Trace the WING seam line and cutting line on a 7 by 8 piece of INTERFACING. Reverse the design and trace a second one.

B. Lay the UPPER WING face down and align the INTERFACING pattern with it. (You will be able to see through both to some extent.) Pin in place. Turn the WING over and align the UNDER WING face to face with UPPER WING. Pin INTERFACING to the back of the UNDER WING to make a four-layer sandwich. Stitch around the seam line on the INTERFACING. Repeat for the other pair of WINGS.

C. Carefully trim the seam allowances to ⅛ inch for smooth edges and clip the inside corners to avoid pulls. Turn the WING and push out the points with the dowel stick.

D. Bend the FLORIST'S WIRE to the shape of the WING and insert the wire inside it with 5 inches of wire sticking out at each end. Top-stitch the edge of the WING part of the way to hold the wire in place. (If this proves too difficult, hand-sew the wire in place.) Repeat for the other WING.

Step 4: Making the Butterfly Body

A. Twist the four 5-inch WING WIRES together firmly. Bend them backward at a right angle and then forward to make a loop for the BODY 1¾ inches long. Leave the ends extended downward for LEGS.

B. Add 4 inches of wire for the ANTENNA, and 3 inches of wire for the third set of LEGS by twisting these wires onto the BODY and aligning them with the other LEGS. Clip the LEGS and ANTENNA to the right length, bend a small loop in the end of each with the pliers, and shape them as shown.

C. Wrap the WIRE BODY with JUMBO BLACK PIPE CLEANERS to make a fuller shape. Make a loop for the HEAD to hold the EYES.

D. If you use EYES with a post, clip off the plastic post with wire clippers. Glue the EYES in place. Paint the LEG and ANTENNA WIRES black and touch up any spots on the wings that need it.

CATS, domestic ones, are all a similar size and have similar appetites and independent characters. But they have many differences. Coats vary considerably from the common shorthair through the elegant longhaired Persians and Angoras to the strange curly-coated cats. The longhairs have short noses and stocky bodies, the better to show off their splendor. Siamese and Abyssinians have slender rangy bodies and long aristocratic noses. The cat shown has kitten proportions with short legs and a large head.

The domestic cat is not a tame version of a wild cat. The wild cat has a more heavily muscled body, wider skull, and convex profile. Wild cats eat differently, gorging rapidly on food and water and then going for days without. Try to get away with that routine with your house pet! Through the ages cats have been considered both deities and demons, valuable for mousing and hated for bewitching.

NOTE: Kitten-sized, this stuffed cat measures 12 inches tall and 6 inches long, not counting the tail. The calico version shows the true shape, while the fur one shows other possibilities. Take special care to sew the face pieces together accurately, maintaining consistent seam allowances for best results. Also use care in sewing the sharp corner at the top of the front leg.

Materials

BODY: 9 by 31 inches gold print calico or gray fur fabric with fur ¾ inches long or less

PATTERN

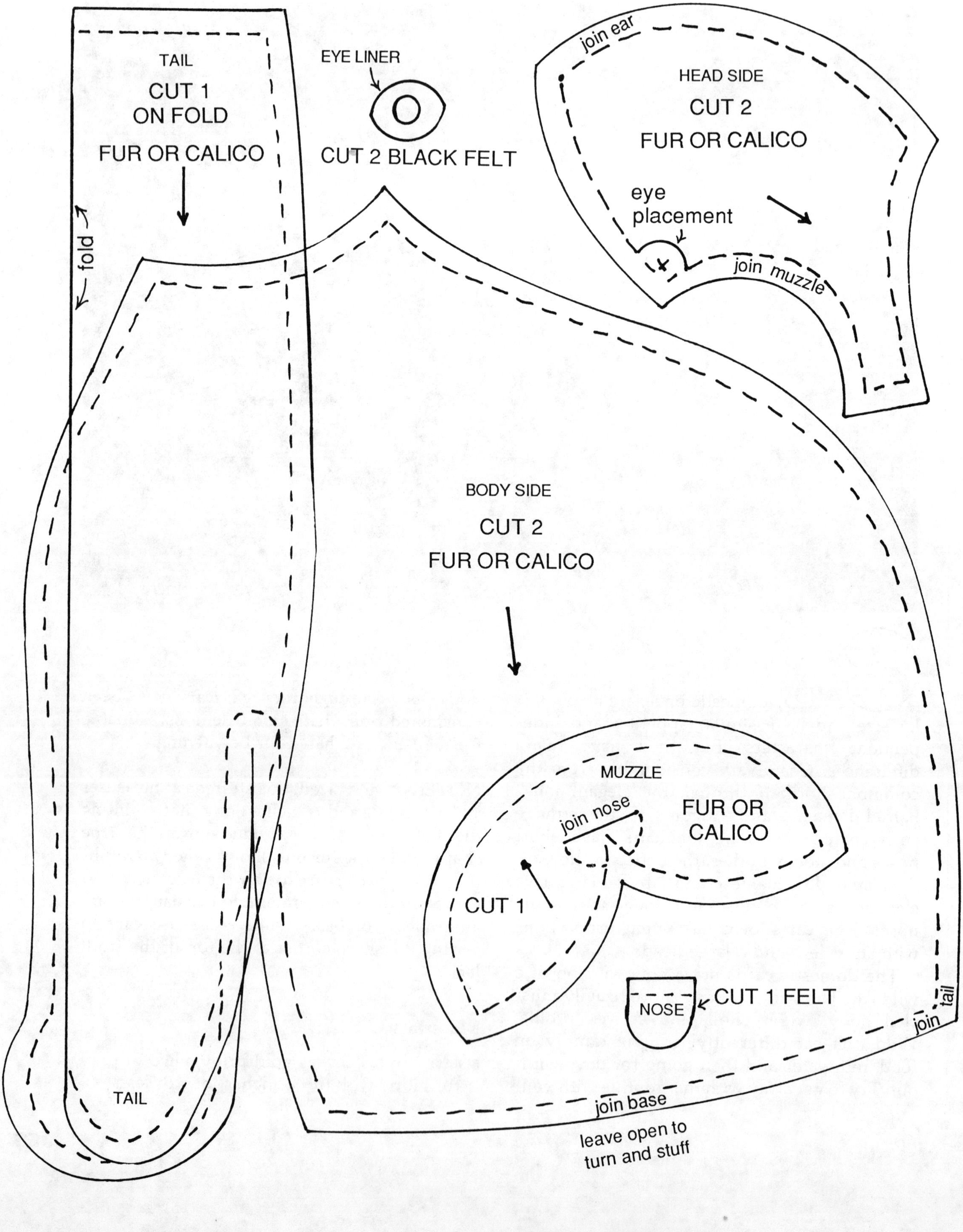

TAIL
CUT 1
ON FOLD
FUR OR CALICO
fold
EYE LINER
CUT 2 BLACK FELT
join ear
HEAD SIDE
CUT 2
FUR OR CALICO
eye
placement
join muzzle
BODY SIDE
CUT 2
FUR OR CALICO
MUZZLE
join nose
FUR OR
CALICO
CUT 1
NOSE
CUT 1 FELT
join tail
TAIL
join base
leave open to
turn and stuff

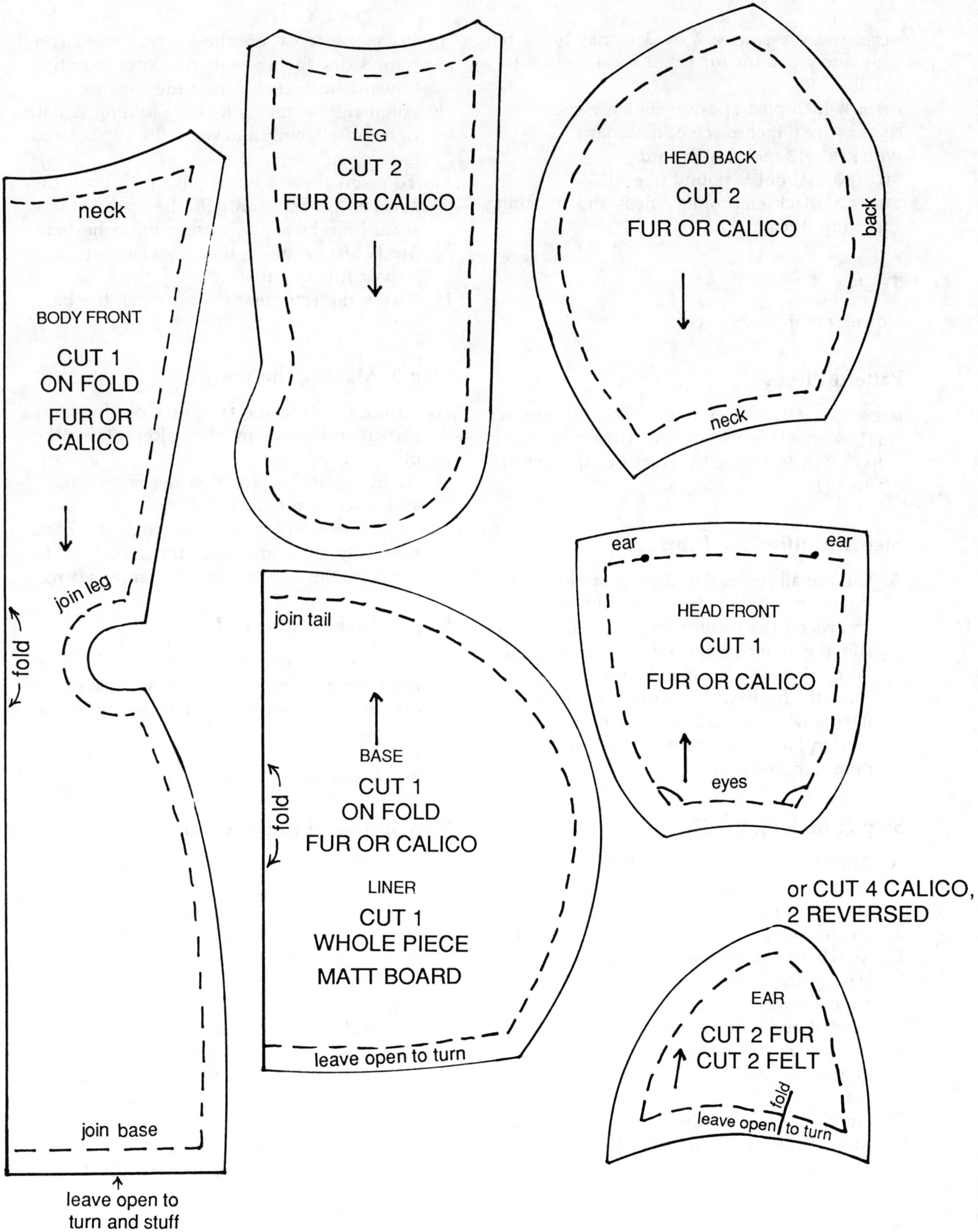

neck
BODY FRONT
CUT 1
ON FOLD
FUR OR
CALICO
join leg
fold
join base
leave open to
turn and stuff
LEG
CUT 2
FUR OR CALICO
join tail
BASE
CUT 1
ON FOLD
FUR OR CALICO
LINER
CUT 1
WHOLE PIECE
MATT BOARD
fold
leave open to turn
HEAD BACK
CUT 2
FUR OR CALICO
back
neck
ear
ear
HEAD FRONT
CUT 1
FUR OR CALICO
eyes
or CUT 4 CALICO,
2 REVERSED
EAR
CUT 2 FUR
CUT 2 FELT
fold
leave open to turn

NOSE and EYE LINERS: 2 by 3 inches black felt
EARS and NOSE for fur cat: 3 by 4 inches gray felt
EYES: ⅜-inch post-and-washer cat eyes
LINER: 4 by 6 inch piece of matboard
WHISKERS: 12 inches stiff cord
STUFFING: About ½ pound fiberfill
THREAD: Black embroidery floss and matching sewing thread

Tools

Dowel, embroidery needle

Pattern Pieces

BODY SIDE (2), TAIL (1), HEAD SIDE (2), MUZZLE (1), NOSE (1), BODY FRONT (1), LEG (2), HEAD BACK (2), HEAD FRONT (1), EAR (4), BASE (1), LINER (1)

Step 1: Cutting the Fabric

A. Cut out all pieces. For the fur cat, match the direction of the fur carefully with the arrows on the pattern. In cutting fur fabric, run the point of the scissors close to the fabric backing to avoid cutting the fur. Tuck the fur in with your fingers or a strong needle when sewing seams. For more information on handling fur fabrics see the section, "Important Tips."

Step 2: Making the Head

A. Align the HEAD SIDE with the HEAD FRONT right sides facing and stitch. Repeat for the other HEAD SIDE.
B. Fit the MUZZLE TOP to the HEAD and stitch.
C. Match two EARS face to face and stitch, leaving the bottom open to turn. Clip the seam allowances closely and turn. Press the EAR flat and stitch across the base. Fold the inner edge vertically ¼ inch from the edge as marked and pin. Repeat for the other EAR.
D. Pin the EARS onto the HEAD so the folded edge of the EAR aligns with the HEAD seam. Baste in place.
E. Place the NOSE on the MUZZLE NOSE-LINE right sides facing with the NOSE pointing upward, and stitch across the flat side.
F. Align the MUZZLE edges by folding it flat, right sides facing, and stitch the MUZZLE and CHIN seam.
G. To insert the EYE POST, push it through the EYE LINER, then through the HEAD at the seam line. Push the washer onto the back firmly after aligning the EYE PUPIL vertically. Repeat for the other EYE.
H. Match the HEAD BACKS and stitch the back seam.

Step 3: Making the Body

A. Fit the LEG into the LEG HOLE on the BODY FRONT and stitch in place. Repeat for the other LEG.
B. Align the HEAD FRONT to the BODY FRONT and stitch at the neck.
C. Align the BODY SIDES, and stitch the back seam. Open flat and stitch the HEAD BACK to the BODY SIDES, matching the center seams.

Step 4: Making the Tail

A. Fold the TAIL face to face and stitch. Trim the seam allowance and turn. For the calico cat, stuff the TAIL lightly. For the fur cat no stuffing is necessary.
B. Fold the TAIL base flat with the seam centered downward, and baste the end shut.

Step 5: Assembling the Cat

A. Open the BODY BACK flat, and baste the TAIL to the bottom edge at the seam line.
B. Align the BODY FRONT SECTION with the BODY BACK SECTION, matching the LEG and NECK seams. Beginning at the bottom corner, stitch the entire seam to the other bottom corner, including the FRONT LEGS. Sew the inside top of the LEG carefully, pivoting the fabric on the sewing machine needle to align the pieces. Clip the seam allowances to the stitch line at the inside corner of the LEGS to avoid pulls.
C. Fit the BASE in place and stitch from the front corner seam around the BACK to the

DIRECTIONS

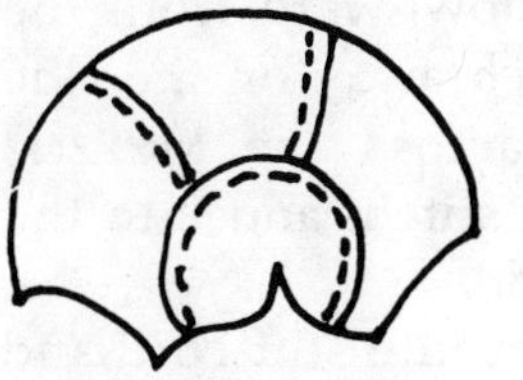
Join head sides to head front. Join muzzle to head.

Sew ears, turn; stitch edge, fold and baste.

Baste ears to head; sew nose to muzzle.

Insert eyes through liners into head, sew muzzle seam.

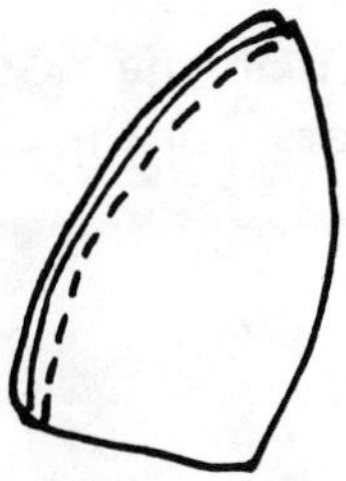
Sew head backs together.

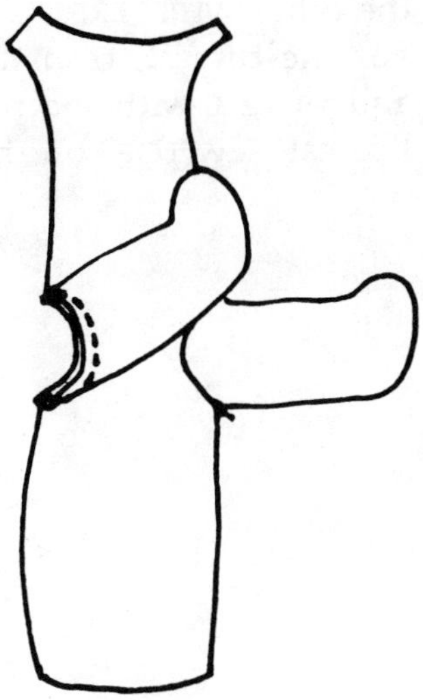
Join legs to body front.

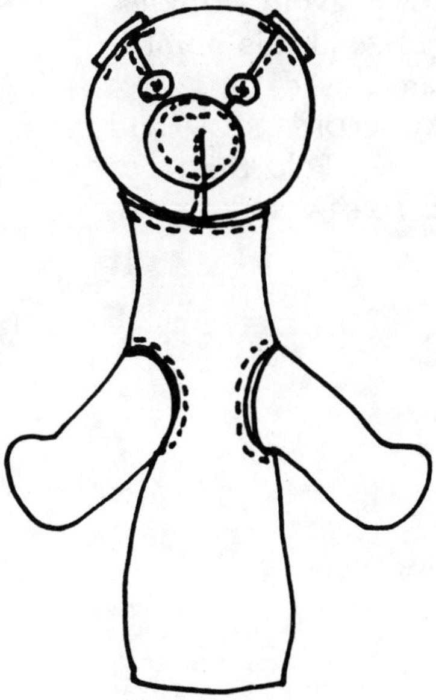
Join head to body front.

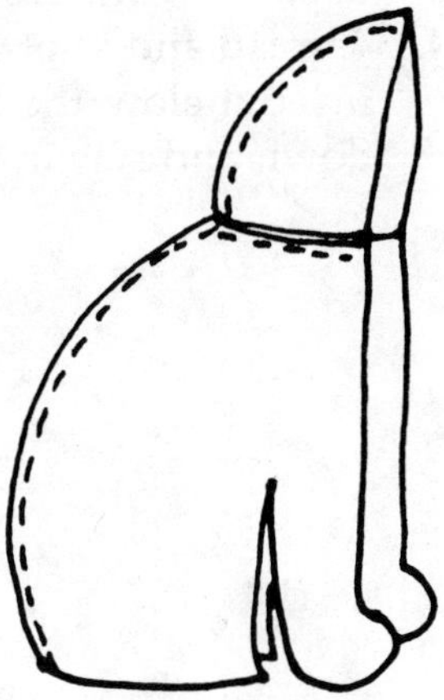
Sew body back seam. Open, join head back to body.

Sew tail, turn, stuff and stitch closed.

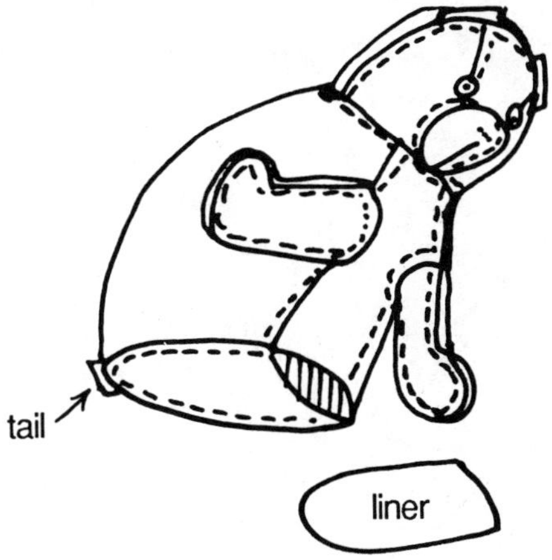

Join front section to back section, baste tail to body. Join base to body.

Sew nose down, sew mouth, knot and sew whiskers.

opposite corner, leaving the front open to turn. This seam includes the TAIL.

Step 6: Finishing the Cat

A. Turn the CAT right side out.

B. Stuff the LEGS first, using the dowel to push small wads firmly into place. Next stuff the MUZZLE. Push wads into the HEAD to hold MUZZLE stuffing in place and continue to stuff the entire cat. Add wads of stuffing at the top of the FRONT LEGS to avoid wrinkles. Insert the MAT BOARD LINER at this point if used. Sew the front seam closed.

C. Thread and knot the EMBROIDERY FLOSS and insert below the NOSE LINE. Fold the NOSE down and sew in place. To sew the MOUTH, continue with the same thread to make a ¼-inch stitch straight downward from the NOSE, coming out ¾ inch away on the side of the MUZZLE. Sew across the MUZZLE, through the downward stitch, and into the MUZZLE on the other side.

D. For the WHISKERS, thread the stiff cord and sew through the MUZZLE from one side to the other. To do this, make a knot two inches from the end and pull the cord until the knot is firm against the MUZZLE. Tie a knot on the other side, tightly against the MUZZLE, and clip off at 2 inches. Repeat for the other WHISKERS.

E. For the fur cat, trim the hair on the NOSE and MUZZLE with sharp scissors. For the calico cat, sew TOES on the feet.

DOGS have been our "best friends" for thousands of years, since the Stone Age. Domestication and breeding of dogs has led to a wide variety of shapes, sizes, and colors bred over the years for different purposes. Dogs range from the tiny "toy" Chihuahua that fits in one hand to the huge St. Bernard, noted for rescuing travelers.

The six recognized groups of purebred dogs include "sporting dogs," handsome setters, retrievers, and spaniels; "working dogs," the well-known collie, sheep dog, husky and German shepherd; "hounds," from the speedy greyhound to the scurrying dachshund; "terriers," with bristly haired Airedales and long-haired Skyes; "toys," little lap dogs like the Pekingese, Chihuahua, pug, and miniature poodle; and the "non-sporting group," with unusual animals like bulldogs, poodles, chow chows, and Lhasa Apsos. The other half of the dog world consists of the everyday mixed breed or mutt.

NOTE: This basic pattern makes a dog 10 by 10 inches. Increasing the pattern size usually makes it easier to sew. Directions given make a Miniature Schnauser, but by varying the color, tail, ear lengths, and type of fur fabric, many variations are possible. The 15-inch black-and-white dog shown portrays our old family pet,

PATTERN

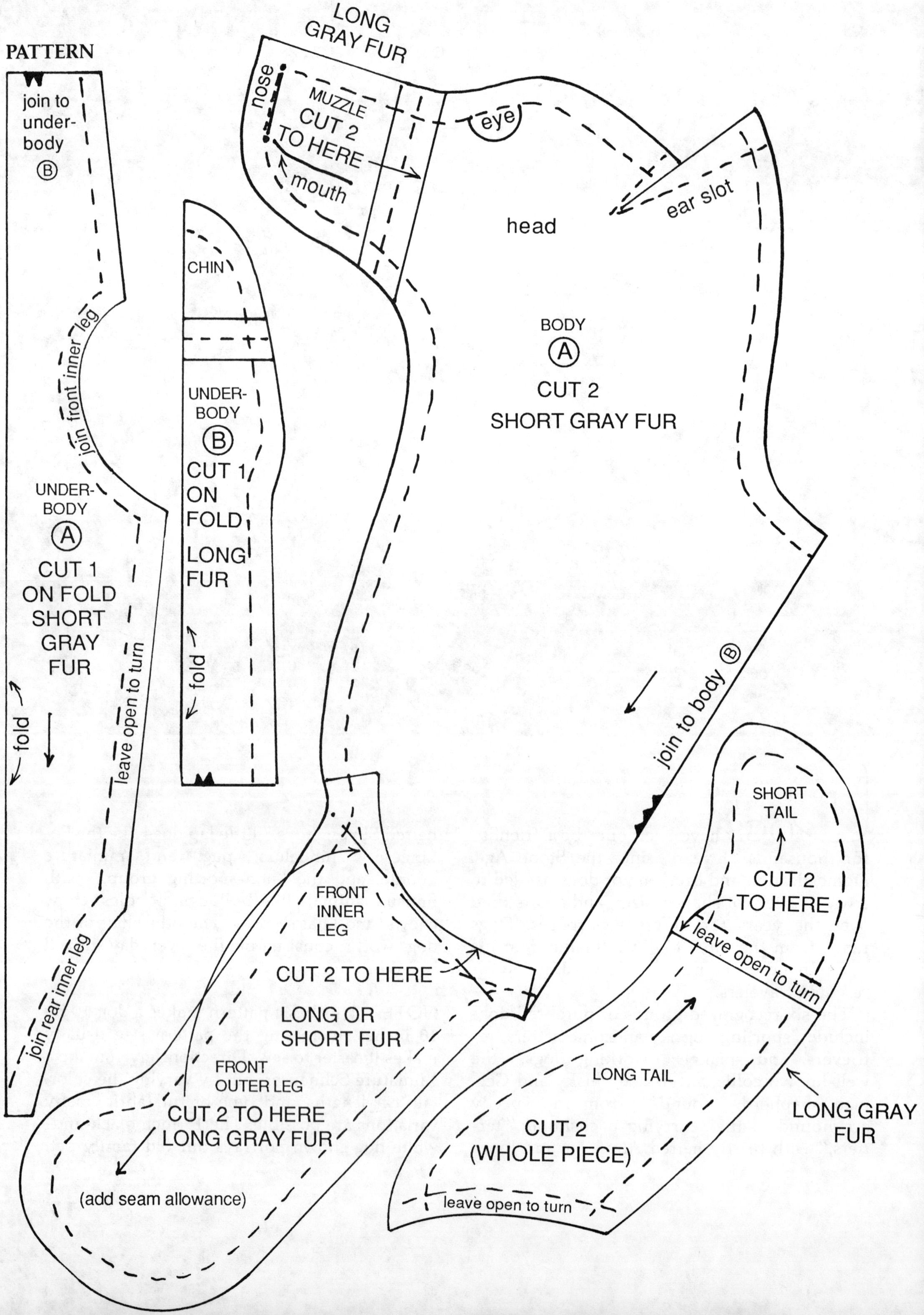

LONG
GRAY FUR
nose
MUZZLE
CUT 2
TO HERE
mouth
eye
ear slot
head
join to
under-
body
B
CHIN
BODY
A
CUT 2
SHORT GRAY FUR
join front inner leg
UNDER-
BODY
B
CUT 1
ON
FOLD
LONG
FUR
fold
UNDER-
BODY
A
CUT 1
ON FOLD
SHORT
GRAY
FUR
fold
leave open to turn
join to body B
SHORT
TAIL
CUT 2
TO HERE
leave open to turn
FRONT
INNER
LEG
CUT 2 TO HERE
LONG OR
SHORT FUR
join rear inner leg
FRONT
OUTER LEG
CUT 2 TO HERE
LONG GRAY FUR
LONG TAIL
LONG GRAY
FUR
CUT 2
(WHOLE PIECE)
(add seam allowance)
leave open to turn

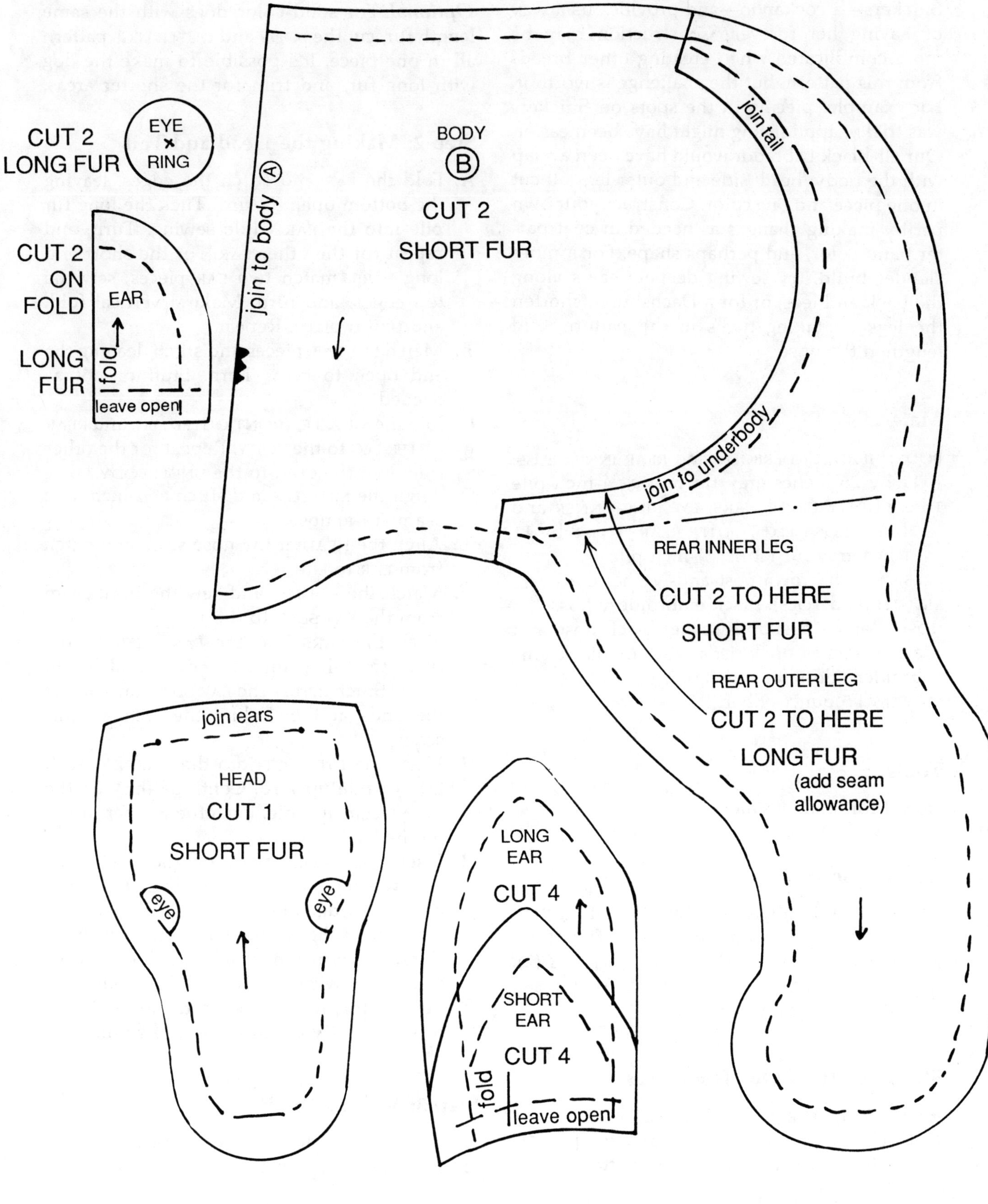
CUT 2
LONG FUR
EYE
×
RING
CUT 2
ON
FOLD
EAR
fold
LONG
FUR
leave open
join to body Ⓐ
BODY
Ⓑ
CUT 2
SHORT FUR
join tail
join to underbody
REAR INNER LEG
CUT 2 TO HERE
SHORT FUR
REAR OUTER LEG
CUT 2 TO HERE
LONG FUR
(add seam
allowance)
join ears
HEAD
CUT 1
SHORT FUR
eye
eye
LONG
EAR
CUT 4
SHORT
EAR
CUT 4
fold
leave open

Snickers—a cockapoo—and provides us a way of having her forever. Construction may be more complicated when creating other breeds from this pattern, but the challenge is worth it. For example, piecing in the spots on Snickers was tricky; appliquéing might have been easier. Our all-black Labrador would have been a snap with the body, head, side and outer legs all cut in one piece and one color. Construct your own pet by making changes as needed in coat pattern and color, and perhaps shape. For a more slender build, try sewing deeper seams along the back and legs; or for a Dachshund, shorten the legs by taking tucks in the pattern, and lengthen the nose.

Materials

BODY, HEAD, UNDERBODY and REAR INNER LEGS: 11 by 26 inches gray fur fabric, ¼-inch pile
TAIL, CHIN, MUZZLE, EARS, EYE RING, INNER and OUTER FRONT LEGS, OUTER REAR LEGS: 8 by 11 inches gray fur fabric, ¾-inch pile
EYES: ⅜-inch brown post-and-washer eyes
MOUTH (and TOES): Black embroidery floss
NOSE: ⅜-inch post-and-washer black nose and a few inches of florist's wire, or black embroidery floss for sewing nose
STUFFING: 5 ounces fiberfill

Tools

Dowel for stuffing, pliers

Pattern Pieces

BODY A and B (2) (given in two pieces), UNDERBODY (2) (also in two pieces), HEAD (1), EAR (2) or (4), REAR INNER LEG (2), REAR OUTER LEG (2), FRONT INNER LEG (2), FRONT OUTER LEG (2), EYE RING (2), MUZZLE (2), CHIN (1)

Step 1: Cutting Out The Pieces

A. Mark the EYE placement.
B. Cut out all pieces. Be sure to match pile direction of fur with arrows on pattern.

Optional: For solid-color dogs with the same length fur, cut the BODY and OUTER LEGS pattern all in one piece. It's possible to make the dog with long fur, and trim for the shorter areas.

Step 2: Making the Head and Tail

A. Fold the EAR and stitch the edges, leaving the bottom open to turn. Tuck the long fur pile into the EAR while sewing. Turn, and repeat for the other EAR. For the short and long EARS, match two EAR pieces, sew the top edges, and turn. Make a vertical fold, and pin in place. Repeat.
B. Match the TAIL pieces and stitch, leaving the end open to turn. Turn. Stuff or not as needed.
C. Join the MUZZLE, FRONT OUTER LEG, and REAR OUTER LEG to the BODY. Repeat for the other side. Join the CHIN to the UNDERBODY.
D. Align the MUZZLES and stitch a ½-inch long seam at the nose.
E. Align the HEAD at the nose seam and stitch from EAR to EAR.
F. Match the BODIES, and sew the back seam from the EAR SLOT to the TAIL.
G. Tuck the EARS into the EAR SLOT on the HEAD top, align the raw edges, and pin in place. Stitch across the EAR SLOT, tapering at the ends and including the EARS in this seam.
H. Insert the EYE POST into the EYE RING with the fur pile upward. Continue through the EYE placement hole. Push the washer firmly on the back.
I. Insert the plastic NOSE on the seam line. The washer may be larger than the nose, causing a ridge in the fabric. If so, bend the top edge of the washer back with the pliers. These noses also have a hole in the post for sewing or wiring in place. To mount the NOSE in this manner, wrap the NOSE thread or wire tightly around a wad of stuffing.

Step 3: Making the Body

A. Baste the TAIL to the REAR INNER LEG.
B. Sew the UNDERBODY to the REAR INNER LEG.

DIRECTIONS

Sew ears, turn and fold.

Sew tail, and turn.

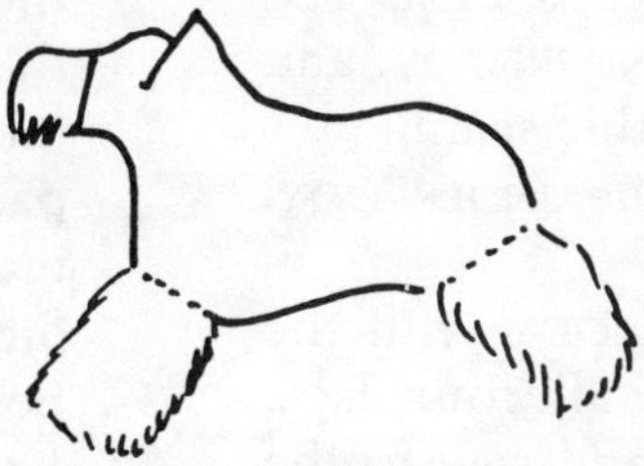

Add long fur sections (or spots) to body, underbody, and legs.

Sew nose seam between dots.

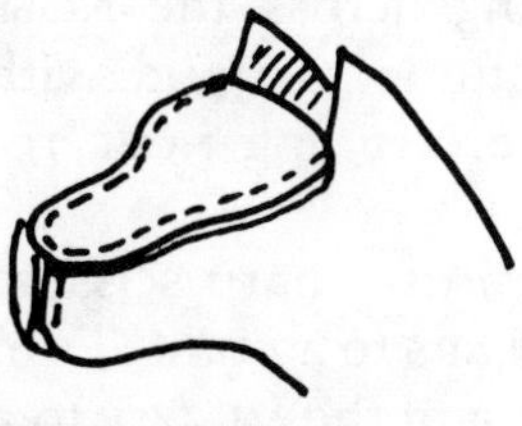

Align head, centered at the nose, and stitch.

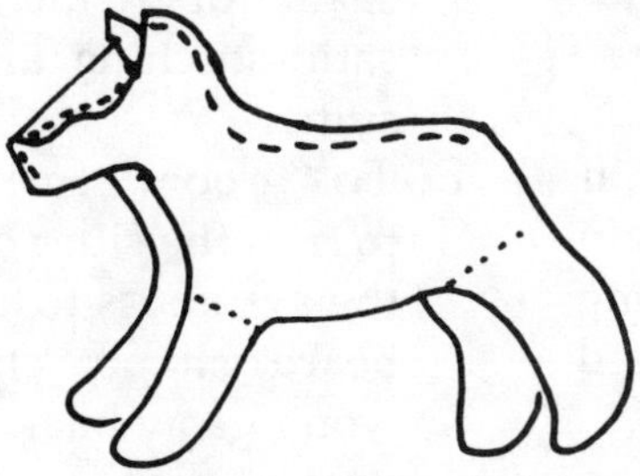

Sew body back seam to tail mount.

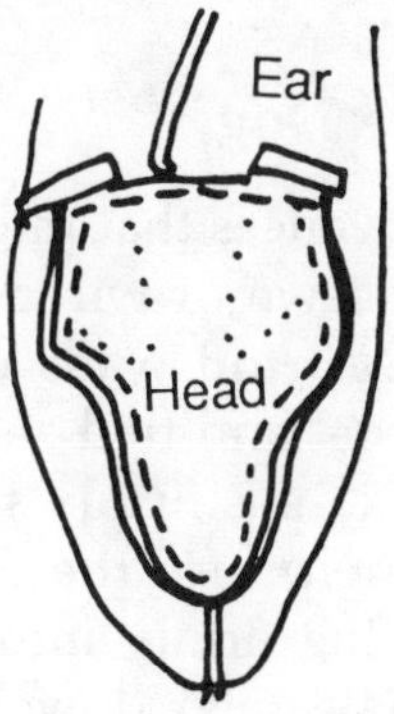

Pin ears into ear slot, stitch.

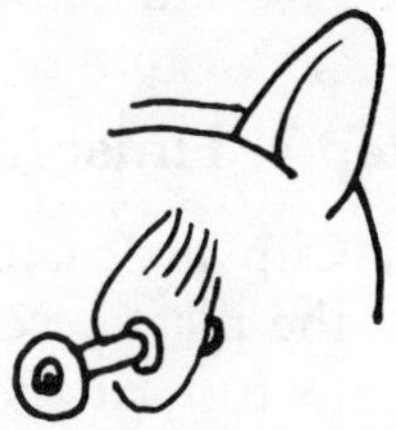

Insert eye through eye ring into head. Insert nose.

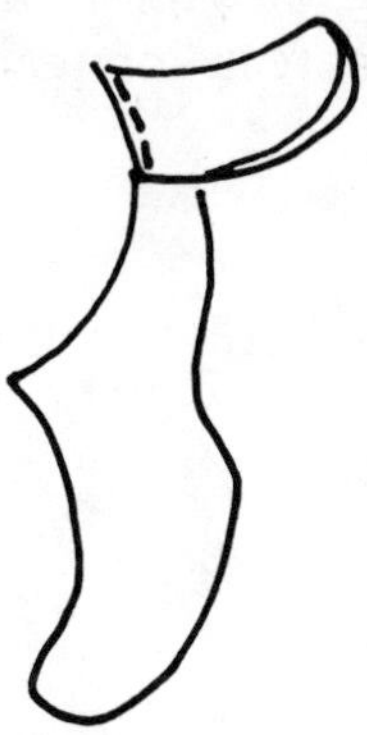

Baste tail to rear inner leg.

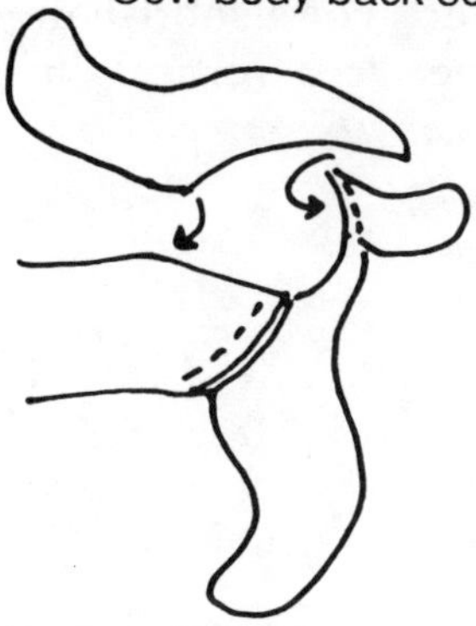

Sew underbody to rear inner leg, join other rear inner leg at crotch.

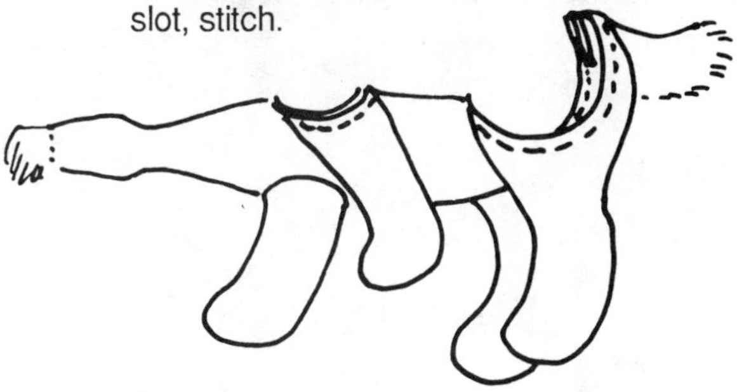

Join front inner legs to underbody.

Join underbody to body including all four legs, turn, stuff.

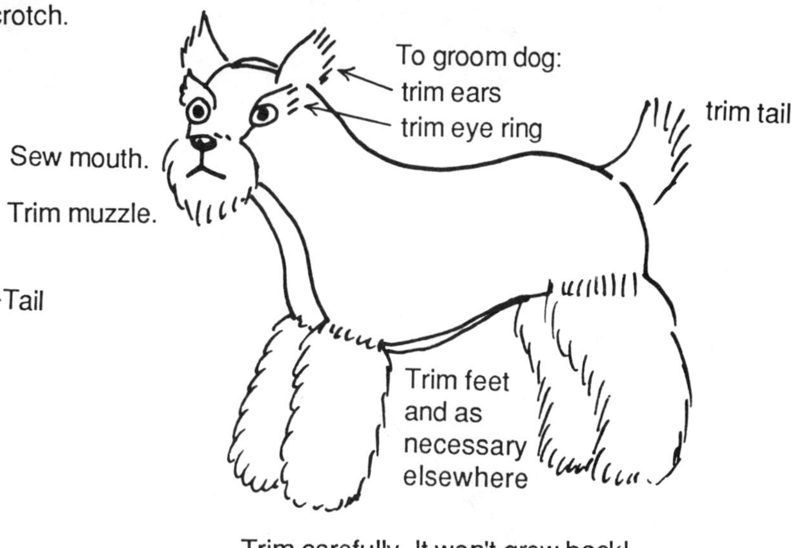

Trim carefully. It won't grow back!

Align the crotch seam of the REAR INNER LEG with the first LEG and the UNDERBODY, and stitch, including the TAIL in this seam.

C. Join the FRONT INNER LEG to the UNDERBODY. Repeat.

D. Align the assembled UNDERBODY with the assembled BODY, matching all four legs. Begin stitching at the CHIN and sew to the TAIL. Repeat for the other side, leaving an opening in the seam for turning the BODY.

Step 4: Finishing the Dog

A. Clip any seam allowances that might pull. If the plastic NOSE is sewn or wired on, begin to turn at the NOSE. Add wads of stuffing around the NOSE post and tied stuffing wad to make sure the NOSE is firmly seated.

B. Use the dowel to help turn the dog and to push wads of stuffing firmly into the LEGS. Scaled-up dogs may need dowel stick armatures in the legs to keep them stiff, but the larger dog is firmly enough stuffed so this isn't necessary (unless he is played with too much and the stuffing shifts or compacts). Continue to stuff the dog until it is modeled to shape and packed full. Add additional packing at the top of each LEG.

C. Sew the opening closed.

D. Use black embroidery floss to sew the MOUTH. For an embroidered NOSE, sew ¼-inch-wide satin-stitching across the NOSE seam for ⅜ inch. Continue to build with satin-stitching until a protruding NOSE results.

E. To "groom" furry dogs, use sharp scissors to trim the sides of the EARS to a point. Trim the EYE RINGS to a point and the MUZZLE to a beard shape, clipping carefully since it won't grow back. Clip FOOT bottoms.

NOTE: For a short-haired dog, or a flat fabric one, sew vertical lines for TOES on each foot.

ELEPHANTS are the biggest quadrupeds on earth (the whale may be the only larger mammal, but it is legless). Since elephants may grow as heavy as seven thousand pounds, they must eat grass, fruit, and leaves for at least 16 hours a day to fill their enormous bulk. In the wild they can only do this in warm climates like Africa and India. Family groups of elephants still roam in a few areas, especially the African game preserves, sometimes shaking trees for food and occasionally uprooting the trees altogether. It's touching to watch so huge a beast gently tending its young (the babies often weigh 200 pounds at birth) with other elephants helping as well.

Elephants are strong, intelligent, and biddable (some kinds more trainable than others), so they have been trained for many jobs from forestry in India to raising the circus tents in the

PATTERN

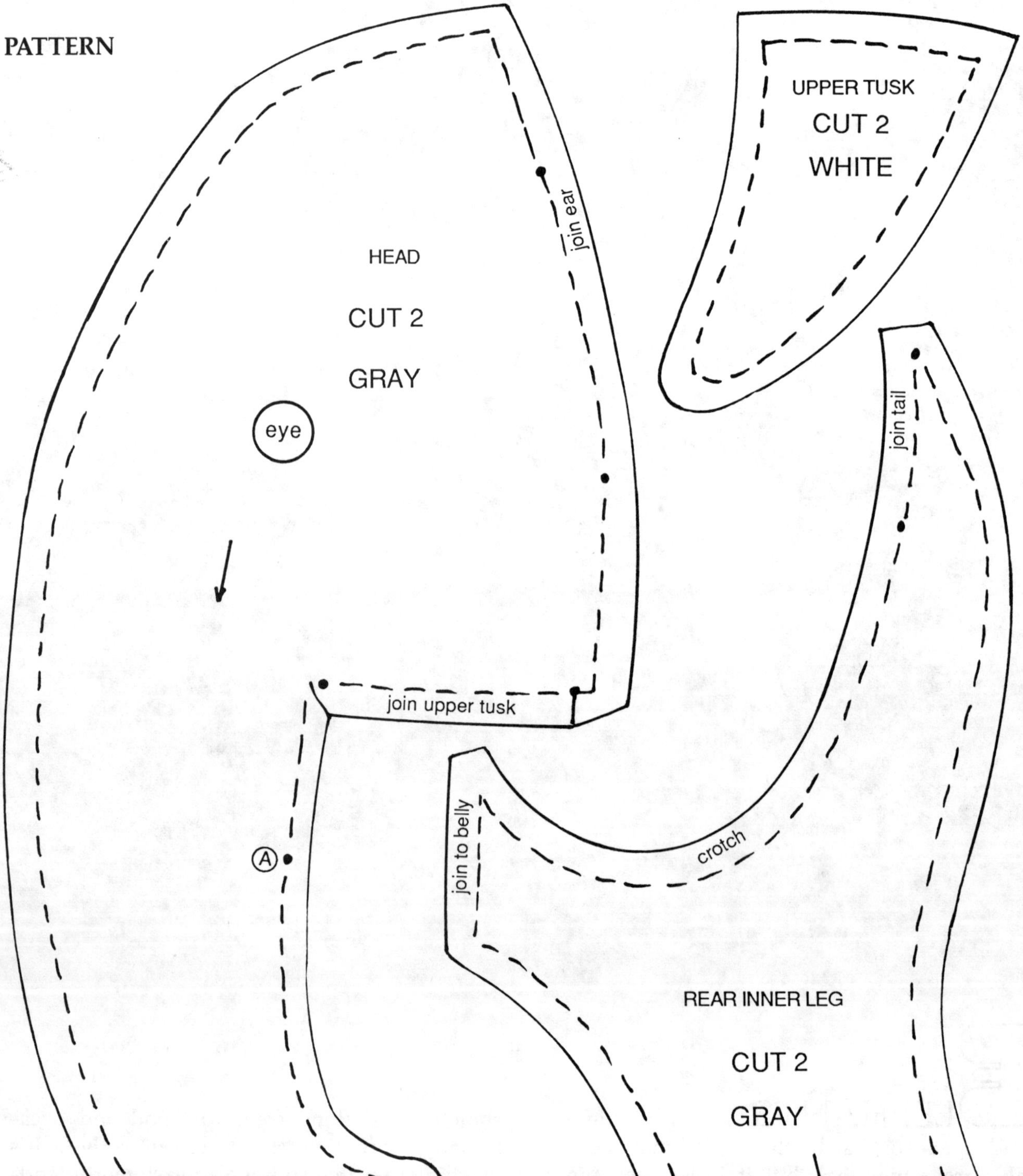
UPPER TUSK
CUT 2
WHITE
HEAD
CUT 2
GRAY
eye
join ear
join upper tusk
A
join tail
join to belly
crotch
REAR INNER LEG
CUT 2
GRAY
toes

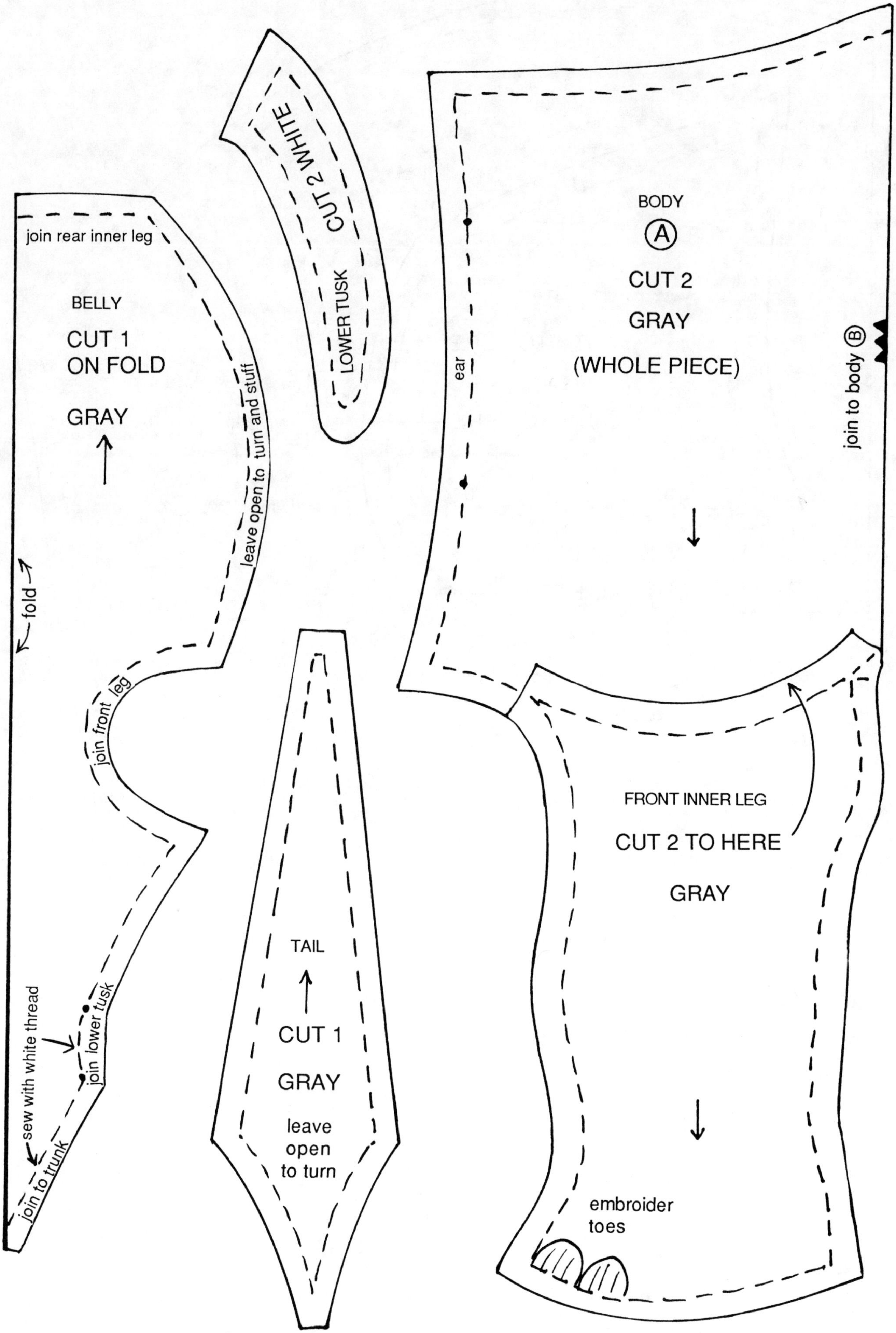

join rear inner leg
BELLY
CUT 1
ON FOLD
GRAY
leave open to turn and stuff
fold
join front leg
sew with white thread
join lower tusk
join to trunk
LOWER TUSK
CUT 2 WHITE
TAIL
CUT 1
GRAY
leave open to turn
BODY
A
CUT 2
GRAY
(WHOLE PIECE)
ear
join to body B
FRONT INNER LEG
CUT 2 TO HERE
GRAY
embroider toes

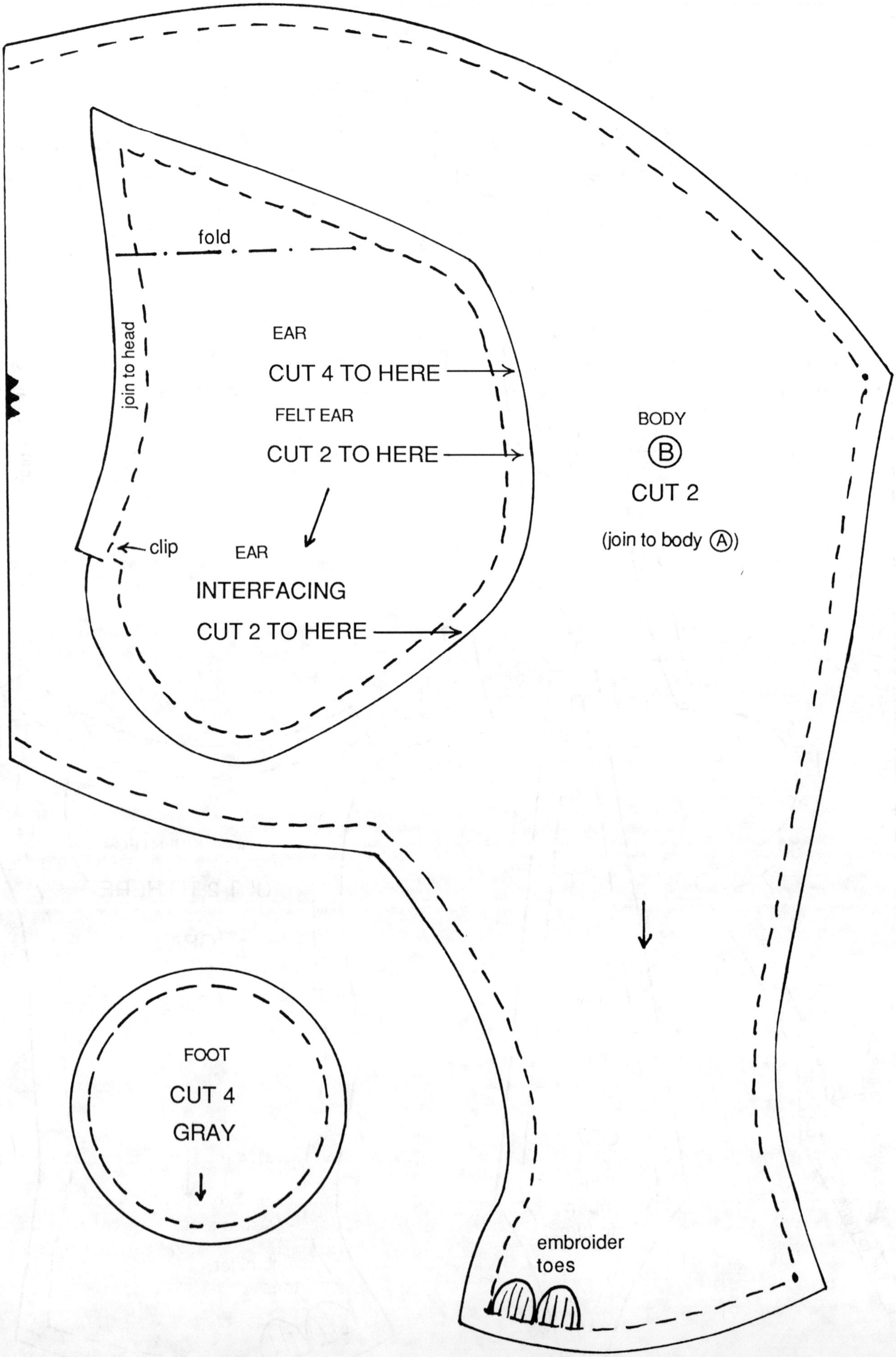
fold
join to head
EAR
CUT 4 TO HERE
FELT EAR
CUT 2 TO HERE
clip
EAR
INTERFACING
CUT 2 TO HERE
BODY
B
CUT 2
(join to body A)
FOOT
CUT 4
GRAY
embroider toes

United States. African pachyderms have larger ears than their relatives in India. Both have thick, wrinkled hides.

NOTE: This toy elephant measures 9 inches high. For a super-sized stuffed animal, enlarge the design 2 or more times. Since children will certainly climb on a large animal, first construct a wooden armature as a base for support.

The elephant shown is made from a stretchy, light-weight velour fabric, ideal in color but unsuitable. To stabilize this flimsy fabric, each piece was backed with a non-stretch fabric. Be careful not to use fabric that is too heavy. It may make some seams like the tusks difficult to sew, and turning the slender tail difficult.

Materials

ALL PIECES EXCEPT THE TUSKS: 20 by 28 inches gray plush, velvet, felt, or velour

TUSKS: 3 by 6 inches white felt, velour, or velvet

EYES: Black or brown ¼-inch post-and-washer eyes

THREAD: Gray sewing thread to match, white for the TUSKS, gray embroidery floss or machine-embroidery thread for the TOES

FOOT LINING: 2 by 8 inches cardboard or, for a washable toy, 1¾-inch plastic disks or buttons

EAR INTERFACING: 5 by 7 inches heavy-weight interfacing

OPTIONAL FELT EARS: 5 by 7 inches felt, use no interfacing

STUFFING: 8 ounces of fiberfill

Tools

A wooden chopstick or similar stuffing tool

Pattern Pieces

HEAD (2), UPPER TUSK (2), LOWER TUSK (2), BODY A and B (2) (given in two pieces), FRONT INNER LEG (2), REAR INNER LEG (2), TAIL (1), BELLY (1), FOOT (4), EAR (2 or 4), EAR INTERFACING (2), FOOT LINING (4)

Step 1: Cutting the Fabric

A. Cut out all pieces.

NOTE: If the fabric is flimsy or stretchy, use a more stable fabric for backing every piece except the ears, which are interfaced, and the tail. To do this, smooth the gray fabric over the backing fabric and cut both together for accuracy. Keep the pieces pinned together with their backing.

Step 2: Assembling the Elephant Parts

A. Lay two EARS face to face. Pin the INTERFACING to one side. Stitch around the EAR, leaving the base open to turn. Clip the inside corner seam allowance and trim away the interfacing seam allowance. Turn the EAR, flatten, and top-stitch close to the edge. Fold the EAR lengthwise ¾ inch from the top edge as marked, and pin.

Optional: For felt ears use a single or double layer. Eliminate the seam allowance. Top-stitch the double layers together.

B. Fold the TAIL flat and stitch. Turn, using the small end of the wooden chopstick to push the narrow end out.

C. Align the OUTER TUSKS with the HEAD and stitch. Align the EAR with the HEAD and baste in place.

D. Insert the post-and-washer EYE, or machine-embroider the EYE. Machine-embroider the TOES, or hand-embroider later.

E. Align the TAIL on the INNER BACK LEG, angling downward, and baste. Match the INNER BACK LEGS, and stitch the crotch seam.

F. Assemble the BELLY section. To do this, sew the INNER TUSKS to the BELLY. Align the FRONT INNER LEGS to the BELLY leg holes and stitch. Align the REAR INNER LEGS to the BELLY and stitch.

Step 3: Making the Body

A. Align the HEAD with the BODY at the neck, and stitch, including the EAR in this seam.

B. Beginning at "A" on the HEAD TRUNK, sew

DIRECTIONS

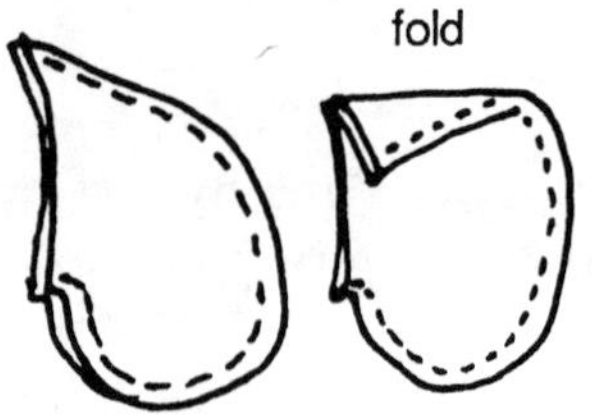

Sew ears, turn; topstitch; fold and baste.

Sew tail; turn.

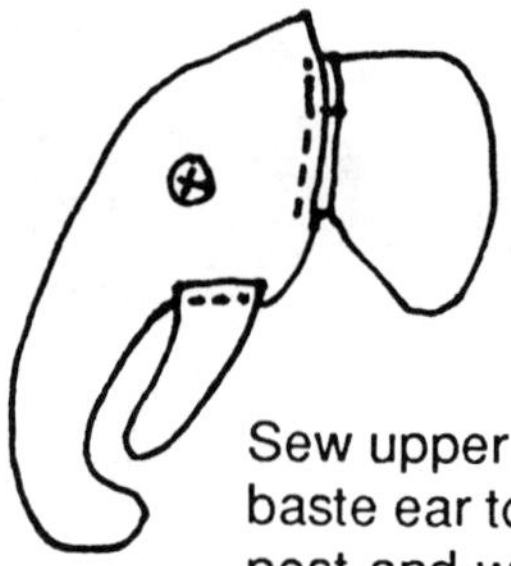

Sew upper tusk to head, baste ear to head, insert post-and-washer eye.

Baste tail to rear inner leg; join rear inner legs at the crotch seam, machine sew toes on all feet.

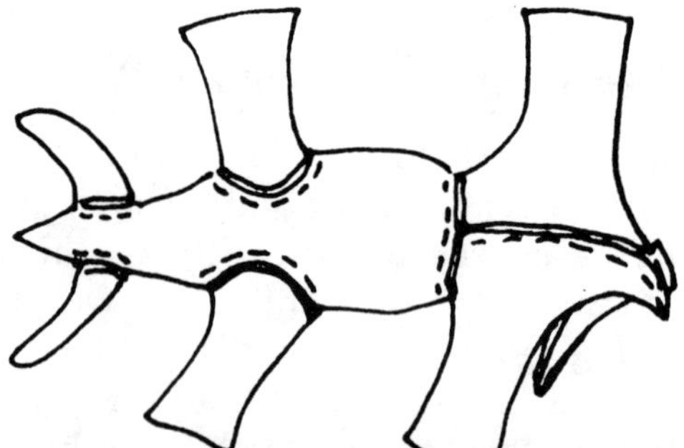

Sew lower tusk, front inner legs, and rear inner legs to belly.

Sew head to body.

Sew from Ⓐ on trunk to tail.

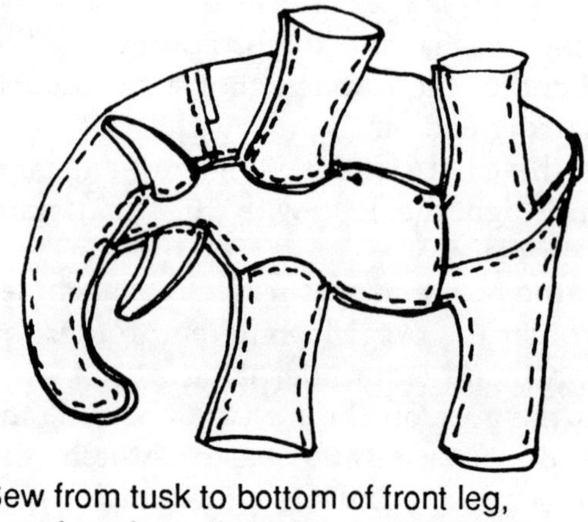

Sew from tusk to bottom of front leg, from front leg to back leg, and back leg to tail. Repeat, leaving 3-inch opening to turn.

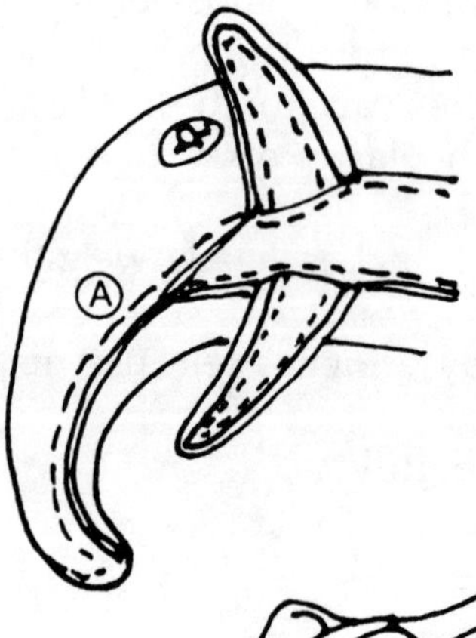

Change to white thread to sew tusks. Sew from tusk to Ⓐ on trunk, repeat.

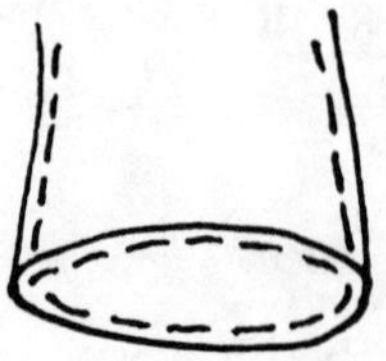

Sew foot to leg on all four legs.

Optional: hand-sew toenails on all feet.

down the TRUNK, around the HEAD, and along the BODY back seam to the TAIL.

C. Fit the assembled BELLY to the assembled BODY, matching the NECK at the TUSKS, the FRONT LEGS and the REAR LEGS and pin. Beginning at the TUSK joining, stitch down the FRONT LEG, leaving the bottom open for the FOOT. (For the TUSKS see the next step.) Sew the back seam of the FRONT LEG and across the BELLY to the REAR LEG, leaving a FOOT opening. Stitch up the REAR LEG to the TAIL. Repeat for the other side, leaving a 3-inch opening on the BODY for turning and stuffing. Join the FOOT to the FOOT OPENING on all four legs.

D. Change the machine thread to *white*, top and bobbin. The TUSK widths do not match, creating the rounded form of the TUSK. Align the back edges of the TUSK and stitch from the top to the tip. Stitch a rounded tip, pivot the fabric on the needle so the front TUSK edges align, and stitch to the TUSK TOP. Continue the seam onto the trunk to "A." Repeat for the other side.

E. Clip any inside corner seam allowances that would pull the fabric when turned. Turn, using the chopstick to push out the TRUNK and TUSKS.

Step 4: Finishing the Elephant

A. Insert the FOOT LINERS.

B. Using small loose wads and the stuffing stick, stuff the TRUNK and TUSKS firmly. Continue adding wads of stuffing to fill the legs. Add stuffing until the animal is well filled and modeled to shape. Be sure to add a large firm wad of stuffing at the top of each leg for proper shape and support. Sew the opening closed with hidden stitching.

C. Hand-sew any details, EYES, or TOES, unless this was done previously.

FROGS come in about two thousand various colors, sizes, and shapes and live all over the world except in very cold climates. In ancient Egypt frogs were considered a symbol of female fertility, linked with the annual overflowing of the Nile so necessary to farming. Eight Egyptian gods had frog heads, representing resurrection, probably because of the frogs' annual reappearance. In Japan frogs are the symbol of energy and perseverance, credited with drawing all the mosquitoes out of a room. All legends highlight the way frogs lay many eggs, hibernate in cold weather, and catch insects on their long, quick tongues.

Most frogs are noted for their large hind legs that allow them to jump as much as six feet in distance. Frog jumping contests, popular in Huck Finn's day, still occur in frog season. Frogs are amphibians who spend half their lives in the water. The frog's webbed feet and quick swimming style have led to human swimmers' use of the "frog kick" and rubber flippers for speed.

NOTE: The completed frog shown measures 18 inches from toe to eye, and 12 inches wide. Only two steps will need special care in making this pattern, sewing and turning the tiny toes, and stitching the final seam around the body with the stuffed legs inside. To avoid problems in either area, use exposed unturned seams to make the frog. Trim them evenly after stitching.

The large person-size frog shown on the cover stands about 6 feet tall. The stuffings are light-weight and the bamboo armatures strong but not sturdy enough for sitting on his lap. Amounts of material are given for the small frog. To determine amounts for the large frog, multiply fabric dimensions by the number of times enlargement in *each* direction. For example, the 4-times-larger frog takes 16 times as much fabric.

Materials for Small Frog

NOTE: This small pattern given is designed for a firmly woven, non-fraying flat fabric such as felt. Pile fabric will make a plumper creature. Felt was used for the small frog and upholstery velvets for the large one. Other possible choices include printed cottons or velveteen, cotton and polyester broadcloth, suede cloth, or terrycloth.

BODY BACK, HEAD, EYES, ARMS, and LEGS: 12 by 24 inches green felt

BODY FRONT, ARMS, and LEGS: 12 by 15 inches light-yellow felt

SPOT: 1½-inch square of bright green felt

THREAD and TRIM: Green poly-cotton sewing thread and yellow on bobbin, gold embroidery floss for MOUTH and NOSE

EYES: ⅞-inch green plastic post-and-washer movable eyes

STUFFING: ½ pound fiberfill

Materials for Large Frog

BODY BACK, HEAD, EYE BACKS, ARMS, and LEGS: 6½ yards of soft green 60-inch-wide upholstery velveteen or fur

BODY FRONT, ARMS and LEGS: 1½ yards of soft yellow 60-inch-wide upholsteıy fabric or fur

EYE PUPIL: 4 by 8 inches dark brown velveteen, white accent

THREAD: matching sewing thread

PATTERN

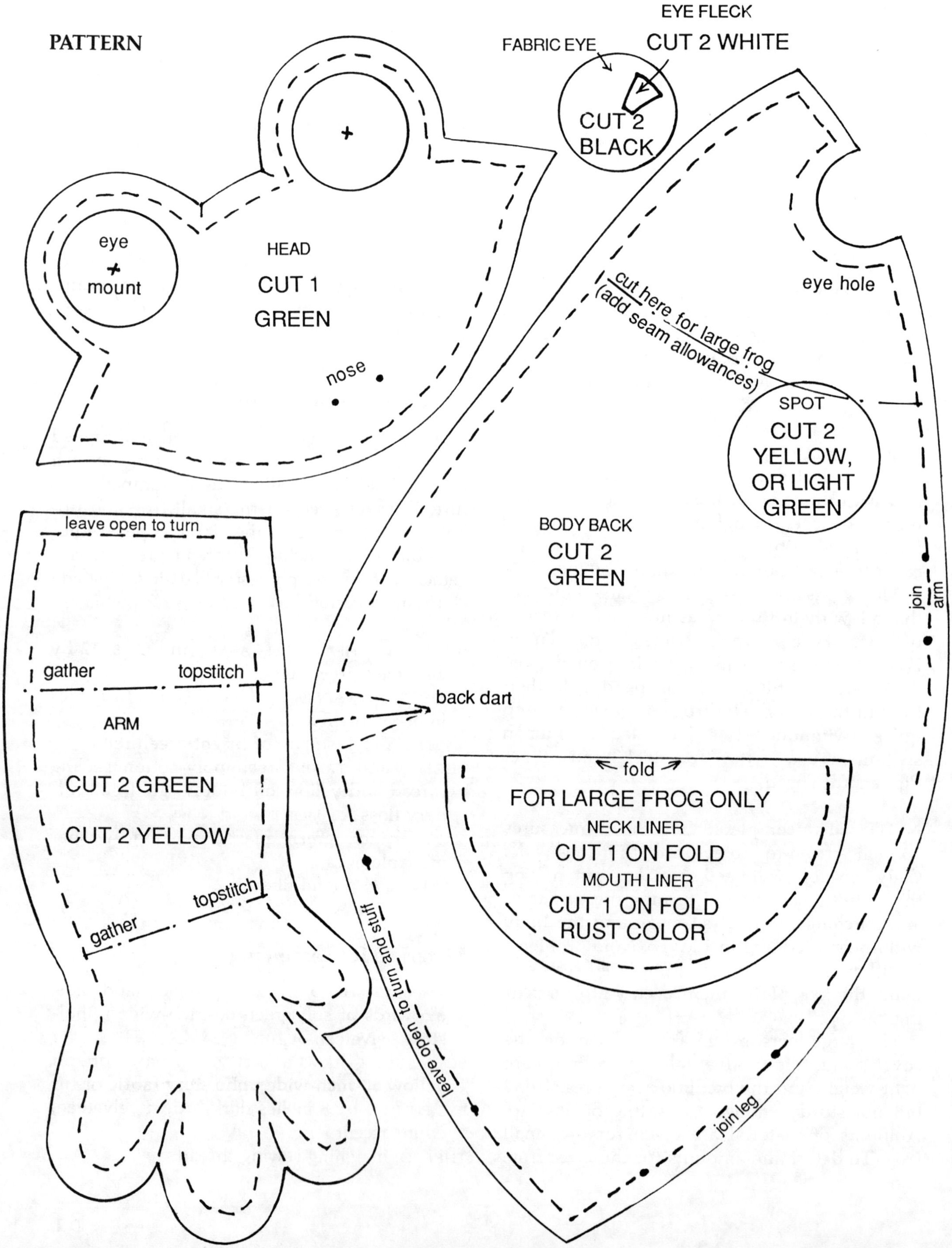
EYE FLECK
CUT 2 WHITE
FABRIC EYE
CUT 2
BLACK
eye
mount
HEAD
CUT 1
GREEN
nose
cut here for large frog
(add seam allowances)
eye hole
SPOT
CUT 2
YELLOW,
OR LIGHT
GREEN
BODY BACK
CUT 2
GREEN
join arm
leave open to turn
gather
topstitch
ARM
CUT 2 GREEN
CUT 2 YELLOW
topstitch
gather
back dart
fold
FOR LARGE FROG ONLY
NECK LINER
CUT 1 ON FOLD
MOUTH LINER
CUT 1 ON FOLD
RUST COLOR
leave open to turn and stuff
join leg

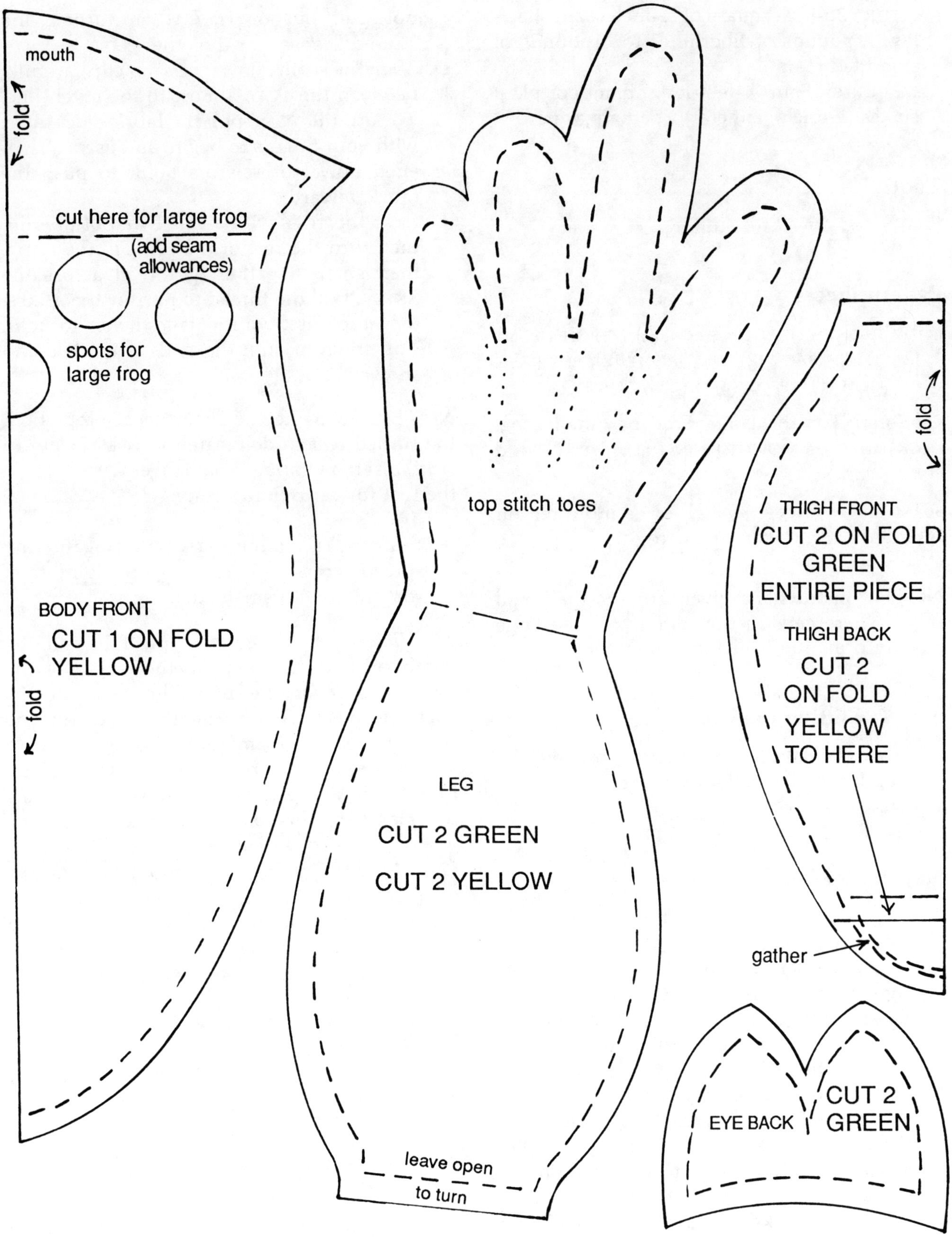
mouth
fold
cut here for large frog
(add seam allowances)
spots for large frog
BODY FRONT
CUT 1 ON FOLD
YELLOW
fold
top stitch toes
LEG
CUT 2 GREEN
CUT 2 YELLOW
leave open
to turn
fold
THIGH FRONT
CUT 2 ON FOLD
GREEN
ENTIRE PIECE
THIGH BACK
CUT 2
ON FOLD
YELLOW
TO HERE
gather
EYE BACK
CUT 2
GREEN

STUFFING: 36-inch square of ½-inch foam sheeting, 2 pounds of fiberfill, 2 to 4 pounds of shredded foam

ARMATURES: Four 4-feet-long bamboo plant stakes (½-inch diameter), coathanger wire

Tools

Sharpened dowel for stuffing

Pattern Pieces

BODY FRONT (1), BODY BACK (2), THIGH FRONT (2), THIGH BACK (2), LEG FRONT (2), LEG BACK (2), HEAD (1), SPOT (2), EYE BACK (2)

Optional: For the Large Frog or Small Frog: NECK LINER or MOUTH LINING (1), EYE (2), and PUPIL (2)

SEAM ALLOWANCES: 3/16-inch or as indicated on pattern, ¾ inch for larger frog

NOTE: Instructions given are for the small frog. Where construction differs for the large frog, information is included in a note.

Step 1: Cutting the Fabric

A. Scale the pattern up or down to make the frog larger or smaller as desired.

B. Cut out all pieces.

Step 2: Making the Legs

A. Pin the THIGH BACK to the LEG BACK and stitch. Repeat for the other LEG.

B. Sew a gathering thread across the lower edge of the THIGH FRONT. Pull the gathering thread to align the THIGH FRONT with the LEG FRONT top. Pin the seam and stitch. Repeat for the other LEG.

C. Pin the assembled LEG FRONT to the LEG BACK, matching the KNEE seams. Use a very short stitch to sew around the entire LEG, leaving the top open to turn. Stitch one or two small stitches across the point between the TOES to make a squared corner so it will not pull out or fray when turned and stuffed. Repeat for the other LEG.

D. Trim the seam allowances and clip carefully between the TOES almost to the stitch line. To turn the TOES, pull the fabric sides apart with your fingers to begin, and use a sharpened dowel or scissors point to push the fabric inward.

E. Stuff the TOES with a small wad of fiberfill, then turn the rest of the LEG. Fill the FOOT, then stitch a gathering thread across the ANKLE. Pull the thread to narrow the ANKLE, then top-stitch with small stitches to hold. Top-stitch to quilt the TOES as marked and shown.

NOTE: To make the LARGE FROG, top-stitch the turned feet to delineate the TOES. Begin to stuff. Insert a wrapped coathanger wire to angle the feet forward. Stuff firmly.

F. Stuff the LEG to the KNEE. Stitch a gathering thread across, pull to narrow the joint, then top-stitch with small stitching.

NOTE: For the LARGE FROG, push the end of a bamboo plant stake, cut to the length of the lower LEG, over the protruding end of the coathanger wire. For a smooth effect, stuff the LEG with ½-inch foam rubber sheeting cut to size and wrapped around the bamboo armature. Fill in any extra space with fiberfill stuffing. Hand-stitch across the KNEE.

G. Fill the LEG nearly to the top, taking care to push a wad into the KNEE. Do not stuff the LEGS too full or they will not bend well. Fold the LEG TOP, matching seam to seam, and pin closed. Repeat Steps 4, 5, and 6 for the other LEG.

NOTE: For the LARGE FROG, fill the THIGH with foam sheeting and a bamboo stake as before. Continue as above and repeat Steps 4, 5, and 6 for the other leg.

Step 3: Making the Arms

A. Pin the ARM FRONT to the ARM BACK. Sew around the entire ARM, leaving the top open

DIRECTIONS

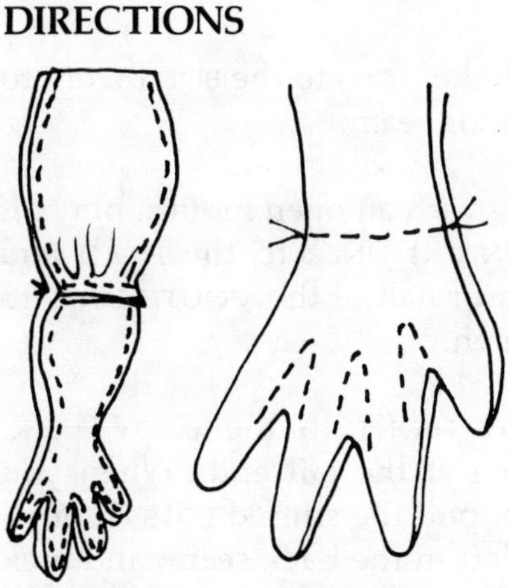

Gather knee, join upper leg to lower, join leg back to leg front, turn and stuff. Top-stitch stuffed ankle and toes (except large frog).

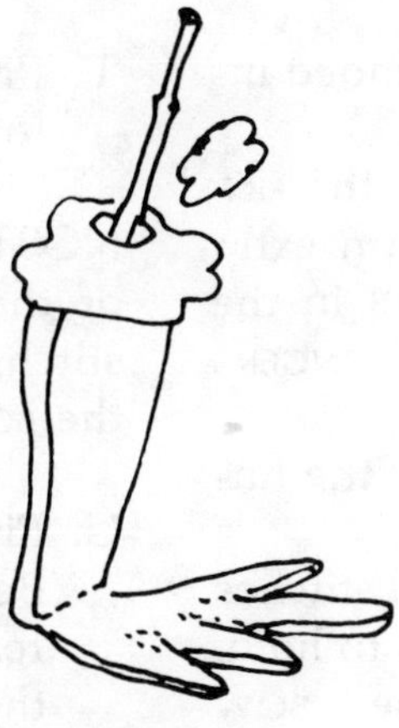

Insert bamboo armature in large frog legs.

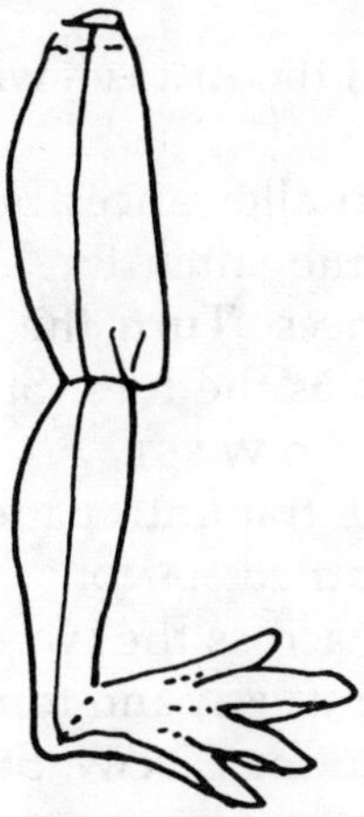

Fold stuffed leg seams to match seams, baste.

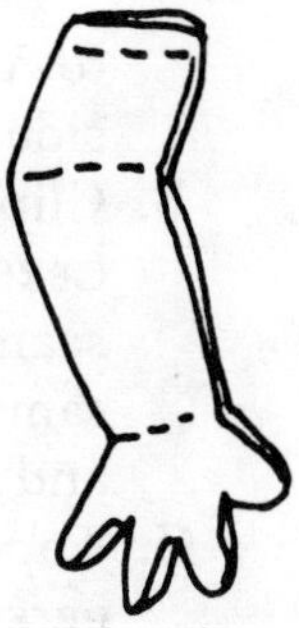

Join arms, stitch, turn, stuff, top-stitch.

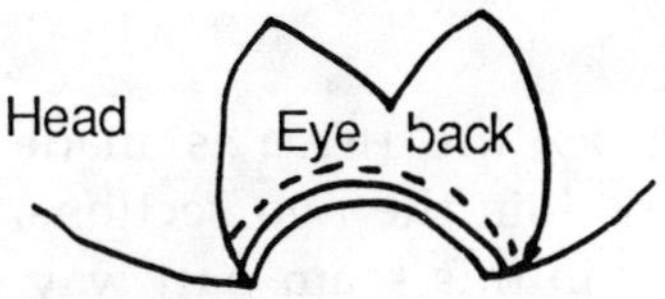

Join eye back to eye hole on body.

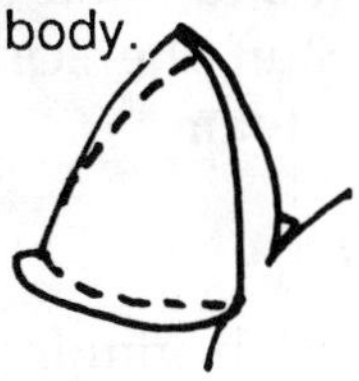

Stitch eye back seam.

Applique fabric eye, or pierce eye hole.

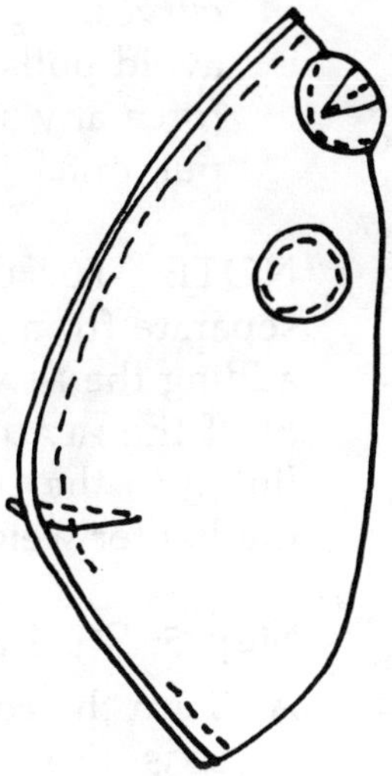

Applique spot, sew back darts and back seam, leave opening.

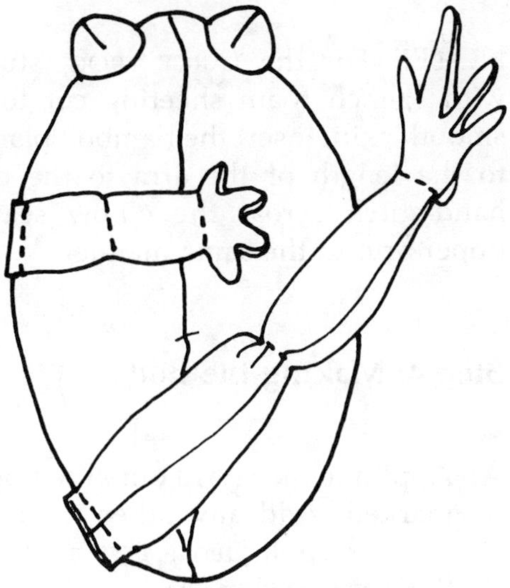

Baste arms and legs to body back.

Optional heads for large frog.

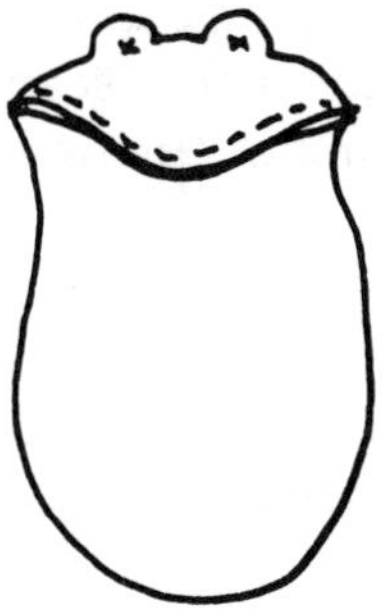

Sew head to body front.

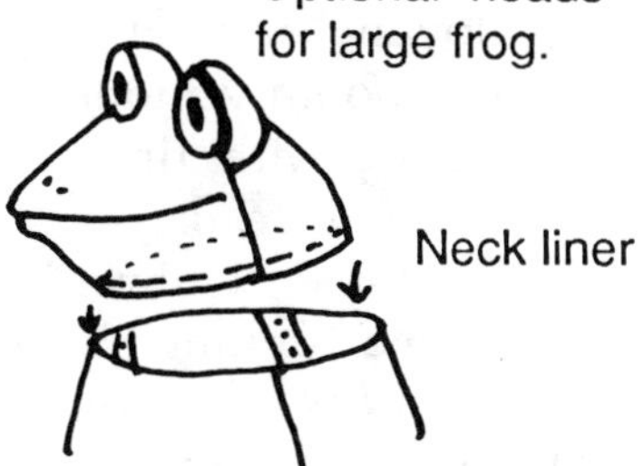

Insert neck liner to hold stuffing in head. Join body.

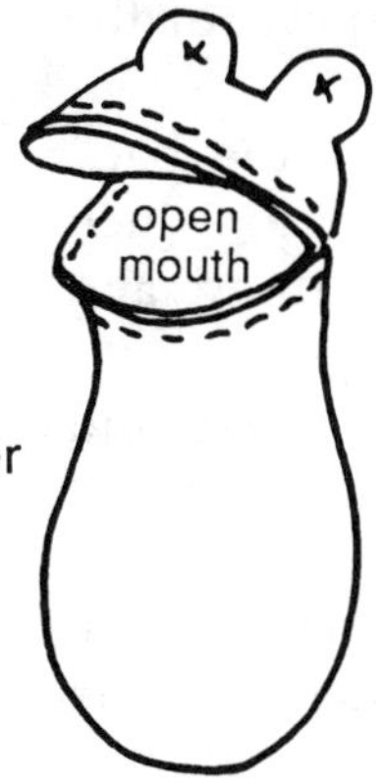

Use neck liner for mouth pattern. Sew mouth to head and body.

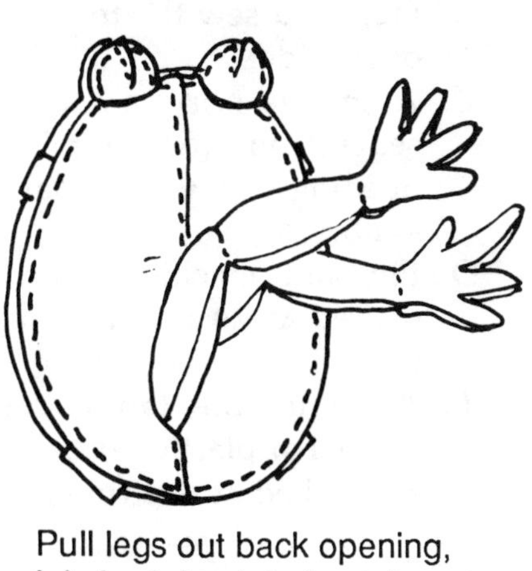

Pull legs out back opening, join body back to front. Insert eyes, turn, stuff, sew closed.

to turn. Stitch the FINGERS with rounded inside corners.

B. Clip the seam allowances between the FINGERS just to the stitch line, and trim extra seam allowances. Turn the FINGERS in the same manner as the toes. Stuff the FINGERS and HAND to the WRIST.

C. Top-stitch the trapunto pattern for the fingers on the turned HAND.

D. Gather-stitch across the WRIST, pull stitches to narrow the WRIST, and top-stitch to hold.

E. Fill the ARM to the ELBOW. Stitch the ELBOW as for the WRIST. Continue to fill nearly to the top and pin the ARM closed. Repeat Steps 1, 2, 3, and 4 for the other ARM.

NOTE: For the LARGE FROG, stuff the ARM with ½-inch foam sheeting cut to shape, for smooth skin. Insert the bamboo plant stake (cut to the length of the arm to the elbow), and hand-stitch across the elbow seam. Fill the upper arm in the same manner.

Step 4: Making the Body

A. Appliqué the SPOTS onto the BODY BACKS as marked. Add any other machine embroidery or appliquéd SPOTS at this time. Sew the BODY BACK darts.

B. Pin and stitch the EYE BACK to the EYE HOLE on the BODY BACK. Fold the EYE BACK face to face, and sew the top seam. Repeat for the other side.

C. Align the BODY BACKS, and sew the back seam from top to tail, leaving a 2-inch opening below the dart for turning and stuffing.

D. Pin and machine-baste the stitched and stuffed ARMS and LEGS in place on the BODY BACK.

E. Appliqué the fabric EYE CIRCLES on the HEAD. For plastic EYES, cut the insertion hole as marked at this time.

F. Pin and stitch the HEAD to the BODY front to form the MOUTH seam.

NOTE: For frog with an open mouth, pin half of the MOUTH (NECK) LINER to the HEAD and stitch. Pin the lower half of the MOUTH LINER to the BODY and stitch.

G. Pin the BODY FRONT to the BODY BACK. Begin to stitch at the tail end. When you reach the top, pull the stuffed LEGS through the opening left in the back seam, and tuck the ARMS inside so you can complete stitching the seam.

H. Carefully clip any seam allowances on curves, especially at the turn of the eyes, to avoid pulls and wrinkles in the skin. Reinforce any stitching that looks as if it might pull out.

NOTE: For LARGE FROG, the HEAD is made separate from the BODY. Join the two sections, adding the HEAD LINING in this seam part way. Stuff the HEAD with fiberfill and hand-sew the lining to the HEAD seam. Stuff the BODY with the lighter weight shredded foam.

Step 5: Stuff and Finish:

A. Turn the completed FROG, beginning at the LEGS. Examine the turned fabric for sturdy seams and accurate placement of pieces. Insert the plastic EYES.

B. Stuff the EYES first. Push soft wads of fiberfill in place with the eraser on the pencil. Fill the HEAD carefully to form the mouth and nose. Completely fill the FROG to overflowing, and pat or work the stuffing until it is smoothly modeled. Sew the BACK seam closed with tiny hidden stitches using a strong thread.

C. To finish, embroider the MOUTH in place with a running chain stitch. Embroider two NOSTRILS with French knots.

D. To keep the FOOT in place, bend the FOOT up to the ANKLE and tack.

GIRAFFES are the tallest animals on earth, growing between 18 and 19 feet tall. The giraffe's long neck helps it to reach the top, most tender leaves of the trees, and its 18-inch-long prehensile tongue pulls the tender shoots into its mouth. In spite of its length, the giraffe's neck has the same number of vertebrae as a mouse. Extremely long legs give the giraffe a graceful floating gallop; however, the legs are so long that the animal must splay its front legs wide so it can lower its head far enough to drink.

With few weapons to defend itself, the giraffe usually chooses to run from attack, although it can deliver a mean kick with its sharp hooves if necessary. At full speed it runs with a fast rocking gallop like a camel.

Not only is the giraffe taller than most, but it is more attractively decorated, with a beautiful mosaic-patterned coat ideal for camouflage in leafy shade, but a real standout on the open veldt in Africa.

NOTE: This pattern makes a stuffed toy 18 inches tall. Armatures are required to keep the legs from sagging; in this case, bamboo plant stakes wrapped in soft fabric. The polyester fabric used has a delightful orange and yellow print, but the loose weave frayed at the edges, complicating construction. Use a firmly woven, non-fraying fabric if you can find a suitable print. If not, stencil, paint, or draw spots with a marker, or appliqué fabric spots on.

Materials

BODY, LEGS, TAIL, BELLY, and EARS: 26 by 22 inches firmly woven flat fabric, yellow with a brown spot pattern, or as you can find or create

FEET and HORNS: 8 by 14 inches brown fabric

OPTIONAL HORNS: 3-inch brown pipe cleaner

EYES: ⅜-inch brown post-and-washer eyes

TAIL and MANE: ¼-ounce brown 4-ply yarn

STUFFING: 6 ounces fiberfill

ARMATURES: 4 bamboo plant stakes (or wooden dowels) 8 inches long and ½ inch diameter; ½ yard cheese cloth

TRIM: Brown embroidery floss

Pattern Pieces

BODY A, B, C, and D (2) (given in four pieces), BELLY (1), TAIL (1), FRONT INNER LEG (2), REAR INNER LEG (2), EAR (4), FEET (8), HORN (4)

Step 1: Cutting the Fabric

A. Note that the BODY has been divided into four pieces to fit on the pages. Assemble the body pattern before using.

PATTERN

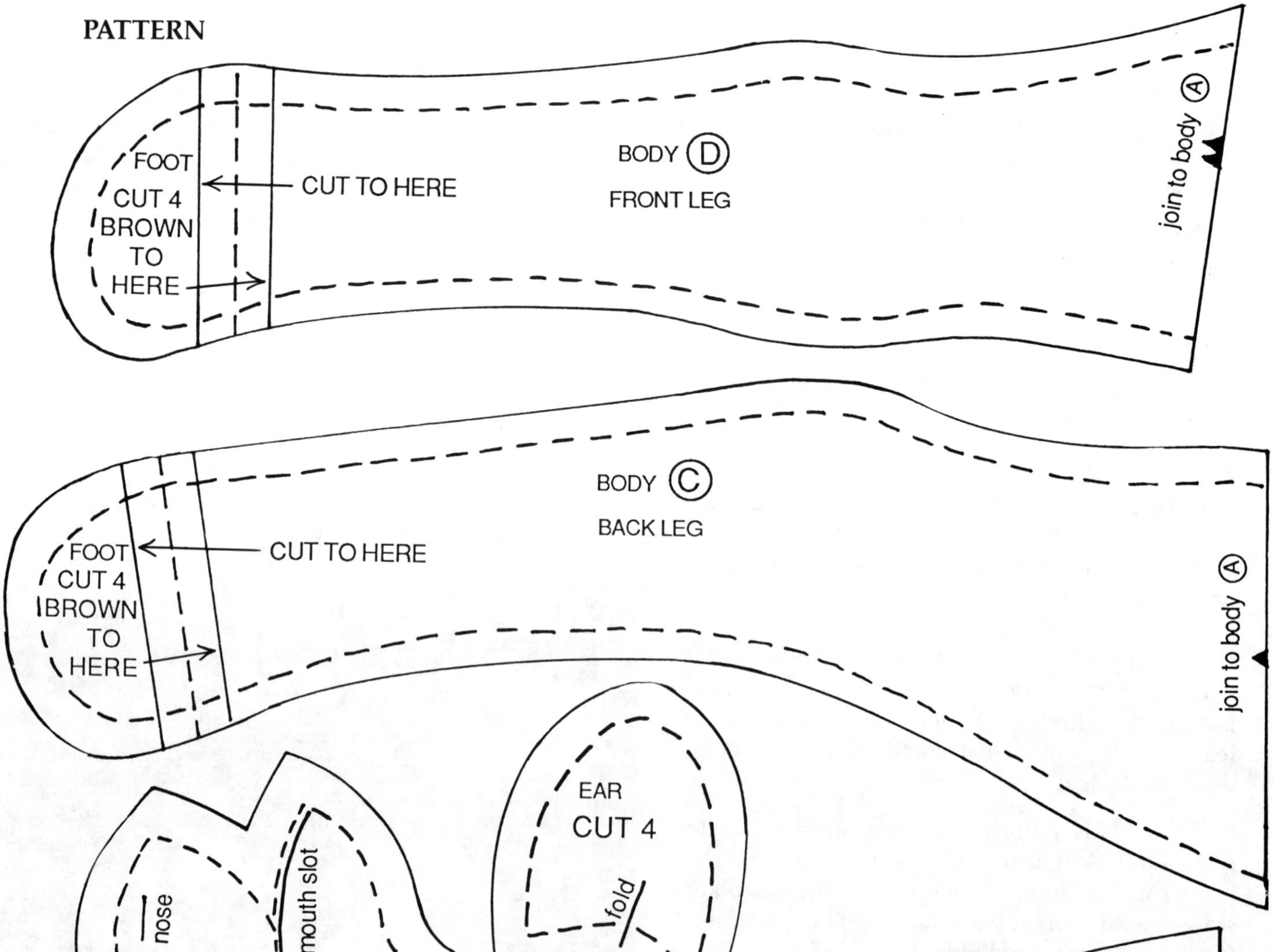
FOOT
CUT 4
BROWN
TO
HERE
CUT TO HERE
BODY D
FRONT LEG
join to body A
FOOT
CUT 4
BROWN
TO
HERE
CUT TO HERE
BODY C
BACK LEG
join to body A
EAR
CUT 4
fold
nose
mouth slot
eye
head
BODY B
NECK
ear slot
sew mane
join to body A

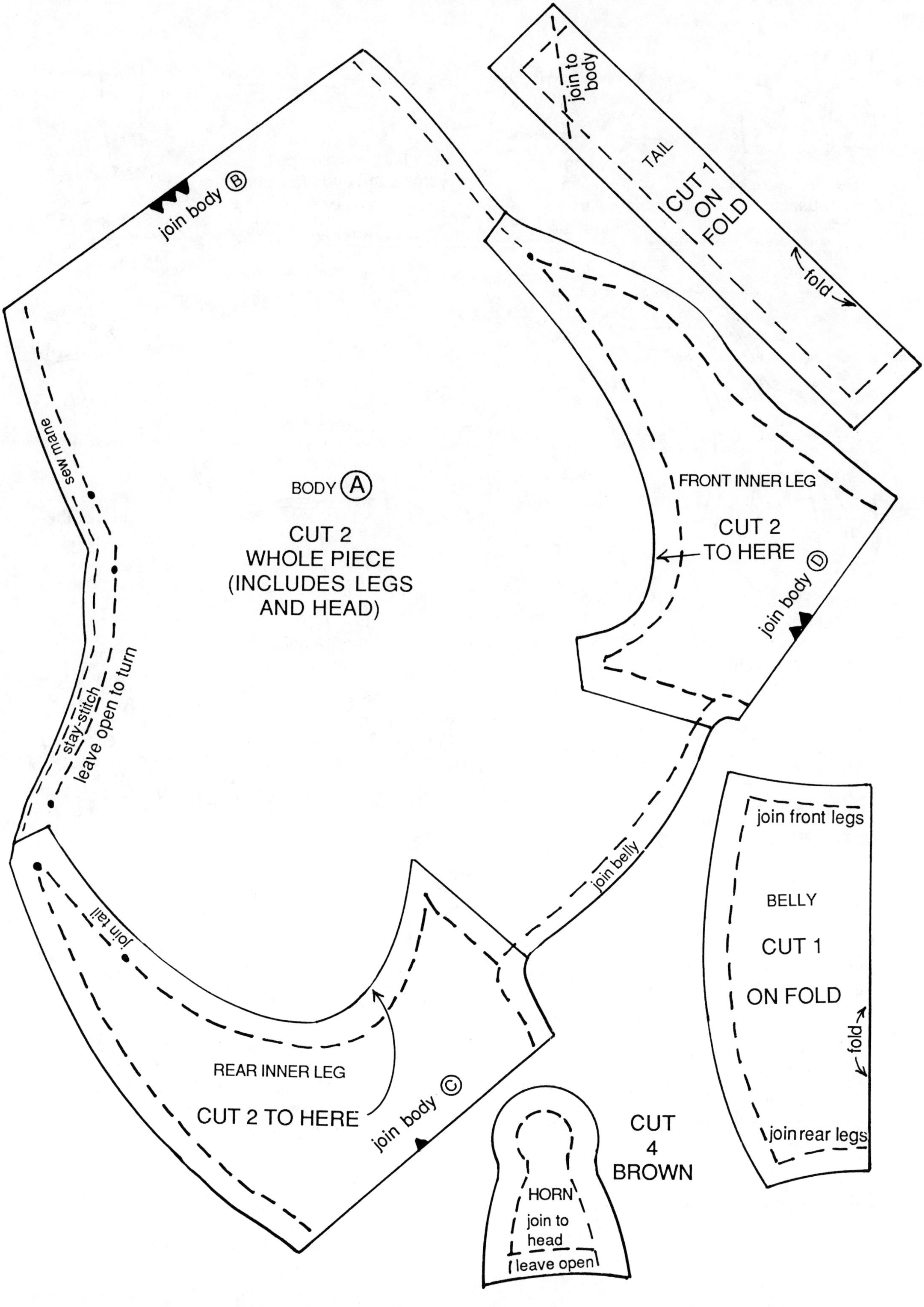
join to body
TAIL
CUT 1 ON FOLD
fold
join body B
sew mane
BODY A
CUT 2 WHOLE PIECE (INCLUDES LEGS AND HEAD)
stay-stitch
leave open to turn
FRONT INNER LEG
CUT 2 TO HERE
join body D
join belly
join tail
REAR INNER LEG
CUT 2 TO HERE
join body C
join front legs
BELLY
CUT 1
ON FOLD
fold
join rear legs
HORN
join to head
leave open
CUT 4 BROWN

DIRECTIONS

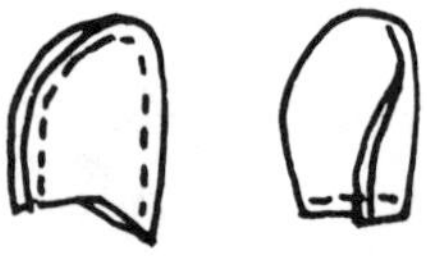

Sew ear, turn,
fold, baste
repeat

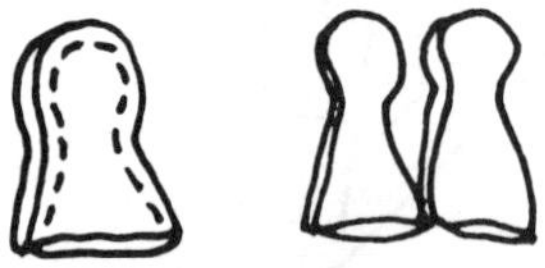

Sew horn,
clip seam
allowances,
repeat, turn

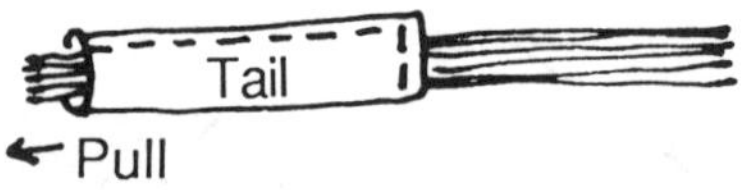

Sew tail over yarn, pull
yarn to turn and stuff, trim yarn.

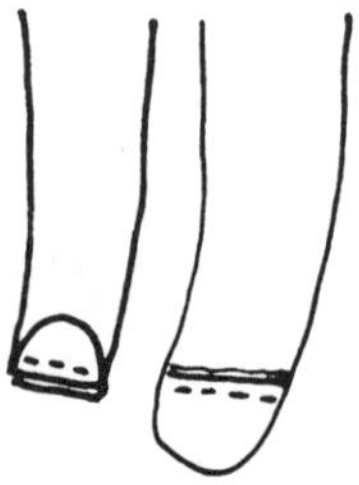

Sew feet to
all eight leg
pieces.

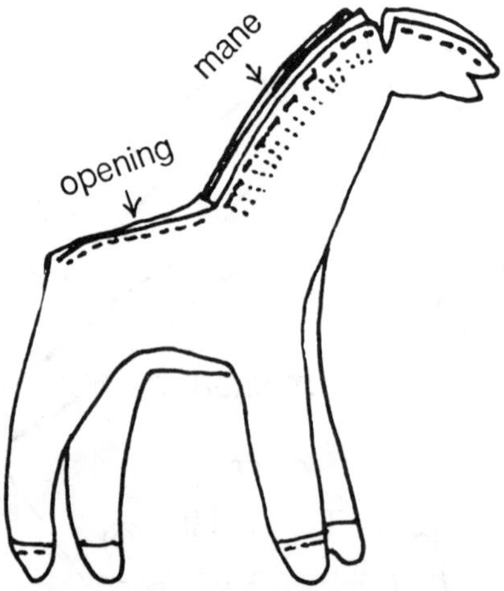

Stay-stitch opening,
baste mane to neck,
sew back seam, leave
opening to turn.

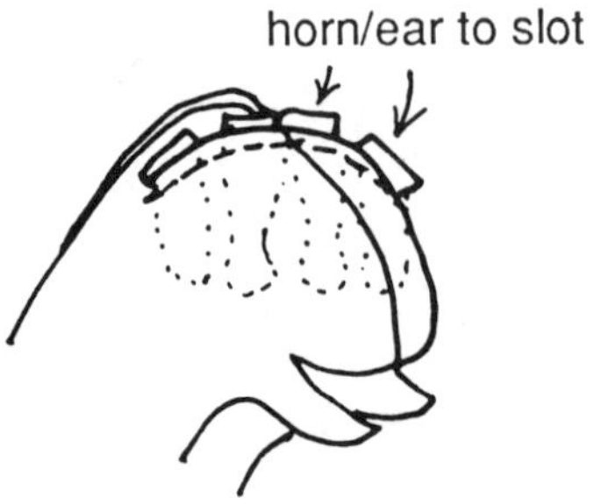

Baste ears, horns
to ear slot, stitch.

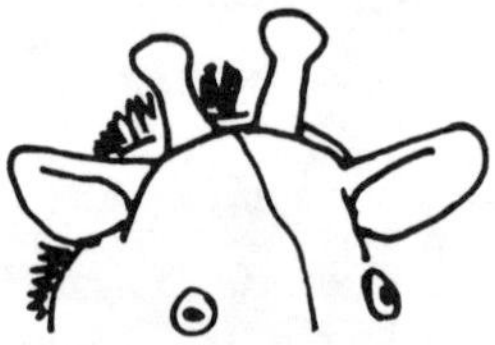

Turned view;
insert eyes.

Sew yarn loops
to mane strip

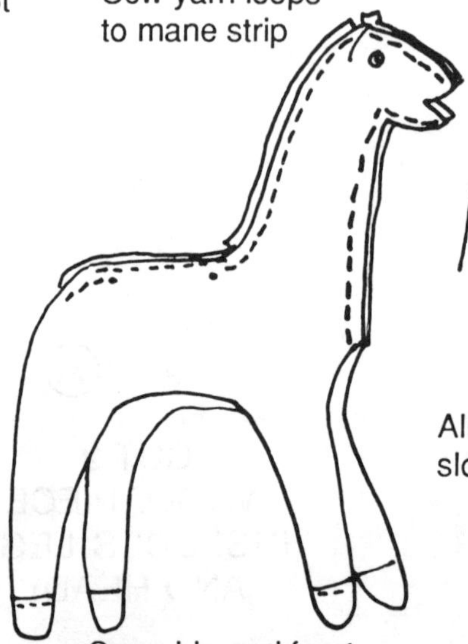

Sew chin and front
neck seam.

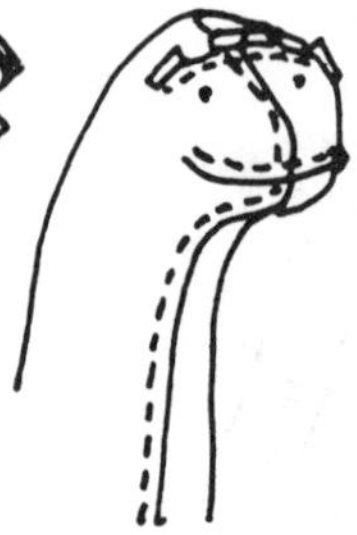

Align mouth
slot, stitch.

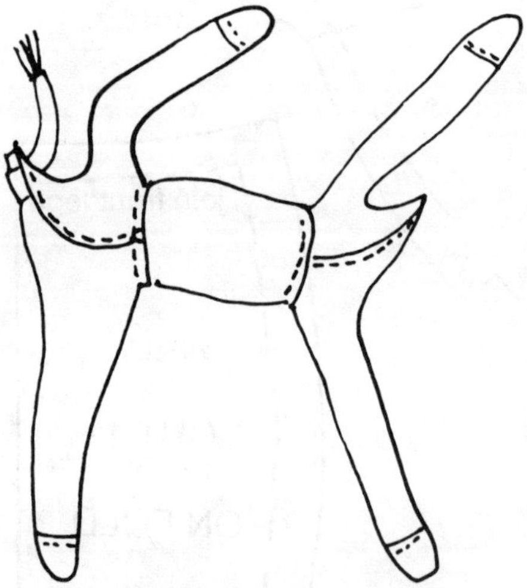

Baste tail to rear inner leg,
sew rear inner leg at crotch,
including tail. Sew front
inner legs at crotch. Join all
inner legs to belly.

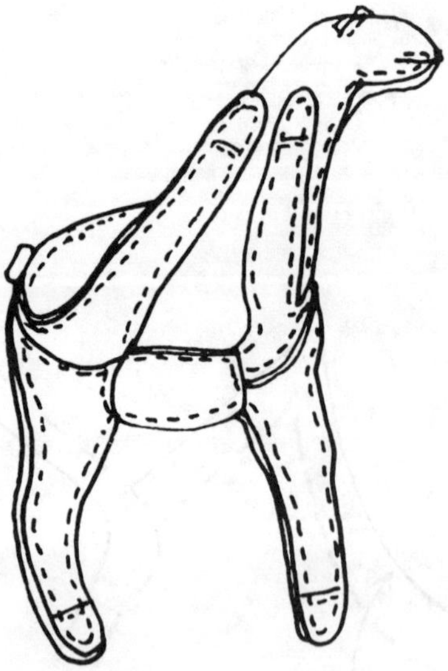

Join assembled underbody
to assembled body, matching
all four legs; turn.

Insert wrapped rods in legs;
stuff firmly.

Embroider mouth, nose.

B. Cut out all pieces.
C. Mark the EYE placement.

Step 2: Sewing the Added Pieces

A. Match EARS, right sides facing, and stitch, leaving the bottom open to turn. Turn, fold the EAR vertically as marked, and align the opening edges. Baste. Repeat for the other EAR.
B. Match two HORNS and stitch. Carefully turn this tiny piece. Repeat for the other HORN.
C. To make the TAIL, begin by cutting 36 inches of brown yarn and fold twice into four strands 9 inches long. Fold the TAIL lengthwise over the yarn, leaving 1 inch of yarn protruding at the top, 5 inches out the end. Sew the TAIL, being careful not to sew the yarn in the seam. Leave one end open to turn. Stitch across the end centered on the yarn several times to anchor the yarns. Pull the short end of the yarn to turn and stuff the TAIL with yarn. Clip off the tassel end to 3 inches. Clip off the open end evenly.
D. For the MANE, cut a strip of fabric 8 inches long and ½ inch wide. Pack 1-inch loops of brown yarn closely together on the strip. Sew the loops to the strip along the edge of the loops. Baste the strip of loops to one side of the NECK BACK as marked with the strip folded out of the seam.
E. Sew all the FEET to the LEGS, eight in all.

Step 3: Making the Body

A. Stay-stitch the edges of the opening on the back of the BODY pieces. Align the BODY pieces, and sew the back seam from the tail for ½ inch, leave an opening for turning, and sew to the EAR SLOT. Include the MANE in this seam. Sew the HEAD top to the MOUTH SLOT.
B. Pin or baste the EARS and the HORNS to the EAR SLOT. Align the EAR SLOT raw edges and stitch, including the EARS and HORNS in this seam.
C. Insert the EYES. Push the eye post through the EYE PLACEMENT HOLE and affix the washer firmly onto the post.
D. Sew the NECK FRONT seam from the MOUTH SLOT to the FRONT LEG joining.
E. Fold the MOUTH SLOT closed, and stitch.
F. Baste the TAIL to the REAR INNER LEG as marked, angling the TAIL downward. Sew the FRONT INNER LEGS together. Sew the REAR INNER LEGS together on the crotch seam, including the TAIL in this seam.
G. Sew the REAR INNER LEGS to the BELLY. Sew the FRONT INNER LEGS to the BELLY.
H. Align the assembled BELLY to the assembled BODY, matching all the LEGS. Sew from the TAIL to the shoulder, including the LEGS, and repeat. Clip inside corner seam allowances and turn.

Step 4: Finishing the Giraffe

A. For the LEG ARMATURES, cut the bamboo plant stake or dowel into four pieces, 8 inches long. Cut the cheesecloth into strips 1½ inches wide. Wrap each armature with two strips of cheesecloth for padding.
B. Wrap a wad of stuffing around the end of a LEG ARMATURE rod. Push the stuffing into one LEG, followed by the padded rod. Push additional stuffing into the LEG around the rod, pushing it in place with a narrow sharpened dowel. Fill the LEG completely and firmly, modeling ankles, knees, and shoulders. Repeat for each leg.
C. Pack small wads of stuffing into the HEAD, shaping it carefully so the EYES face forward a little. Fill the NECK firmly. Fill the entire animal, making sure to pack stuffing around the RODS inside the body so the LEGS angle outward properly. Sew the opening closed with invisible stitching. Use great care since this is an exposed seam.
D. If pipe-cleaner HORNS are used, bend little knobs on each end. Position the HORNS straight upward.
E. Using brown embroidery floss, embroider the MOUTH and NOSE.

HOGS are raised on farms all over the world and are prized for their usefulness. Hogs' smart noses are used by the French to sniff for underground truffles, a mushroomlike delicacy. They provide bacon (however unwillingly), ham, pork, and sausage meat; fat for lard, skin for leather, and bristle for brushes; and soap, glue, medicines, and more.

Hogs aren't stupid just because they like to wallow in the mud; they rank as smarter than horses, cattle and sheep in animal intelligence. Pink hogs have sparse bristly hair and little pigmentation in their skin, so wallowing in mud keeps the bright sun off.

Not all hogs are pink. The Berkshire and Poland China breeds are black with white or brown feet. Durocs are rusty red, Spotted Poland Chinas have large black spots on white, and Hampshires are black with a white "jacket" on their shoulders.

A hog less than ten weeks old is called a pig. Piglets can make affectionate pets, but grown up you may have an 800-pound hog in the house.

NOTE: This pattern makes up readily, requiring special care only for turning the tail and making the divided hoof. Instructions are given for making both a simple and a cleft hoof. The small hog measures 11 inches long and 6½ inches high. The big one twice the size takes 4 times as much fabric, 8 times as much stuffing, and is much easier to sew because of wider seam allowances and larger pieces.

Materials

BODY, UNDERBODY, FRONT INNER LEG, REAR INNER LEG, TAIL, EARS, HOOVES, and SNOUT: 11 by 17 inches pink felt, printed cotton, or velveteen. (For velveteen or any fraying fabric, staystitch along the edges of the opening or along all raw edges before cutting out. Also reinforce corners that might pull out.)

EYES: ⅜-inch (9 mm) pink or amber plastic post-and-washer eyes

THREAD: Matching sewing thread, dark pink embroidery floss

TAIL: 12 inches matching yarn to turn and stuff

STUFFING: 6 ounces fiberfill

EARS: 4 by 4 inches contrasting fabric for ear fronts

Optional: 4 by 4 inches Pellon interfacing

PATTERN

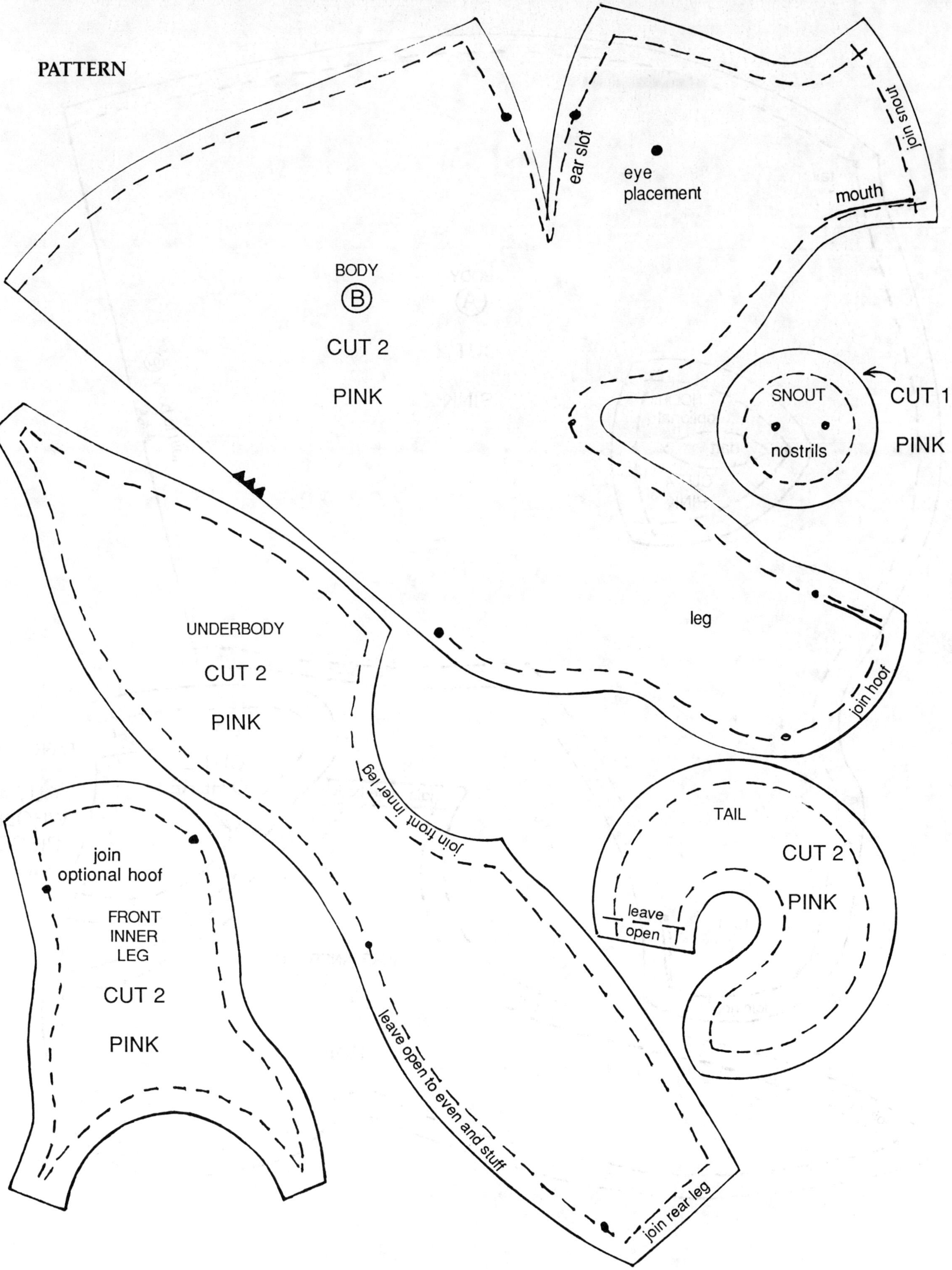

ear slot
eye placement
join snout
mouth
BODY
B
CUT 2
PINK
SNOUT
nostrils
CUT 1
PINK
leg
join hoof
UNDERBODY
CUT 2
PINK
join front inner leg
leave open to even and stuff
join rear leg
join optional hoof
FRONT INNER LEG
CUT 2
PINK
TAIL
CUT 2
PINK
leave open

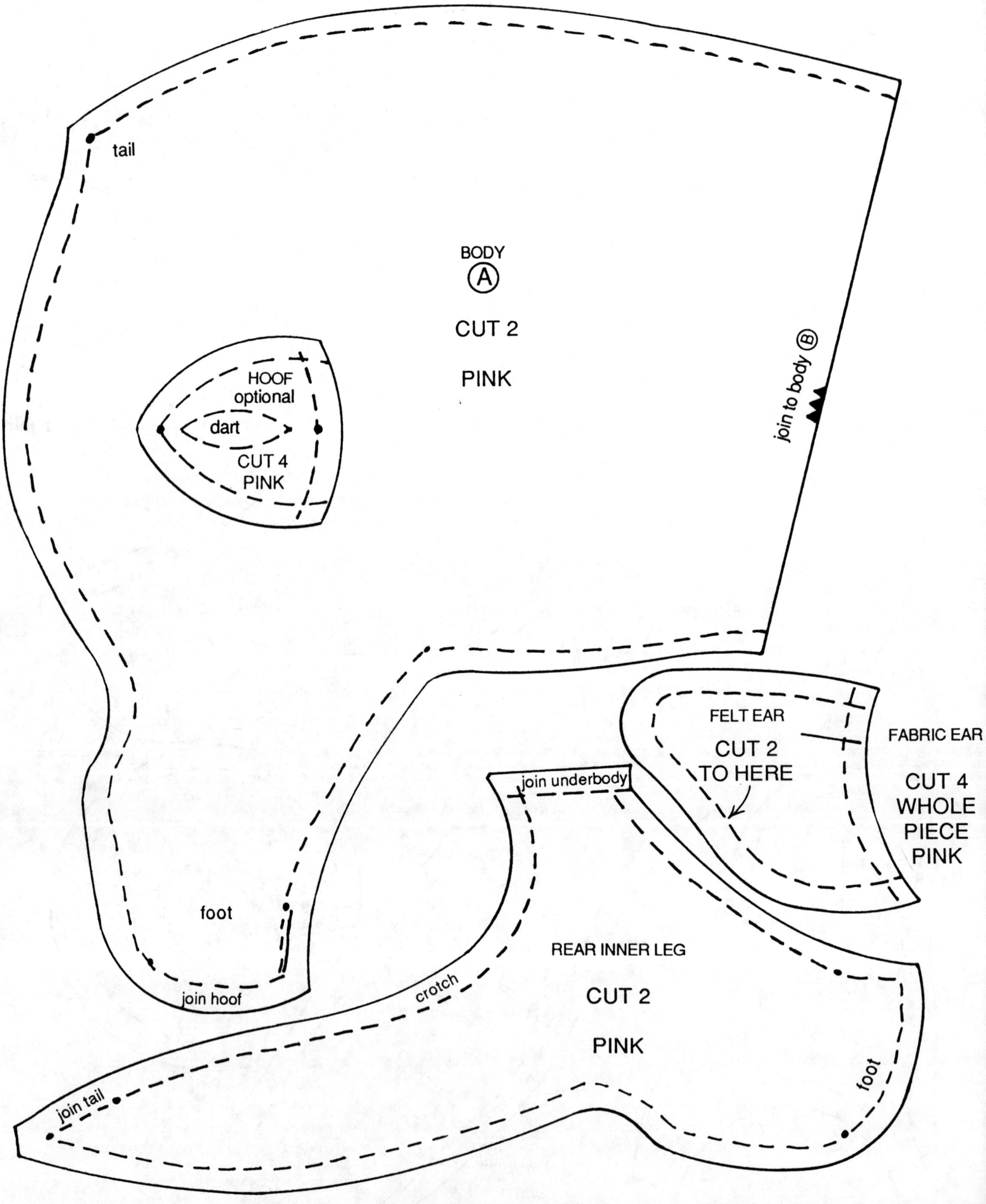
tail
BODY
A
CUT 2
PINK
join to body B
HOOF
optional
dart
CUT 4
PINK
FELT EAR
CUT 2
TO HERE
FABRIC EAR
CUT 4
WHOLE
PIECE
PINK
join underbody
foot
REAR INNER LEG
CUT 2
PINK
join hoof
crotch
join tail
foot

Tools

A chopstick or dowel, embroidery needle

Pattern Pieces

BODY A and B (2) (given in two pieces), UNDERBODY (2), FRONT INNER LEG (2), REAR INNER LEG (2), TAIL (2), SNOUT (1), EAR (2 or 4), HOOF (4)

Step 1: Cutting the Pieces

A. Cut out all pieces. Cut only two ears for single layer felt ears. For velveteen or pile fabric cut each piece unfolded and separately to avoid mistakes.

B. Mark EYE placement.

Step 2: Sewing the Hog

A. Place two EAR pieces together face to face. Stitch, leaving the end open to turn. If INTERFACING is used, pin to the back of one EAR before stitching and sew into the seam. Trim the seam allowances, and turn. Repeat for the other EAR. Fold the EAR vertically as marked and pin or baste.

B. Pin the TAILS together and stitch, leaving the end open. This piece is difficult to turn. To help turn and stuff at the same time, sew the TAIL over yarn as shown. To do this, fold the yarn into a 6-inch piece and place it on the TAIL, face up, with 3 inches extending from the tip end. Lay the other TAIL piece on top, face down, matching the edges. Stitch around the TAIL without stitching the yarn in the seam (except at the tip), and leave the end open. Pull on the yarn sticking out the open end of the TAIL to turn. The yarn at the tip will follow and become stuffing. Clip off the exposed yarn.

C. Place the BODY pieces face to face, and stitch the back seam from TAIL to SNOUT.

Optional: For machine-embroidered EYES, sew them before sewing the BODIES together.

D. Pin the EARS in the EAR SLOT with the fold toward the center seam and facing the SNOUT. Sew the SLOT closed, tapering carefully over the EARS at each end.

E. Pin the TAIL to the REAR INNER LEG. Align the REAR INNER LEGS and stitch the crotch seam.

F. Stay-stitch the edges of the UNDERBODY at the opening to avoid fraying. Match the UNDERBODY pieces face to face, and stitch the center seam, leaving the 3-inch opening for turning.

G. Join the FRONT INNER LEG to the UNDERBODY. Repeat. Sew the UNDERBODY to the REAR INNER LEGS.

H. Pin the BODY to the UNDERBODY, face to face, matching the LEGS carefully. For simple FEET, sew from the TAIL to the SNOUT around each leg. Repeat for the other side.

I. Join the SNOUT to the BODY.

J. Clip a tiny hole and insert the EYES.

Optional: To make cleft HOOVES, do not stitch between the dots marked on the feet when joining the UNDERBODY to the BODY. Open the FOOT and align the edges with the HOOF. Stitch the HOOF to the FOOT. Fold the HOOF along the DART line and stitch. If the dart is too difficult to do by machine, hand-stitch. Repeat for all four feet.

Step 3: Finishing the Hog

A. Clip the seam allowances to the stitch line at sharp corners or inside curves. Turn, using the chopstick or dowel to push out the hooves.

B. Begin to stuff by pushing small wads into the HOOVES with the chopstick. For the CLEFT HOOVES, fill each side carefully and fully. If the HOOF spreads, tack a few stitches to pull it inward. Fill the rest of the LEGS very firmly so they won't wrinkle. Fill the SNOUT firmly. Continue to stuff, adding small soft wads to build the hog shape. Stuff each end fully before filling the middle. Use the chopstick to adjust or add filling as you stuff. Push firm wads into the tops of each LEG for strength. Stuff very firmly. Remember, it's a pig!

C. Use invisible stitching to sew opening closed.

D. Embroider the MOUTH with a chain stitch. Sew two large French knots for NOSTRILS. If you made simple FEET, embroider a half-inch verticle line for the cleft in the HOOF.

DIRECTIONS

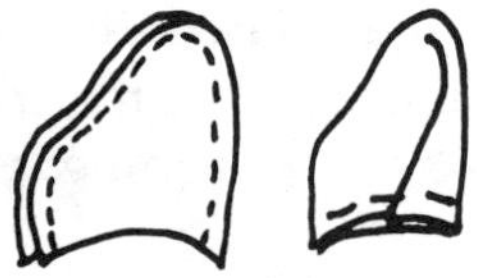

Sew ears, turn and fold.

Lay tails over yarn;
sew tail. Pull yarn
to turn and stuff.

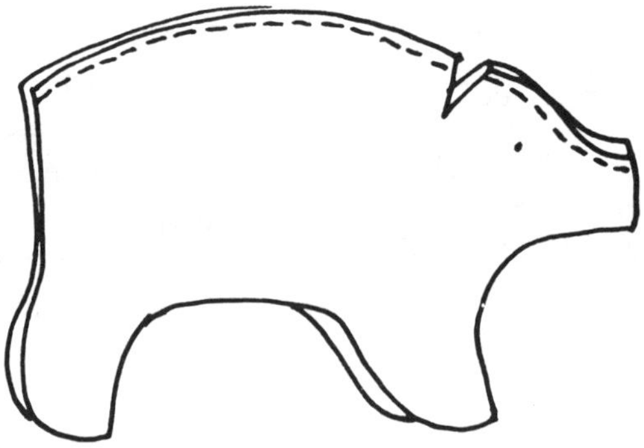

Sew back seam to snout.

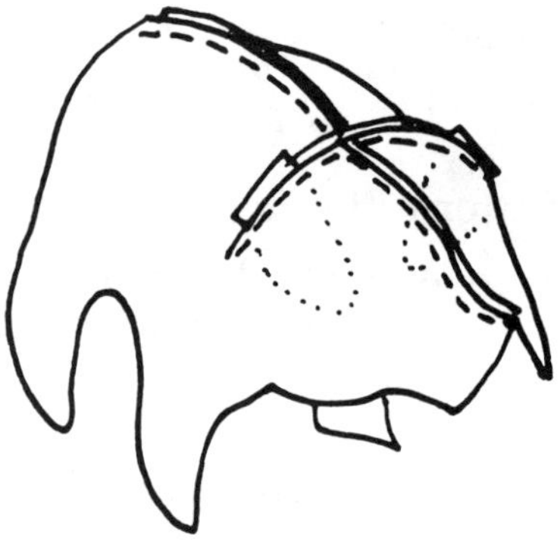

Pin folded ears in slot, sew,
tapering seam carefully.

Pin tail on rear
inner legs, sew crotch.

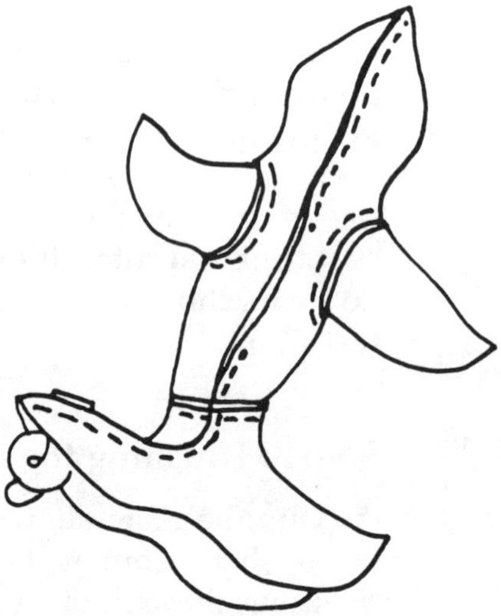

Stay-stitch center underbody
seam. Join underbody, leaving
a 3-inch opening to turn. Join
front inner legs and rear inner
legs to underbody.

Sew underbody to body, joining
all legs. Sew feet closed or add hooves.

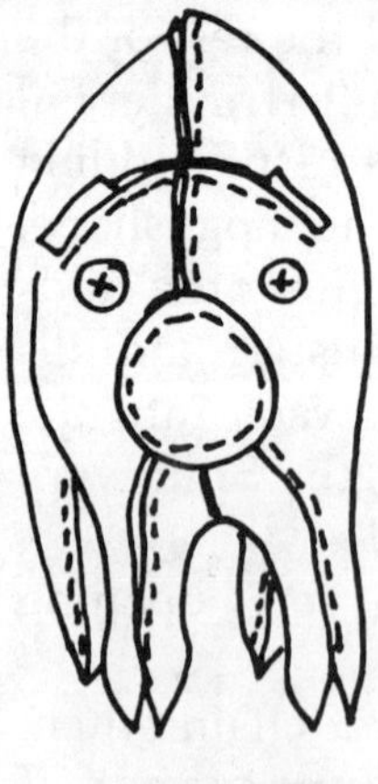

Insert eyes,
join snout.

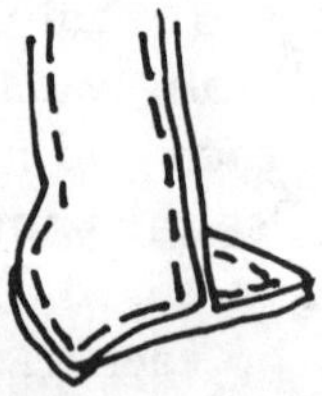

Optional hooves:
Leave feet open as marked.
Align foot to hoof, sew.

Fold hoof
dart and sew.

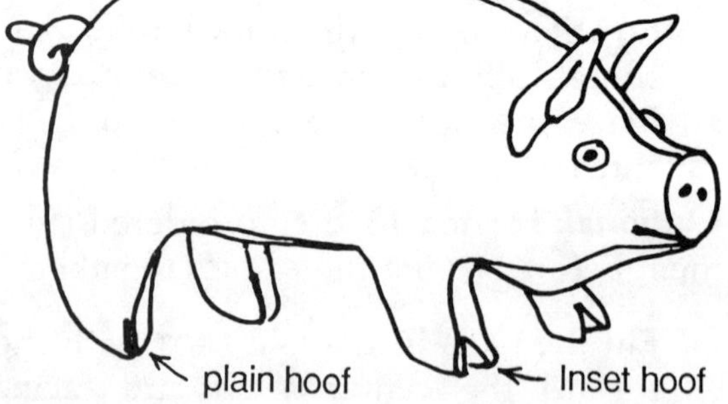

Turn, stuff, embroider mouth, nostrils
and hoof cleft.

IGUANAS are lizards that like it hot. These reptiles live in warm areas of the Eastern and Western Hemispheres. Although they resemble dragons or TV monsters with their scaly comblike crest down the back and large flap of skin on the throat, iguanas would rather run (or swim) than fight. The common iguana, found in the forests of tropical America, is a slow, timid creature that is easy to catch. It's common to see Mexican children dangling fat iguanas by the roadside for sale. Some common iguanas may grow to 5 feet, too long to dangle!

The several varieties of iguana have different characteristics. The rare Rhinoceros Iguana from Haiti has three blunt horns on his snout. The tiny Zebra-Tailed Lizard who lives in our southwest desert has a thick body with a zebra-striped tail. The Marine Iguana, native to the Galapagos Islands, is the only lizard known to feed in the sea surf.

NOTE: Close to life-size (for some iguanas), this one measures 17 inches long and 3 inches high. Those tiny toes may be difficult to turn and the fin tricky to attach, so three options are given. Of course it will be much easier to make if you double the size, or sew in a fabric such as felt, calico, or even velveteen rather than this unusual sequin-covered fabric. It's an elasticized knit fashion fabric with a continuous string of sequins tacked to the surface, making it difficult to cut accurately, machine-stitch, or turn. For best results, stitch seams with a narrow zig-zag stitch to avoid pulled seams, and anchor sequin thread ends. Although the sew-

PATTERN

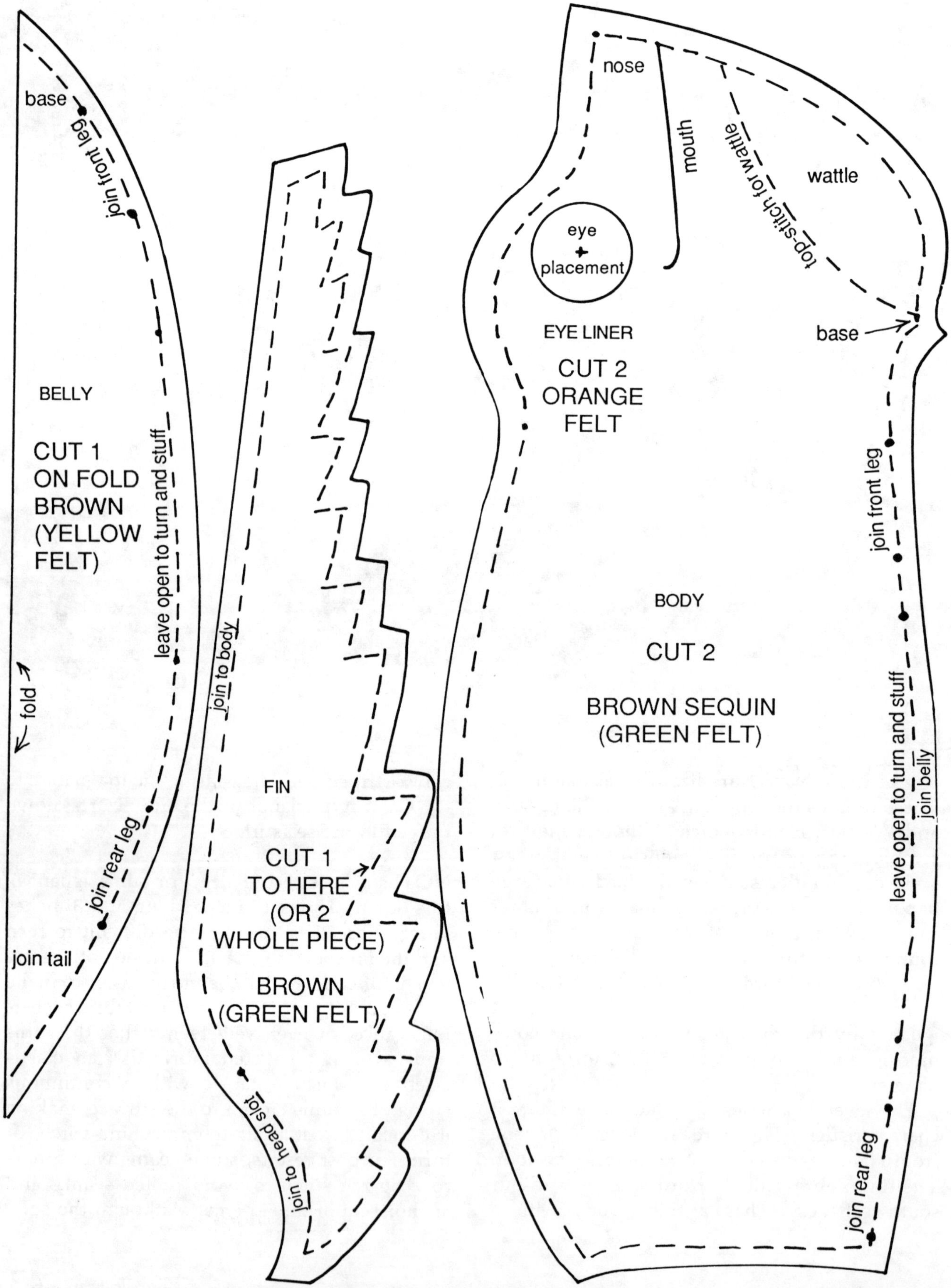

base
join front leg
BELLY
CUT 1
ON FOLD
BROWN
(YELLOW
FELT)
leave open to turn and stuff
fold
join rear leg
join tail
join to body
FIN
CUT 1
TO HERE
(OR 2
WHOLE PIECE)
BROWN
(GREEN FELT)
join to head slot
nose
mouth
top-stitch for wattle
wattle
eye
placement
base
EYE LINER
CUT 2
ORANGE
FELT
BODY
CUT 2
BROWN SEQUIN
(GREEN FELT)
join front leg
leave open to turn and stuff
join belly
join rear leg

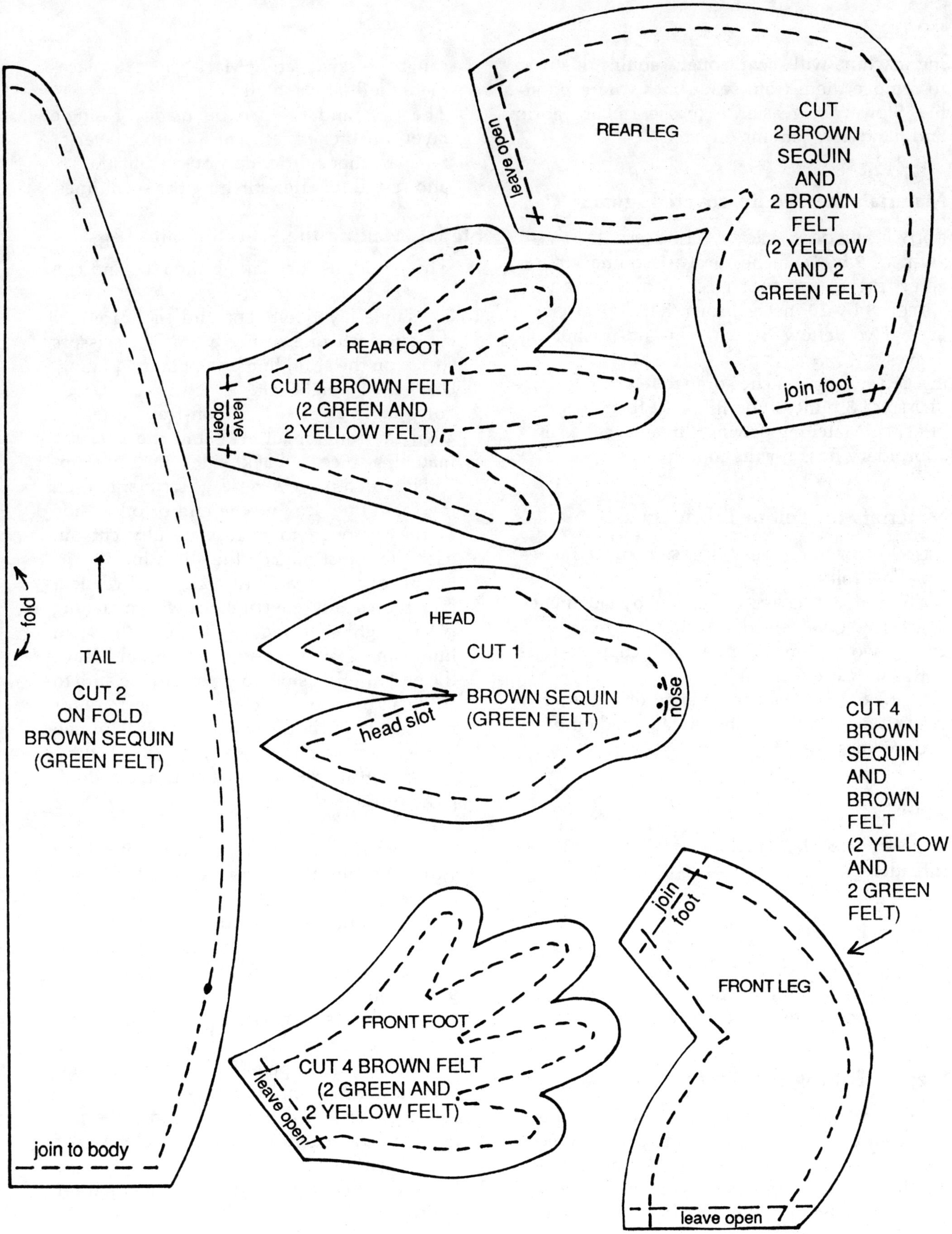
REAR LEG
CUT
2 BROWN
SEQUIN
AND
2 BROWN
FELT
(2 YELLOW
AND 2
GREEN FELT)
leave open
join foot
REAR FOOT
CUT 4 BROWN FELT
(2 GREEN AND
2 YELLOW FELT)
leave open
fold
TAIL
CUT 2
ON FOLD
BROWN SEQUIN
(GREEN FELT)
join to body
HEAD
CUT 1
BROWN SEQUIN
(GREEN FELT)
head slot
nose
CUT 4
BROWN
SEQUIN
AND
BROWN
FELT
(2 YELLOW
AND
2 GREEN
FELT)
FRONT LEG
join foot
leave open
FRONT FOOT
CUT 4 BROWN FELT
(2 GREEN AND
2 YELLOW FELT)
leave open

ing machine will sew through sequins, it's best to remove them from seam lines where possible. Slower, but easier, is to use a plain fabric and hand-sew sequins on later.

Materials for Sequin-covered Iguana

BODY, TAIL, UPPER FRONT LEG, UPPER REAR LEG, HEAD: 9 by 20 inches brown sequined fabric

BELLY, FIN, UNDER FRONT LEG, UNDER REAR LEG, FEET: 8 by 20 inches brown felt

EYES: Two yellow ½-inch post-and-washer cat eyes

EYE LINER: 1 by 2 inches orange felt

STUFFING: 3 ounces fiberfill, yarn for toes

THREAD: Matching sewing thread, yellow embroidery floss for the mouth

Materials for Felt or Fabric Iguana

BELLY, UNDERLEGS, FEET SOLES: 8 by 9 inches yellow felt

BODY and ALL OTHER PARTS: 9 by 30 inches green felt, velveteen, or calico

EYES: Two yellow or green ½-inch post-and-washer cat eyes

EYE LINER: 1 by 2 inches orange or yellow felt

THREAD: Matching sewing thread, gold embroidery floss

Tools

Tapestry needle, crochet hook, and needle threader

Pattern Pieces

BODY (2), FIN (1 or 2), BELLY (1), EYE LINER (2), TAIL (2), REAR LEG (4), FRONT LEG (4), HEAD (1), REAR FOOT (2 or 4), FRONT FOOT (2 or 4)

Step 1: Cutting the Pieces

A. For the sequin-covered fabric with a knitted elasticized backing, trace the pattern pieces with tailor's chalk on the back side. Cut out the pieces carefully, using strong sharp scissors. Sequins will be cut and fall off, but can be resewn later. Mark the EYE placement, and clip a small hole.

B. The FEET and FIN can be made of single layer, unstitched felt. For a double layer of felt, or other fabric, do not cut out the FIN and FEET until after stitching the seam lines.

Step 2: Making the Feet, Fin, and Legs

A. Three options for making the FEET and FIN:

1. For single-layer felt FEET and FIN, carefully cut out each one, using a smooth scissors stroke on the seam line except at the joining. Use heavy-weight felt.
2. For double layer felt or non-fraying fabric, align the four uncut FEET and the FIN with matching pieces, back sides facing. Topstitch with a narrow zig-zag (satin stitch) on the seam line, leaving the end or other side of the FIN open to turn. Carefully cut out each piece just outside the stitch line.
3. For turned FEET and FIN, align four uncut FEET pieces and one FIN piece with matching pieces, right sides facing. Stitch on the seam line using a short straight stitch, and leave the end or other side open to turn. Be sure to stitch across the inside angle of the TOES for turning. Trim the seam allowances, clipping to the seam line between the TOES and turn. Use a knitting needle to help turn, but don't poke through the fabric.

B. To stuff double-layer FEET, thread matching yarn in a blunt tapestry needle. Insert the needle into the open end of the FOOT, emerging out the TOE end. Clip off the yarn and pull the ends back into the TOE. Repeat for each TOE until the FEET are stuffed to your liking.

C. Match the REAR UPPER LEG with the REAR UNDER LEG. Stitch the side seams, leaving the top and bottom open. Turn right side out. Turn a narrow hem and tuck it inward. Insert the completed REAR FOOT into the LEG hole and stitch across the joining. Repeat for the other LEGS.

D. Stuff the LEGS, leaving the top unstuffed for seaming.

DIRECTIONS

Three ways to sew feet (or fins).

1. Single layer.

Cut foot (for fin) from thick felt on seam line.

2. Double layers

Stitch foot (or fin) on seam line right side up. Cut outside, stitch line, and stuff.

3. Double layers

Sew seam on reverse side, trim, turn. Sew stuffing with yarn on tapestry needle.

Sew both leg seams; turn.

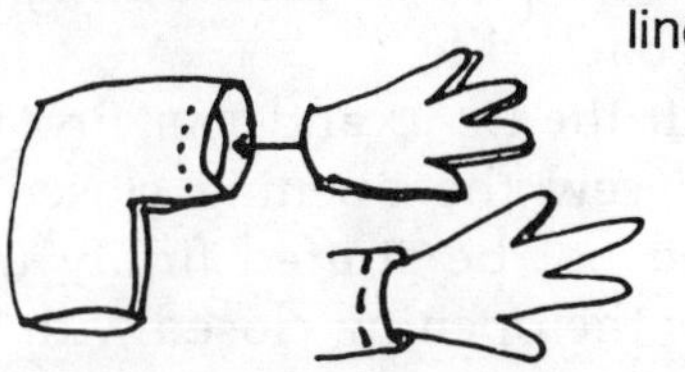

Turn small hem, insert foot and top-stitch joining; stuff.

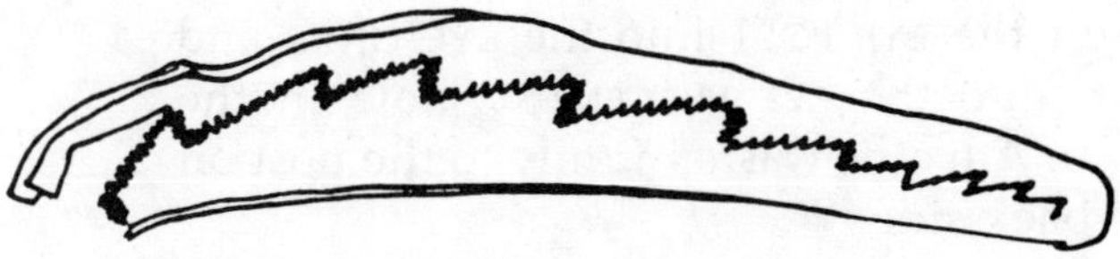

For fin, seam and turn or top-stitch and trim.

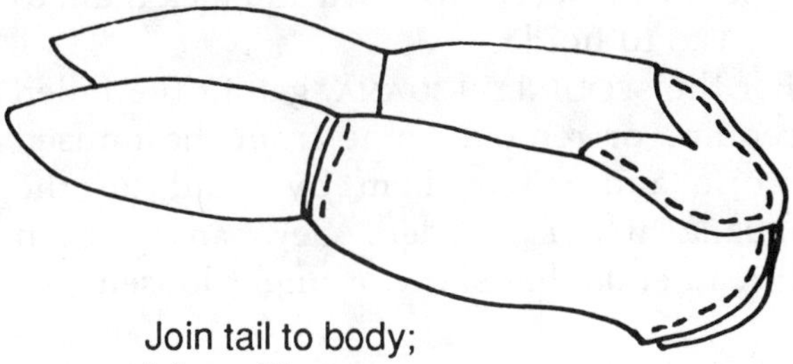

Join tail to body; join wattle seam; join head to body.

Insert fin into head slot and back seam, and stitch.

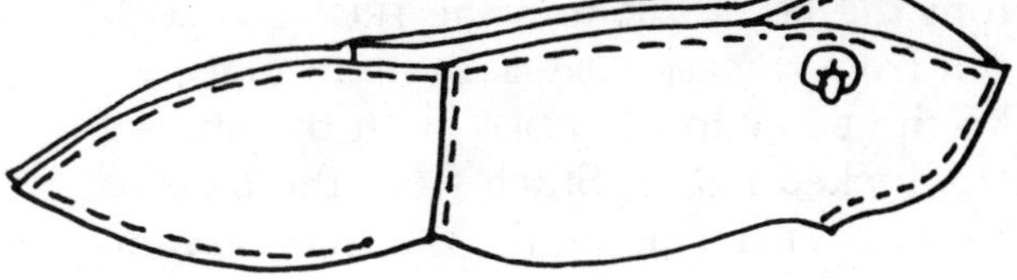

Sew tail seam.

Baste stuffed legs to belly.

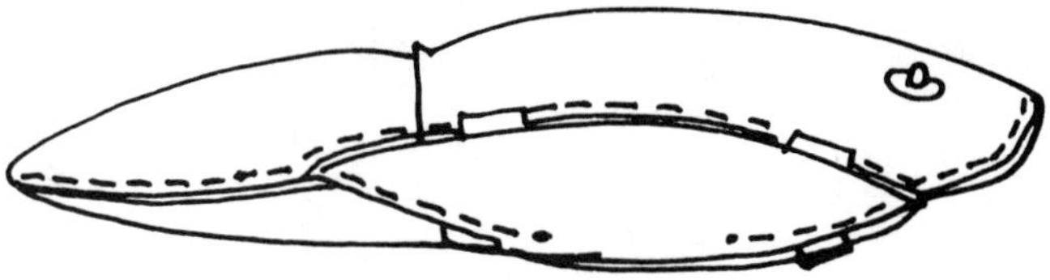

Tuck in legs; join belly to body; leave opening.

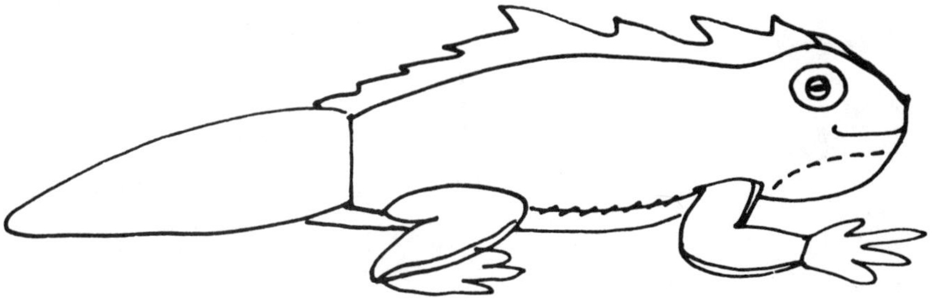

Turn, top-stitch wattle, stuff. Sew foot to leg; sew opening closed; embroider mouth, nostrils.

Step 3: Making the Body

A. Align the TAIL with the BODY, and stitch. Repeat for the other side.

B. Align the BODY pieces at the WATTLE seams and stitch from the BASE to the NOSE.

C. Open the joined BODY pieces and align the HEAD at the NOSE. Stitch the HEAD to the BODY.

D. Pin the completed FIN into the HEAD SLIT and continue to align with the BODY BACK to the TAIL. If the seam is difficult to pin, baste it to one side. Stitch the HEAD SLIT and BODY BACK seam, including the FIN.

E. Insert the EYE POST into the EYE LINER and then into the EYE PLACEMENT hole in the HEAD. Affix the washer firmly to the post on the back side.

Step 4: Attaching the Legs

A. Align the stuffed LEGS on the BELLY as marked, pinning the REAR LEGS 1¼ inches from the BELLY TIP, and the FRONT LEGS ¾ inch from the BELLY BASE. Baste in place.

B. Pin the BELLY to the BODY with the stuffed LEGS tucked inside. Stitch from the BASE to the BELLY TIP including the LEG in this seam. Repeat for the other side, leaving a three-inch opening for turning and stuffing.

Step 5: Finishing the Iguana

A. Trim and clip any seam allowances to avoid pulls. Turn. Top-stitch by hand or machine to make the WATTLE, sewing from ½ inch below the MOUTH to the BASE.

B. For the SEQUINED IGUANA, use the crochet hook or the wire needle-threader to pull the loose sequin threads through the fabric to the back side.

C. Stuff the HEAD and TAIL first. Fill the BODY, and sew the opening closed. This animal need not be stuffed firmly unless desired. Sew the opening closed with hidden stitching.

D. Use the yellow EMBROIDERY FLOSS to chain-stitch the MOUTH. Sew two French knots for the NOSTRILS.

E. Fold the REAR FEET forward and tack them to the LEG to hold.

F. For the SEQUINED IGUANA, gather the fallen sequins or remove some from the unused fabric and stitch them by hand on the iguana where needed. Sew any sequin thread ends that show or might loosen.

JAGUARS once roamed the American Southwest, but now live only in Mexico, and Central and South America. Jaguars and pumas are the largest of the New World cats, slightly smaller but heavier than the bobcat, and close in strength to the larger African tiger and lion. A male can grow to about eight feet long including his 30-inch tail, and weigh nearly 300 pounds. The jaguar, "El Tigre," as the Mexicans call him, is considered the fiercest big cat in the Western Hemisphere.

Some South American jaguars are coal black, like the toy animal shown. Most have a spotted pattern of black rings on their tawny fur, similar to a leopard, but the jaguar's rings have a spot in the center. This marking so resembles a design daubed on with fingertips that an old African legend says the cat got his spots that way. Jaguars are becoming increasingly rare because they require a specialized tropical habitat. Their favorite food seems to be river caymen, South America's alligator.

NOTE: The finished jaguar measures 6½ by 3 by 14 inches. This pattern can be used to make several different big cats since they are similar in shape. To make a tiger, for example, paint, embroider, or appliqué black stripes on orange body fabric with white for the belly and muzzle. For a lion, add a long-haired brown mane on the neck of a tan body with a white muzzle. For a leopard, make the same pattern as follows without the center spot in the ring of spots. A panther is all black. A puma is tan with a white chin.

PATTERN

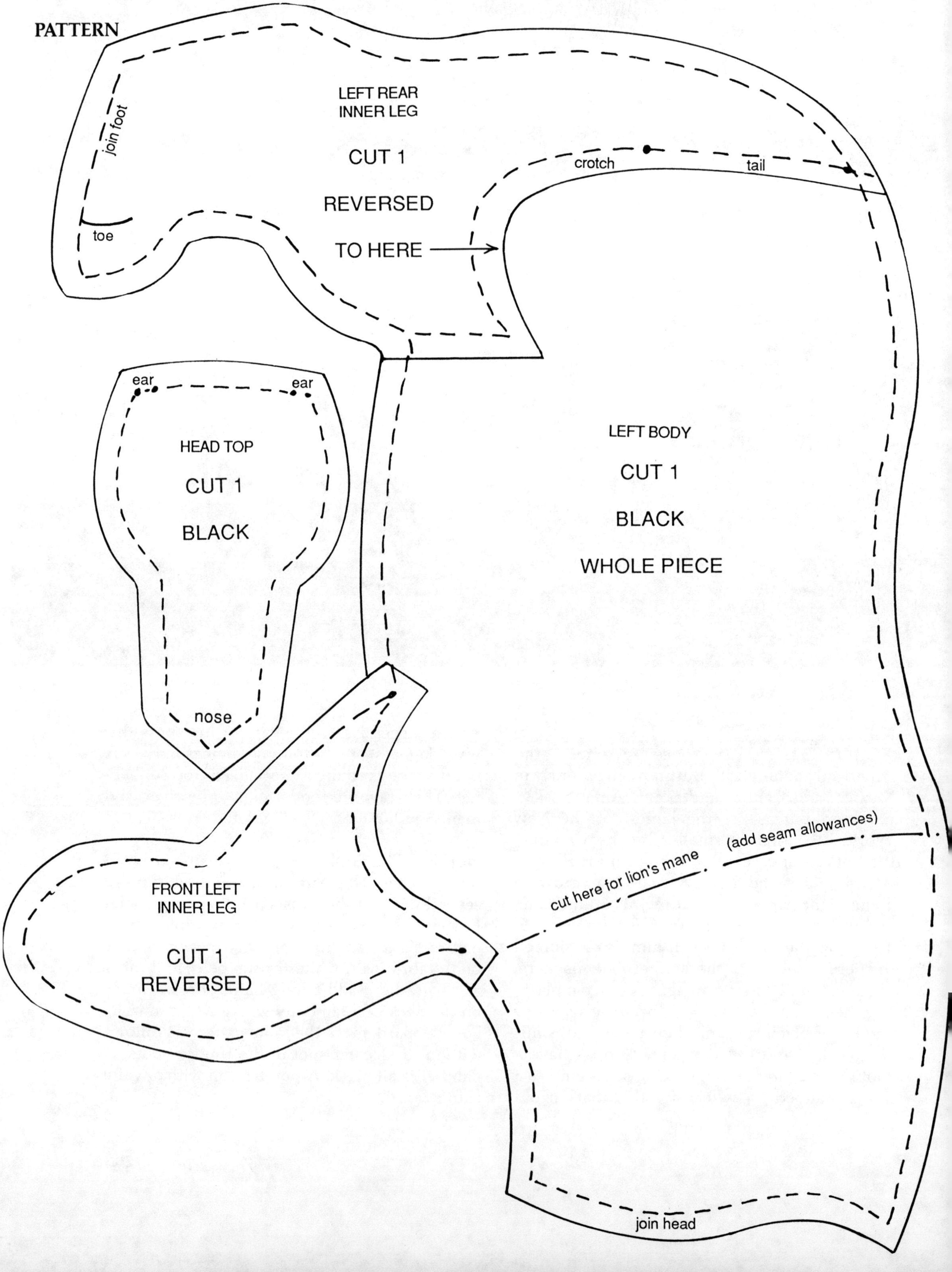

LEFT REAR INNER LEG
CUT 1
REVERSED
TO HERE
join foot
toe
crotch
tail
ear
ear
HEAD TOP
CUT 1
BLACK
nose
LEFT BODY
CUT 1
BLACK
WHOLE PIECE
(add seam allowances)
cut here for lion's mane
FRONT LEFT INNER LEG
CUT 1
REVERSED
join head

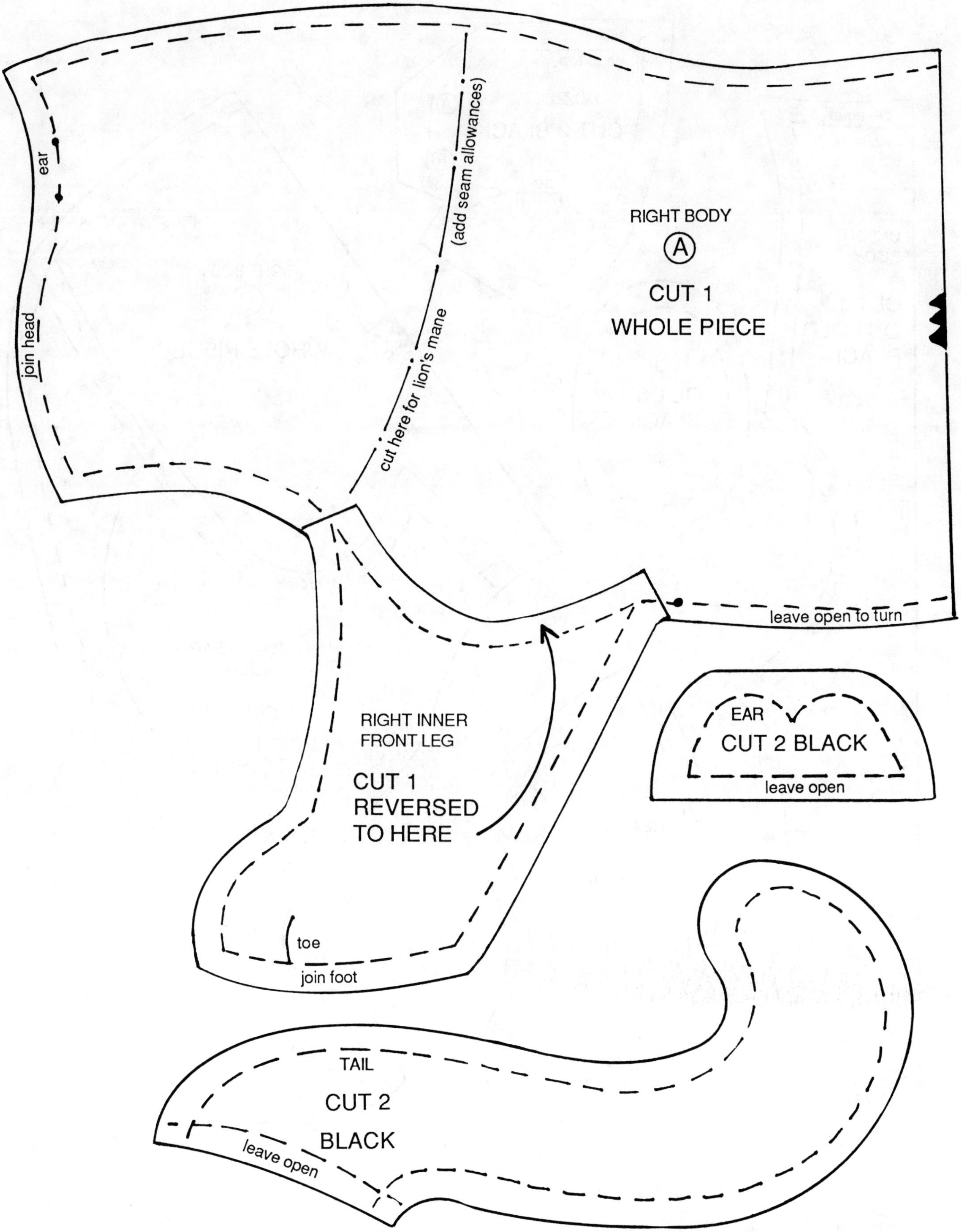
ear
join head
(add seam allowances)
cut here for lion's mane
RIGHT BODY
A
CUT 1
WHOLE PIECE
leave open to turn
RIGHT INNER
FRONT LEG
CUT 1
REVERSED
TO HERE
toe
join foot
EAR
CUT 2 BLACK
leave open
TAIL
CUT 2
BLACK
leave open

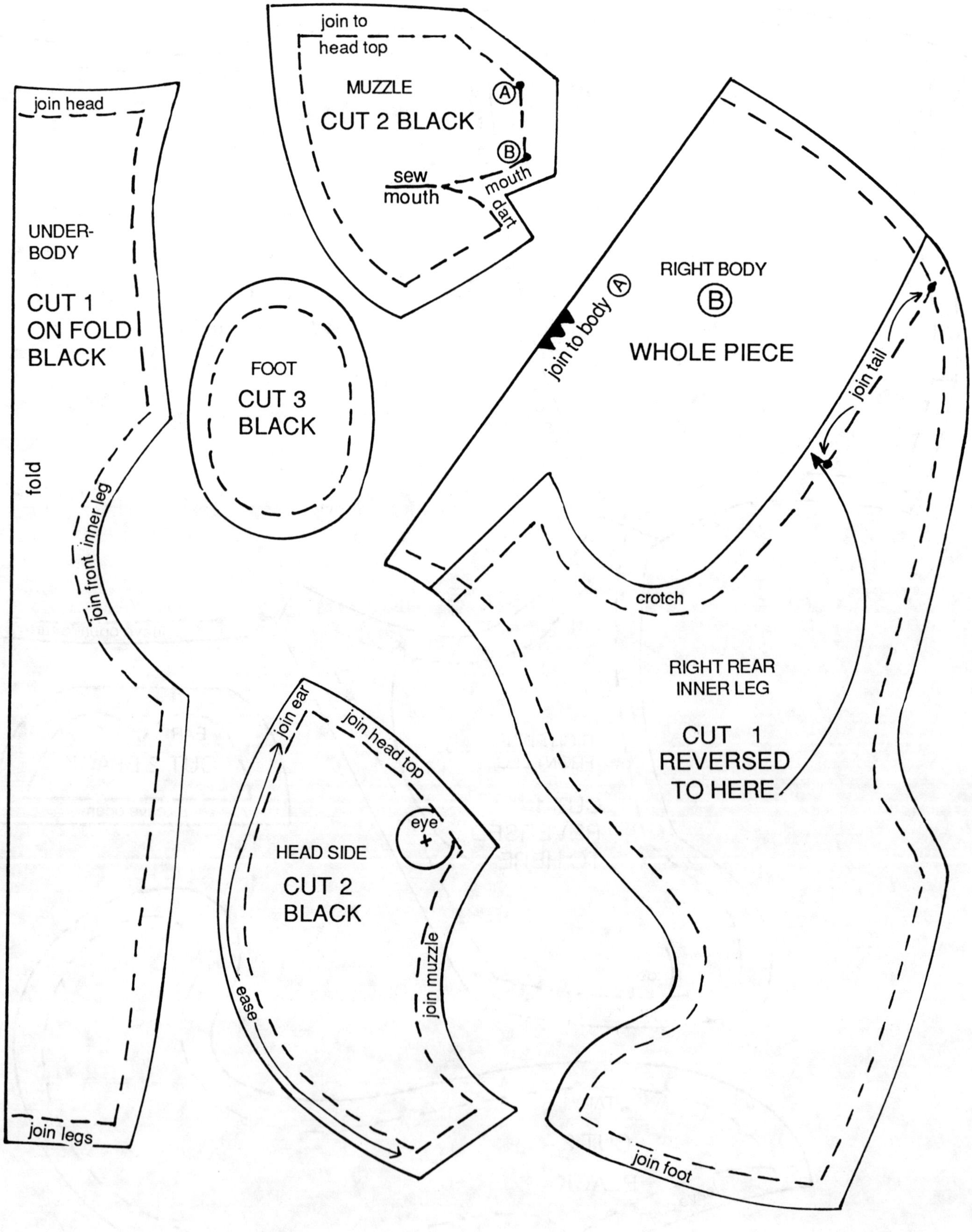

join to
head top
MUZZLE
CUT 2 BLACK
A
B
sew
mouth
mouth
dart
join head
UNDER-
BODY
CUT 1
ON FOLD
BLACK
fold
join front inner leg
join legs
FOOT
CUT 3
BLACK
join to body A
RIGHT BODY
B
WHOLE PIECE
join tail
crotch
RIGHT REAR
INNER LEG
CUT 1
REVERSED
TO HERE
join foot
join ear
join head top
eye
HEAD SIDE
CUT 2
BLACK
join muzzle
ease

Materials for Black Jaguar

BODY: 15 by 30 inches black velveteen or short-piled fur fabric
EYES: Two yellow ½-inch post-and-washer cat eyes
STUFFING: 6 ounces fiberfill
THREAD: Matching sewing thread, same for whiskers

Materials for Spotted Jaguar

BODY: 15 by 30 inches tawny pile fabric
SPOTS: Machine-embroider or print spots with black acrylic paint or textile paint using a pencil eraser to make a circle of five dots with one in the center (see directions)

Materials for Tiger

BODY 15 by 24 inches orange pile fabric
UNDERBODY, INNER LEGS, MUZZLE: 8 by 12 inches white matching fabric
STRIPES: Machine-embroider, paint, or appliqué black stripes

Materials for Male Lion

BODY: 15 by 30 inches tawny velveteen for most of animal
MANE AND TAIL TIP: 4 by 6 inches long-haired brown fur fabric
MUZZLE AND CHIN: 2½ by 5 inches white fur fabric
NOSE: Embroider a triangular black nose and a black mouth

Pattern Pieces

RIGHT BODY A and B (1) (given in two pieces), LEFT BODY (1), RIGHT INNER FRONT LEG (1), RIGHT INNER REAR LEG (1), LEFT INNER FRONT LEG (1), LEFT INNER REAR LEG (1), TAIL (2), EAR (2), HEAD SIDE (2), MUZZLE (2), UNDERBODY (1), FOOT (3), HEAD TOP (1)

Step 1: Cutting the Fabric

A. This pattern is not symmetrical. Be sure to reverse the INNER LEG pieces when cutting the pattern. Cut out all pieces. For fur fabrics trace the pattern on the reverse side. For pile fabrics like velveteen, make generous seam allowances since this fabric frays and pills.
B. Mark the EYE placement.

Optional: For the LION, cut across the BODY pattern as marked for the MANE and add seam allowances. For other animals cut pattern pieces from various colors as noted in the materials listing. For machine-embroidered stripes or spots, pin the pieces to be decorated to Pellon backing and embellish before assembly.

Step 2: Assembling the Small Pieces

A. Fold the EAR face to face and stitch. Taper the seam end on the fold smoothly, and leave the other end open to turn. Repeat for the other EAR.
B. Match the TAILS and stitch, leaving the end open to turn. Clip the seam allowances, turn and stuff lightly.
C. Run basting stitches along the curved HEAD SIDE seam allowance to ease. Align the MUZZLE with the HEAD SIDE and stitch. Repeat for the other side.
D. Sew the HEAD SIDE to the HEAD TOP, ending at point A on the MUZZLE. Join the other HEAD SIDE, ending at point B on the MUZZLE.
E. Match the HEAD SIDES and stitch from C to the MOUTH DART. Align the edges of the MOUTH DART and stitch. Baste the EARS to the HEAD. Insert the EYES.

Step 3: Making the Body

Optional: To make the LION sew the MANE to the BODY on each side.

A. Stay-stitch the seam allowance on the RIGHT BODY opening. Align the RIGHT AND LEFT BODY pieces and stitch the back seam from the TAIL to the HEAD.
B. Stay-stitch the seam allowances on the UN-

DIRECTIONS

Sew ears; trim, turn.

Sew tail; trim, turn, stuff.

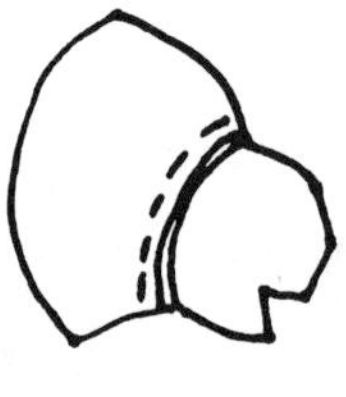

Sew muzzle to head side; repeat.

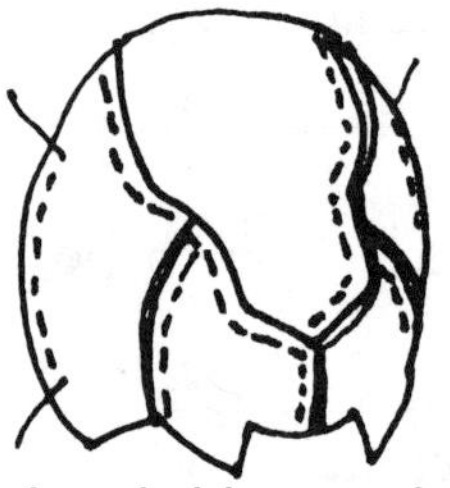

Sew head side muzzle to head top to Ⓐ, (nose). Sew other head side to Ⓑ (mouth). Sew gathering threads.

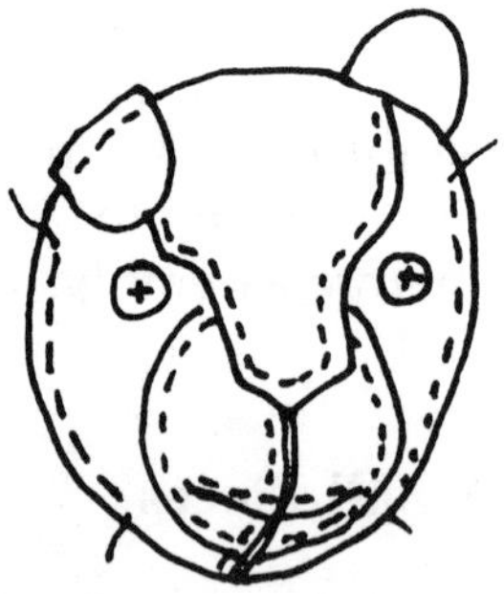

Sew chin seam to mouth dart. Align mouth dart and stitch; baste ears to head; insert eyes.

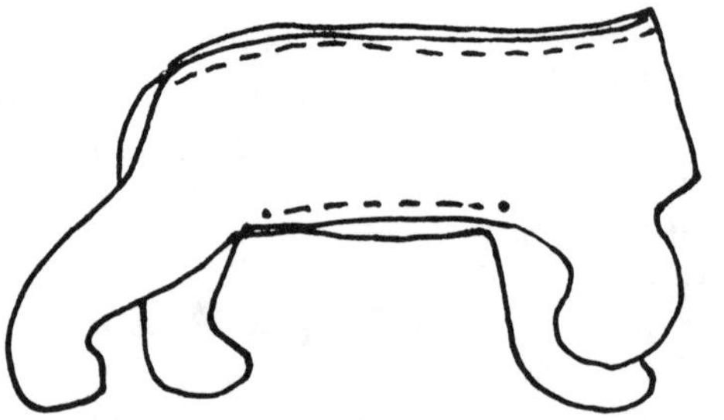

Stay-stitch opening, sew back seam from head to tail.

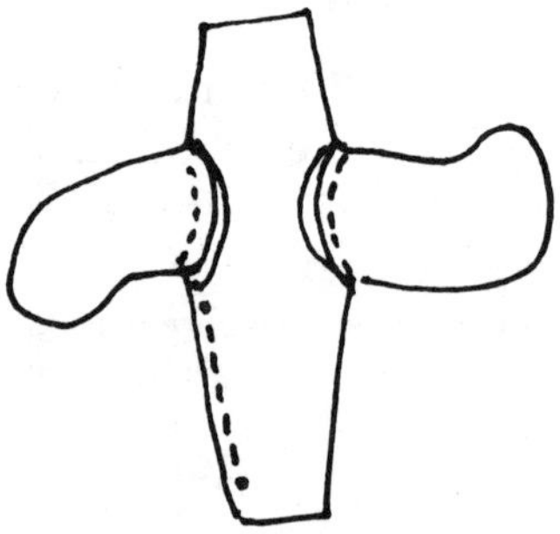

Stay-stitch opening, join front legs to underbody.

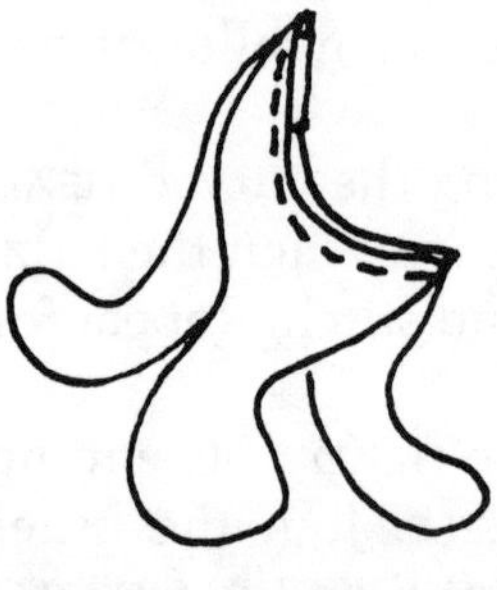

Baste tail to rear inner leg, join inner back legs at crotch, including tail.

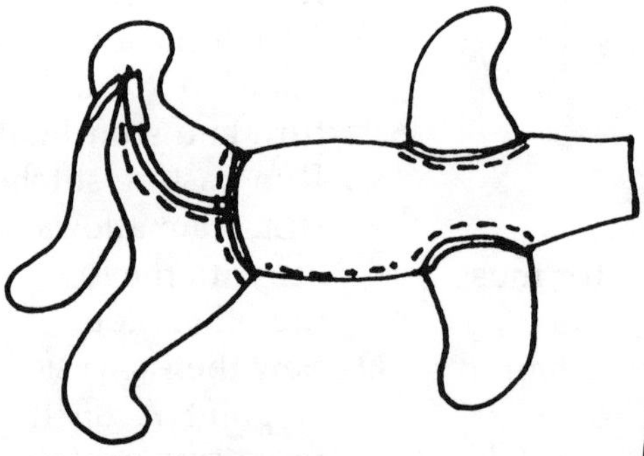

Sew inner back legs to underbody.

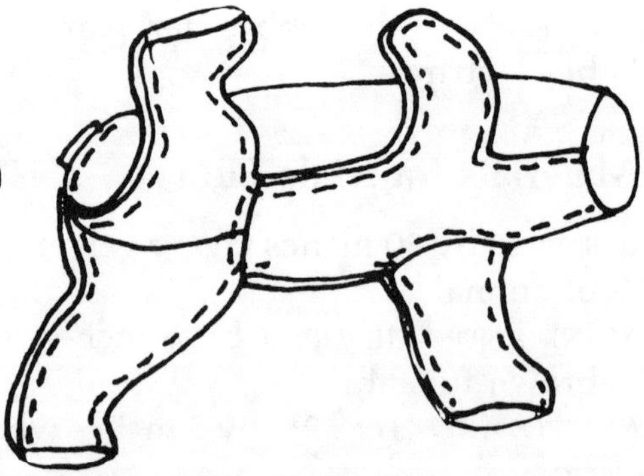

Join underbody to body, including legs.

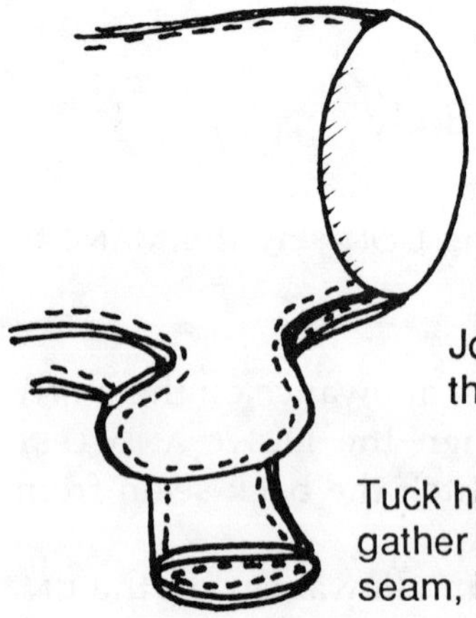

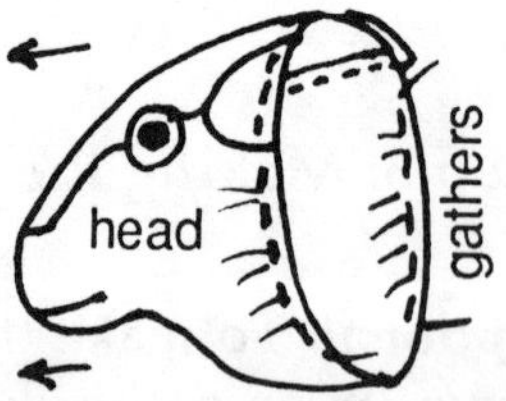

Join foot soles to three open legs.

Tuck head into neck, gather head, stitch neck seam, including ears.

Jaguar spot pattern

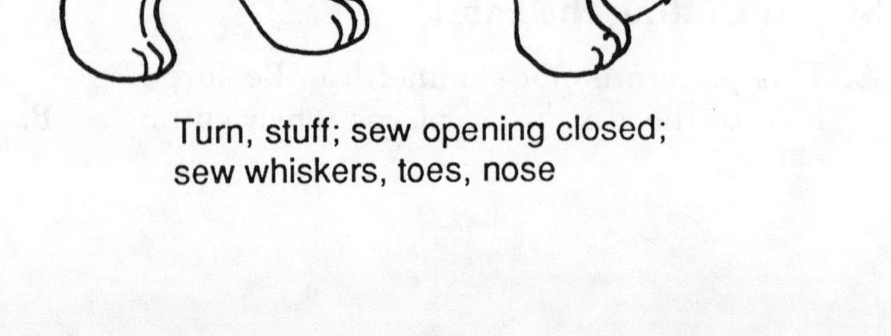

Turn, stuff; sew opening closed; sew whiskers, toes, nose

DERBODY right side opening. Join the FRONT INNER RIGHT LEG to the UNDERBODY and stitch. Join the FRONT INNER LEFT LEG to the UNDERBODY and stitch.

C. Baste the TAIL to one REAR INNER LEG as marked. Align the RIGHT and LEFT REAR INNER LEGS at the crotch and stitch including the TAIL in this seam.

D. Open the REAR LEGS flat, align with the UNDERBODY and stitch.

E. Align the UNDERBODY with the BODY, matching all four LEGS. Pin and stitch, leaving the stay-stitched opening for turning.

F. Turn the HEAD right side out and tuck it into the BODY aligning the neck edges. (No seams align.) Pull the HEAD SIDE ease threads to adjust the fit. Sew the HEAD to the BODY.

G. Match the FOOT to the opening at the bottom of the LEG and stitch. Repeat for the other two LEG openings.

Step 4: Finishing All the Big Cats

A. Clip any seam allowances that might pull when turned. Turn right side out.

B. Begin to stuff the LEGS first. Use small looses wads of fiberfill and push them in place with a stuffing rod or your fingers. Continue to fill the entire animal bit by bit, sculpturing the shape as you stuff. Pack the top of the LEGS firmly so they won't wrinkle. Sew the opening closed.

C. To make WHISKERS sew into the MUZZLE with a double thread knotted 1 inch from the end. Sew through the MUZZLE and knot the thread again tightly to the MUZZLE. Clip off at 1 inch. Repeat for four whiskers.

Optional: For light-colored cats embroider a triangular black NOSE. To make TOES use black thread to sew from the FOOT to the TOE, making three parallel vertical stitches. Pull firmly to form TOES.

KOALAS live only in Australia and eat only one certain kind of eucalyptus leaf. They spend their lives in the trees and have paws strangely adapted to climbing, with three toes forward and two opposed like our thumbs. Their technical name *Phascolarctos* means pouched bear, and they look as cuddly as teddy bears. Even so, koalas are not bears but marsupials. The koala has a pouch to carry its young like the kangaroo, but its pouch seems to be on upside down. However, even tiny baby koalas can hang on tightly and don't fall out. A full-grown koala may reach the size of a bulldog, and can consume 2½ pounds of leaves a night. These adorable animals are slow moving and seemingly unafraid, but have few

PATTERN

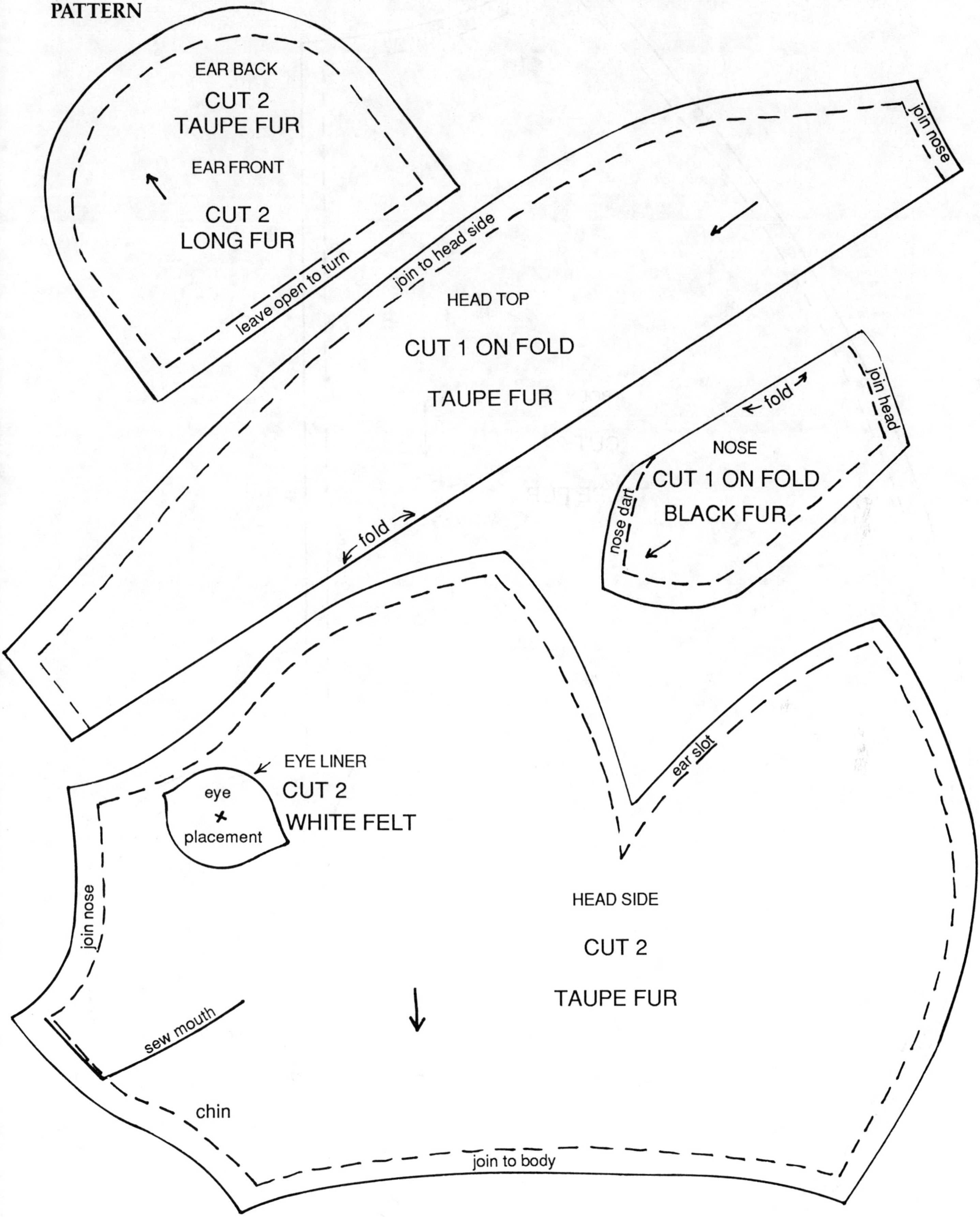

EAR BACK
CUT 2
TAUPE FUR
EAR FRONT
CUT 2
LONG FUR
leave open to turn
join to head side
join nose
HEAD TOP
CUT 1 ON FOLD
TAUPE FUR
fold
join head
fold
NOSE
CUT 1 ON FOLD
BLACK FUR
nose dart
EYE LINER
CUT 2
WHITE FELT
eye
placement
ear slot
join nose
HEAD SIDE
CUT 2
TAUPE FUR
sew mouth
chin
join to body

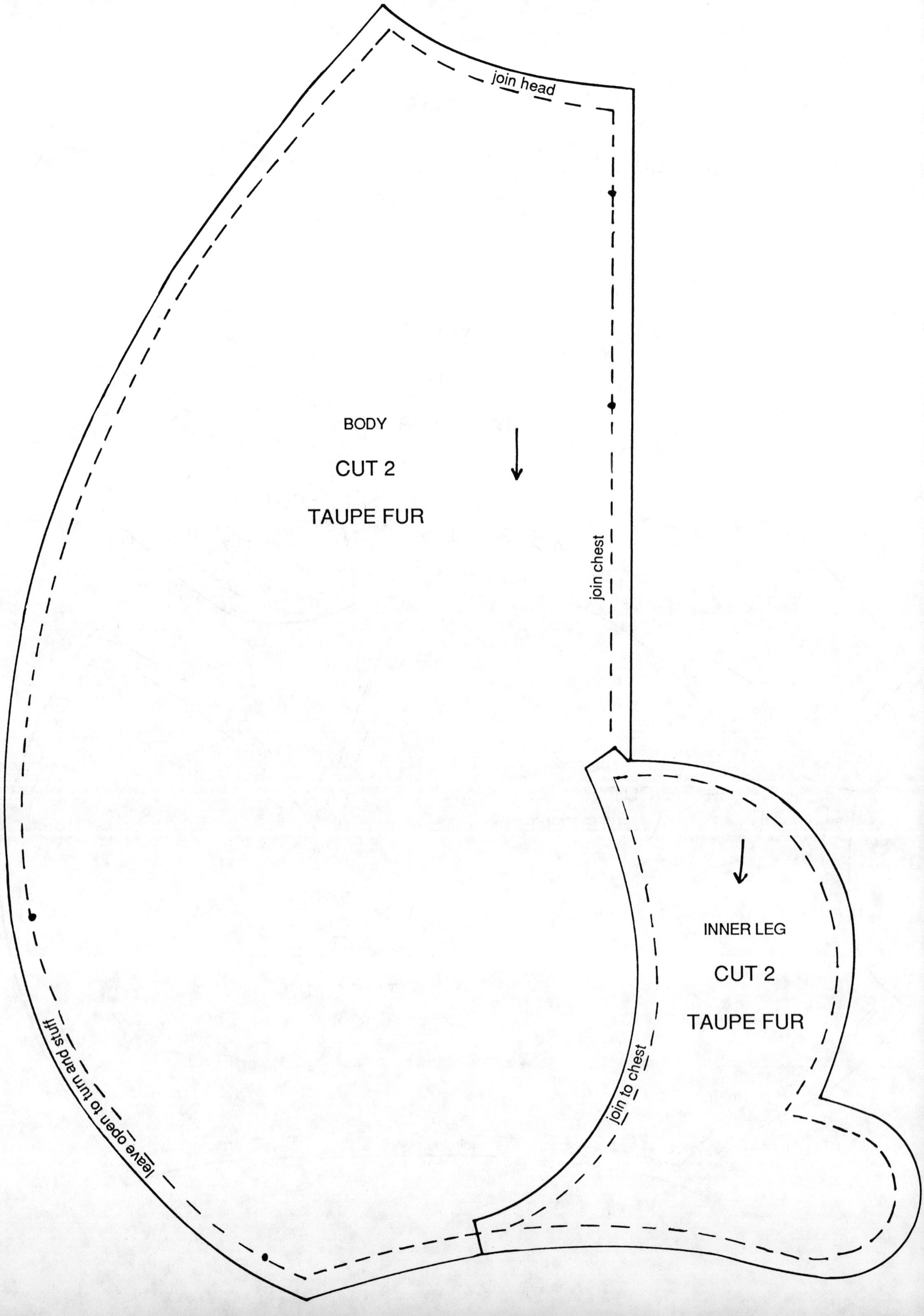
join head
BODY
CUT 2
TAUPE FUR
join chest
leave open to turn and stuff
INNER LEG
CUT 2
TAUPE FUR
join to chest

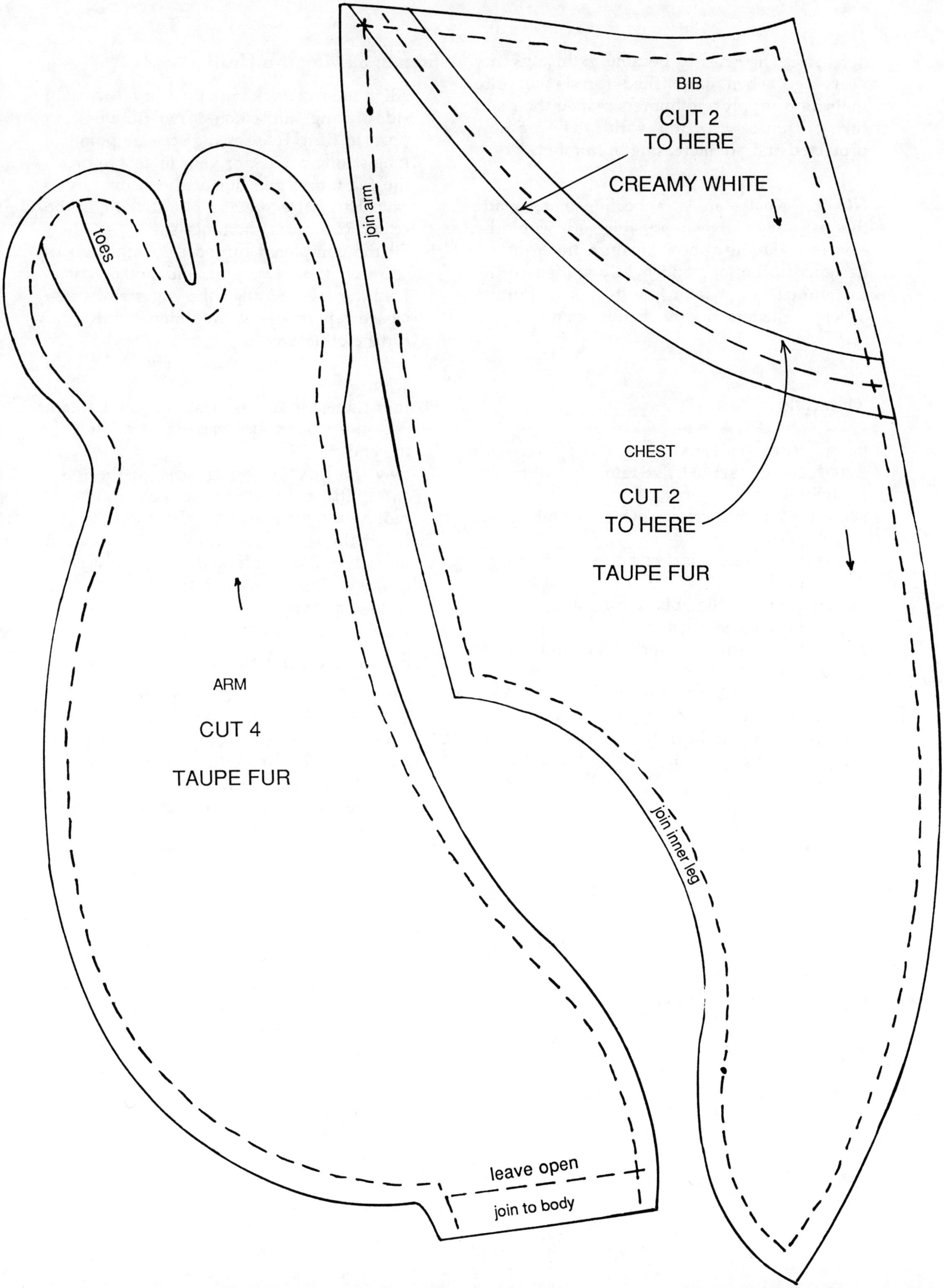
BIB
CUT 2
TO HERE
CREAMY WHITE
join arm
toes
CHEST
CUT 2
TO HERE
TAUPE FUR
ARM
CUT 4
TAUPE FUR
join inner leg
leave open
join to body

defenses. They nearly became extinct twenty years ago when diminished forests cut into their food supply and hunters reaped their soft furs. Fortunately for the world, they are now protected and are increasing in number.

NOTE: Koalas are so appealing that I made this pattern as large as possible so it would be easy to make. As a special feature, the arms are designed to be long and lightly stuffed so the toy animal can pose or hug its owner. Putting Velcro fasteners on the hands increases the grip.

Materials

BODY, HEAD, EAR BACK, ARMS, INNER LEG, HEAD TOP, and CHEST: 20 by 28 taupe fur fabric, ⅜-inch pile
BIB: 5 by 7 inches creamy white fur fabric, ⅜-inch pile
EAR FRONTS: 3 by 5 inches taupe fur fabric, 1-inch pile
NOSE: 3 by 3 inches black fur fabric, ¼-inch pile; or black velveteen
EYES: Two brown ⅝-inch post-and-washer plastic eyes
EYE LINERS: 1 by 2 inches white felt
PAWS: Tan 1-inch Velcro circles
STUFFING: 1 pound fiberfill
THREAD: Matching strong sewing thread, black embroidery floss

Pattern Pieces

BODY (2), INNER LEG (2), HEAD SIDE (2), EYE LINER (2), HEAD TOP (1), NOSE (1), EAR FRONT (2), EAR BACK (2), CHEST (2), ARM (4), BIB (2)

Step 1: Cutting the Fabric

A. When laying out the pattern, match the pile direction arrows with the nap on the fur. Cut out all pieces from the back side.
B. Mark the EYE placement.

Step 2: Sewing the Head

A. Align the EAR BACK with the EAR FRONT right sides facing, and stitch, leaving the bottom open to turn. Use sewing scissors points, a long strong needle, or your fingers to brush the fur fabric pile out of the seam as you sew. This helps prevent pile sticking in the seam. Repeat for the other EAR.
B. Fit the completed turned EAR into the EAR SLOT on the HEAD SIDE and pin or baste. Fold the SLOT to align the edges and stitch closed tapering it at the inner end. Repeat for the other EAR.
C. Align the HEAD SIDES and stitch the chin seam.
D. Join the NOSE to the HEAD TOP and stitch. Sew the NOSE DART, tapering smoothly at the end.
E. Sew the HEAD TOP and NOSE to the HEAD SIDES, fitting the NOSE carefully in place as indicated by the seams and corners.
F. Insert the EYES through the EYE LINERS and into the HEAD as marked. Push the washer firmly on the back when the EYE LINERS are aligned as marked.

Step 3: Sewing the Body

A. Match the ARM pieces, right sides facing, and stitch, leaving the end open to turn. Trim the seam allowances, especially between the fingers. Turn and stuff lightly. Repeat for the other ARM.
B. Join the BIB to the CHEST and stitch. Repeat for the other side.
C. Sew the INNER LEG to the CHEST. Repeat.
D. Baste the stuffed ARM to the CHEST. Repeat.
E. Sew the two assembled sides of the CHEST together.
F. Sew the BODY pieces together along the back seam, leaving an opening for turning.
G. Join the assembled BODY with the assembled CHEST. Begin to stitch at the neck and include the basted ARM in the seam. Stitch around the LEG, ending at the back seam. Continue to stitch up the other side in the same manner. Clip seam allowances at sharp turns.

DIRECTIONS

Sew ears, turn.

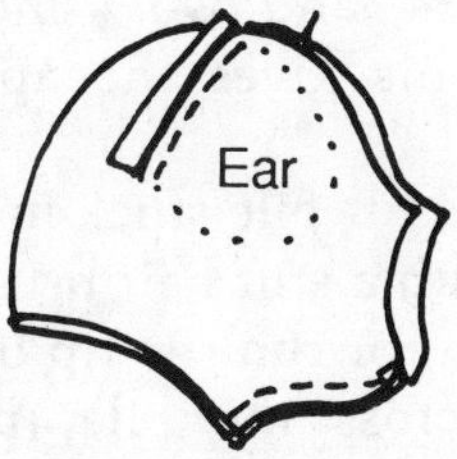

Sew ear into ear slot on head; repeat. Sew chin seam.

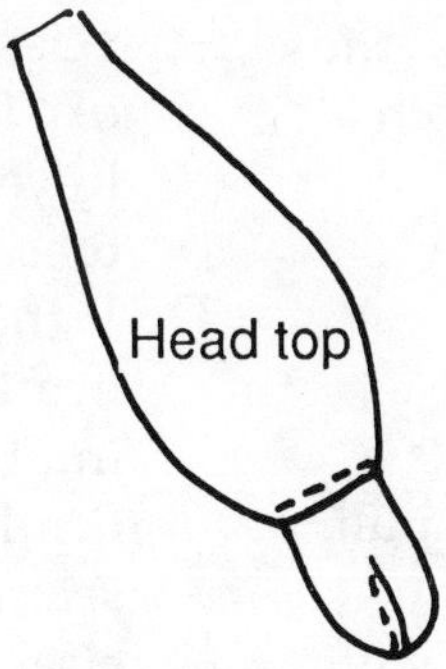

Sew nose to head top. Sew nose dart, tapering ends.

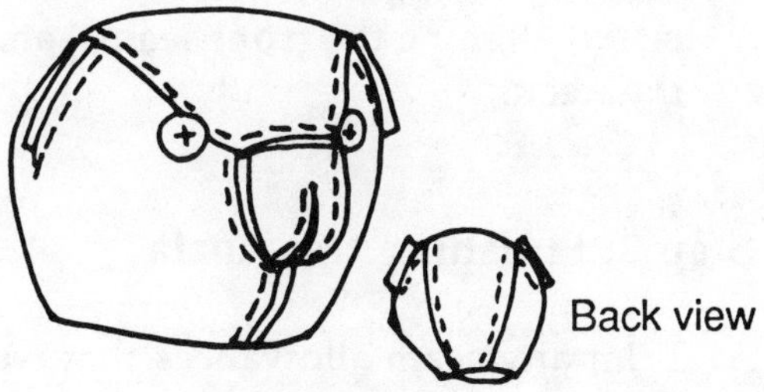

Sew head top/nose to head sides; insert eyes/eye liners.

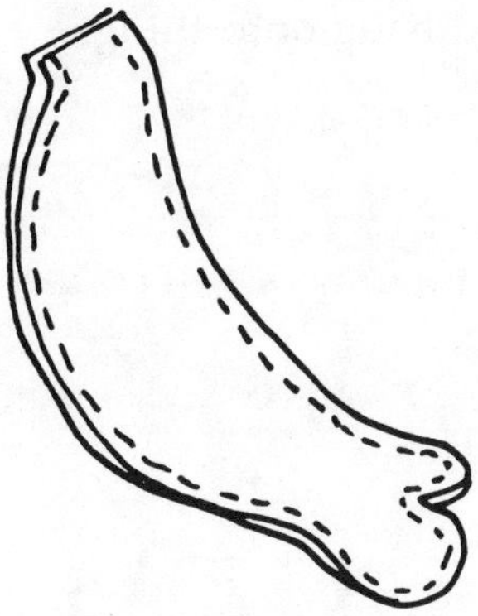

Sew arm, leave top open to turn. Trim, turn and stuff lightly.

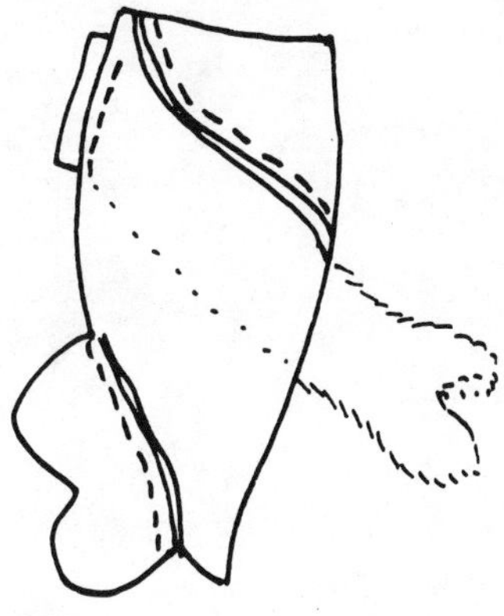

Sew bib to chest; sew inner leg to chest; baste arm to chest; repeat.

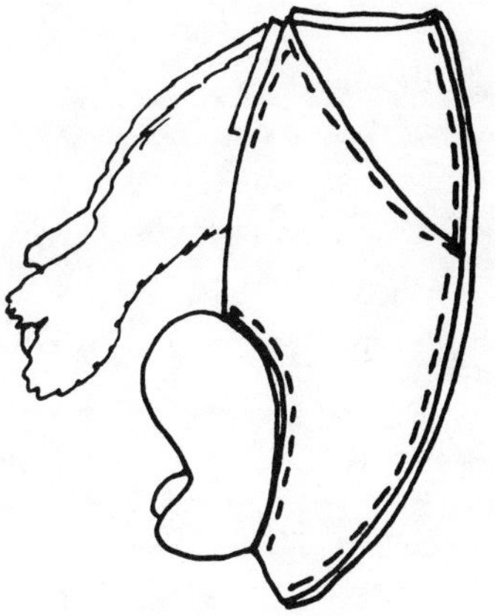

Sew chest to chest.

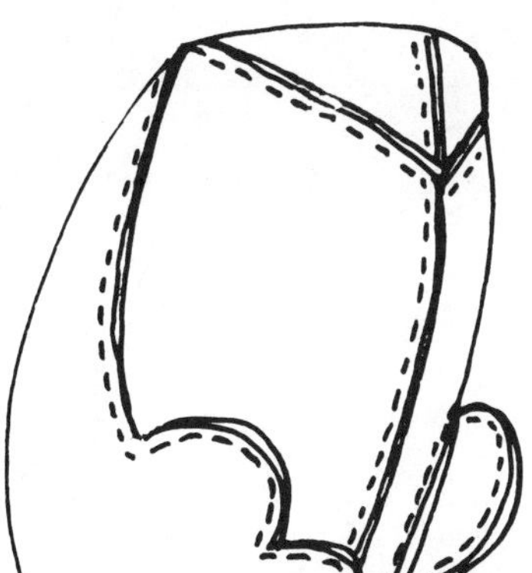

Sew body back seam, leave opening to turn. Join body to chest.

Tuck right-side-out head into body; sew neck seam; turn, stuff.

Sew opening closed. Sew mouth, sew toes. Sew velcro buttons onto paws.

H. Insert the right-side-out HEAD into the BODY, aligning the front seams, and stitch at the neck.

Step 3: Finishing the Koala

A. Trim any seam allowances that would pull. Turn the koala.
B. Begin to stuff at the NOSE. Continue to stuff until the animal is firm. Stitch opening closed with hidden stitching.
C. Embroider the MOUTH as shown. For the TOES, sew one ¾-inch stitch on the top pair of "fingers" and two ¾-inch stitches on the lower. This gives the appearance of five toes.
D. If there is fur pile stuck in the seams, brush firmly with a stiff hair brush or dog grooming brush, or run the tip of a strong needle firmly across the pile (parallel with the seam) several times to loosen. This is more effective for removing pile from the seam than trying to pick it out.
E. Sew tan Velcro fasteners to the paws so the koala can "climb" and hang onto things.

LIONS are known as the Kings of Beasts, not only because they rank among the strongest and fiercest of all wild creatures, but also because of the long-maned male's proud and kingly appearance. The tiger is more fierce than the lion, but they are so similar physically and genetically that they can mate and produce an offspring. A grown lion may measure 9 feet long, 45 inches high, and weigh 900 pounds. Lions can overpower a cape buffalo or catch an antelope. The female lions hunt for the family group, called a pride, occasionally assisted by the males, who dine first.

In early times lions lived in Europe, Asia, and Africa, but civilization has driven them back into the wild. The handsome, fluid form and strength of the lion has impressed people for ages, and many countries still use this animal as their symbol. England has a curly-maned elegant lion, Thailand has a stylized upright lion, and Singapore's lion, called a Merlion, is half fish!

NOTE: This lion measures 10 inches high and 16 inches long plus an 8-inch tail. It is posed sitting, which makes an unusual seam at

PATTERN

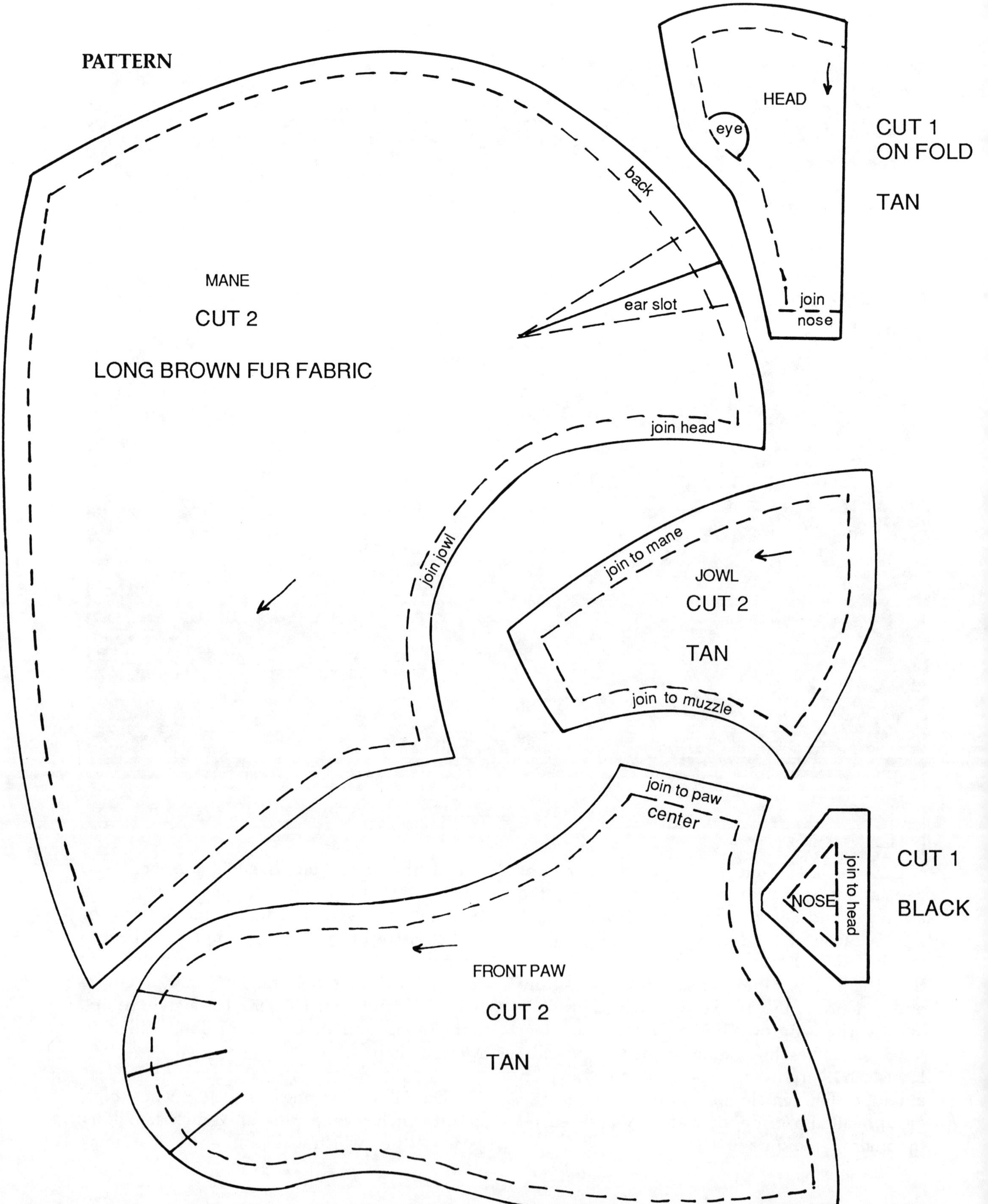
HEAD
eye
join
nose
CUT 1
ON FOLD
TAN
back
MANE
CUT 2
LONG BROWN FUR FABRIC
ear slot
join head
join jowl
join to mane
JOWL
CUT 2
TAN
join to muzzle
join to paw
center
NOSE
join to head
CUT 1
BLACK
FRONT PAW
CUT 2
TAN

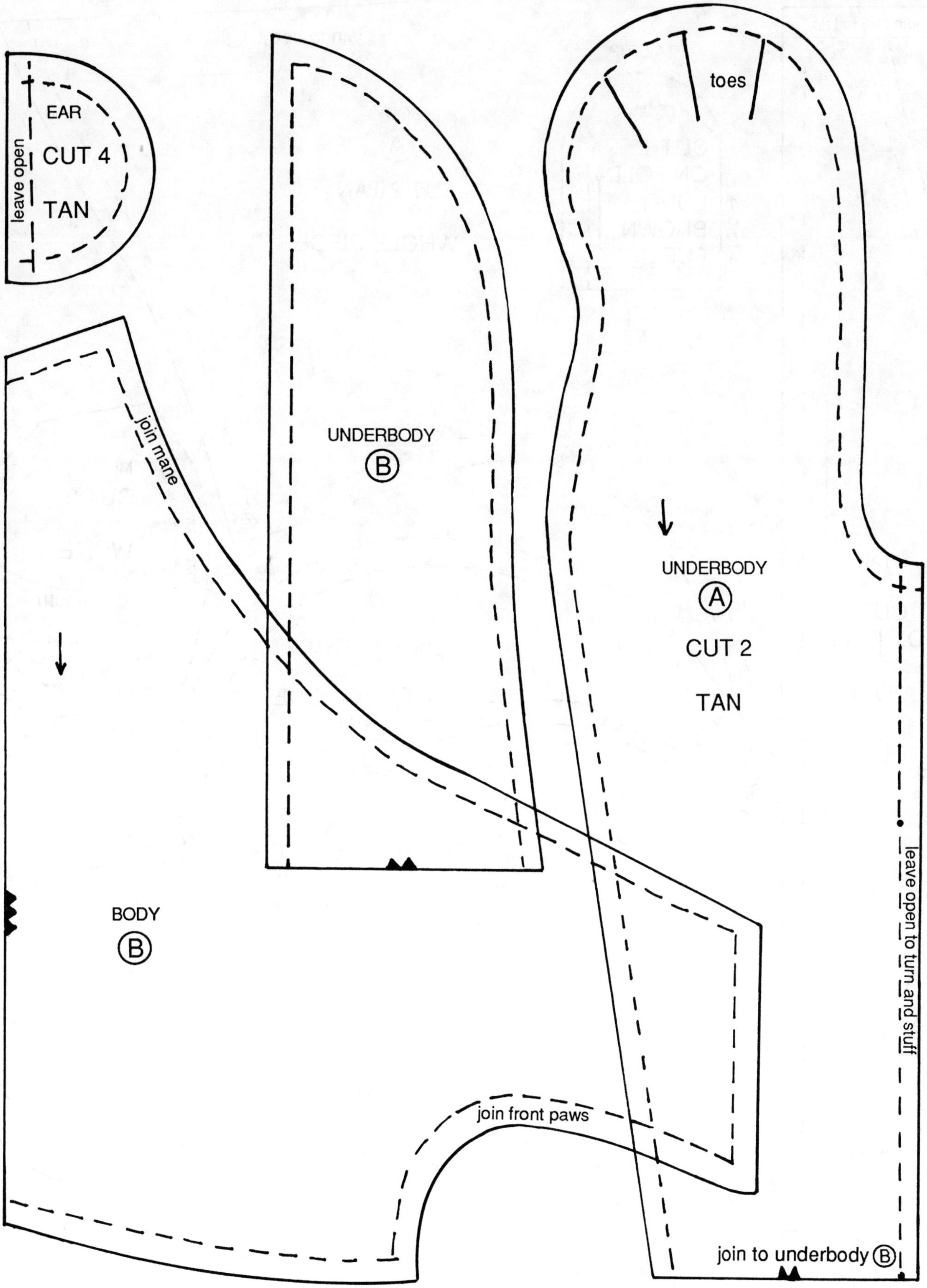

EAR
CUT 4
TAN
leave open
UNDERBODY
B
UNDERBODY
A
CUT 2
TAN
toes
leave open to turn and stuff
join to underbody B
join mane
BODY
B
join front paws

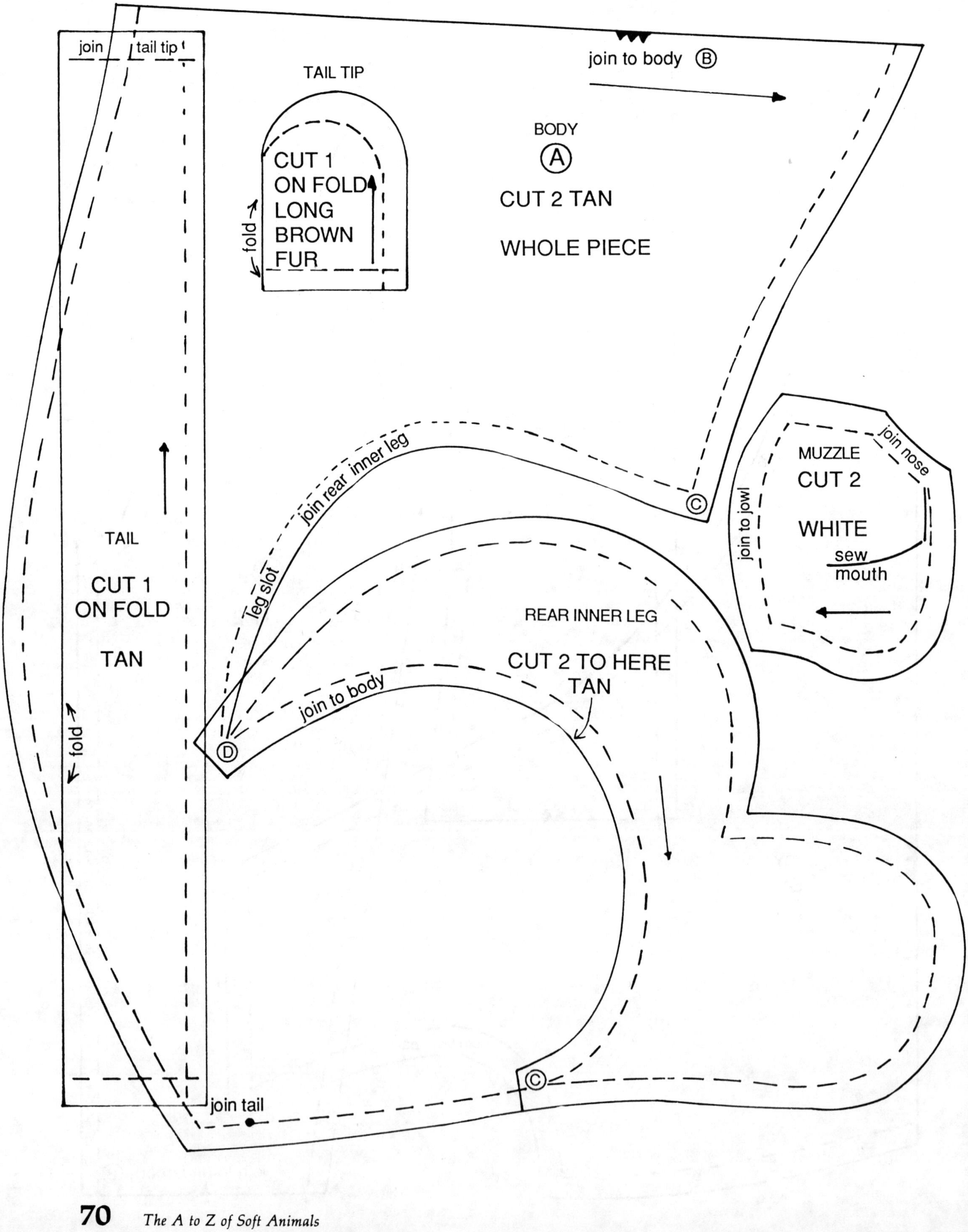
join
tail tip
TAIL TIP
CUT 1
ON FOLD
LONG
BROWN
FUR
fold
join to body B
BODY
A
CUT 2 TAN
WHOLE PIECE
join rear inner leg
C
leg slot
TAIL
CUT 1
ON FOLD
TAN
fold
MUZZLE
CUT 2
WHITE
join nose
join to jowl
sew
mouth
REAR INNER LEG
CUT 2 TO HERE
TAN
join to body
D
C
join tail

the rear inner leg. Since lions and tigers are so similar, this pattern can also be used for a tiger with appropriate stripes added to an orange back and white chest. For a prowling lion, use the jaguar pattern and add a mane as marked. For a simpler nose combine it with the head pattern, and embroider the nose in place later.

Materials

BODY, LEGS, EARS, HEAD, JOWL, TAIL, and UNDERBODY: 20 by 26 tan fur fabric, ¼-inch pile
MANE and TAIL TIP: 8 by 10 inches brown fur fabric, 1½-inch pile
MUZZLE: 3 by 4 inches white fur fabric, ¼-inch pile
NOSE: 1-inch square of black fabric
EYES: Two brown ½-inch post-and-washer plastic eyes
TRIM: Black embroidery floss
STUFFING: 1 pound fiberfill

Pattern Pieces

BODY A and B (2) (given in two pieces), TAIL (1), TAIL TIP (1), MUZZLE (2), REAR INNER LEG (2), EAR (4), UNDERBODY–A and B (2) given in 2 pieces, MANE (2), HEAD (1), JOWL (2), NOSE (1), FRONT PAW (2)

Step 1: Cutting the Fabric

A. Cut out all pieces. Cut the long fur fabric from the back and avoid clipping off pile.
B. Mark eye placement. Notice that the tail must be extended to 8½ inches.

Step 2: Making the Head and Tail

A. Match EARS right sides facing and sew, leaving the bottom open to turn. Turn.
B. Sew TAIL TIP to TAIL. Fold the TAIL to align the raw edges and sew length of it. Turn, using a dowel stick. Stuff lightly or not as you wish.
C. Sew the NOSE to HEAD. If the NOSE piece seems too small to handle, cut the NOSE and HEAD in one piece and embroider the nose later.
D. Sew the MUZZLE to the JOWL and repeat for the other side.
E. Align and sew the JOWL/MUZZLE piece to the HEAD, ending at the base of the NOSE. Repeat for the other side.
F. Baste the EARS to the MANE EAR SLOT. Match the raw edges of the EAR SLOT and sew it closed, including the EARS in this seam. Repeat for the other side. Align the MANES at the back seam, brush the long hairs out of the seam and stitch.
G. Join the assembled HEAD to the MANE. Align the MUZZLE, JOWL, and MANE raw edges, and beginning at the base of the NOSE sew to the end of the MANE to complete the chin/neck seam. Insert the EYES.

Step 3: Assembling the Lion

A. Join the REAR INNER LEG TO THE BODY. To do this, match the REAR INNER LEG HEEL (C) with the BODY (C), aligning the seam from (C) to (D). Begin at the HEEL and stitch the REAR INNER LEG to the BODY At the end of the leg slot (D), pivot the fabric on the sewing machine needle to align the REAR INNER LEG with the LEG cut as part of the BODY. Continue to stitch back to the HEEL. Repeat for the other side.
B. Align the BODY pieces and stitch the back seam and the front of the chest seam. Baste the TAIL to the BODY.
C. Insert the right-side-out HEAD into the neck of the BODY and stitch the MANE to the BODY. Be sure to brush the long MANE hair out of the seam before stitching.
D. Match the FRONT PAWS at the center and sew. Stitch the assembled FRONT PAWS to the BODY.
E. Align the UNDERBODY pieces and stitch the center seam, leaving the opening for turning.
F. Match the UNDERBODY with the BODY, aligning the seams carefully at the HEEL (C), and including the basted TAIL in this seam. Stitch the UNDERBODY to the BODY. Clip any seam allowances that would pull.

DIRECTIONS

Sew ears, turn.

Sew tip to tail, seam tail, turn.

Sew nose to head, or cut all in one piece.

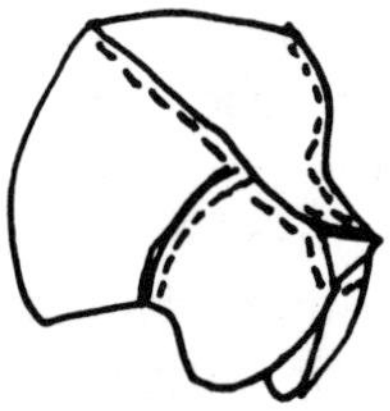

Sew muzzle to jowl, repeat. Sew both to head including nose.

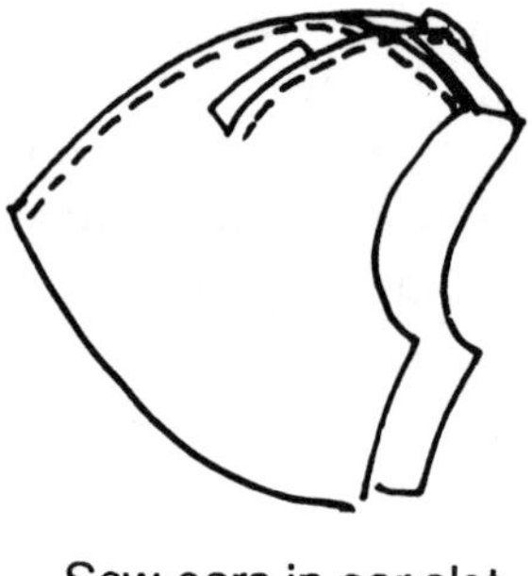

Sew ears in ear slot; repeat; sew mane back seam.

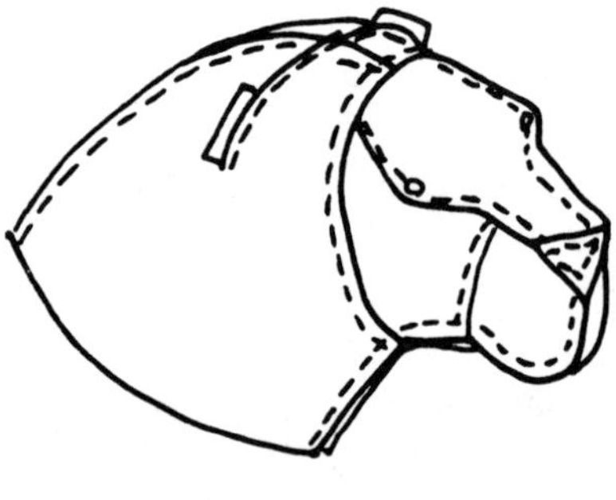

Join head to mane, sew chin/neck seam; insert eyes.

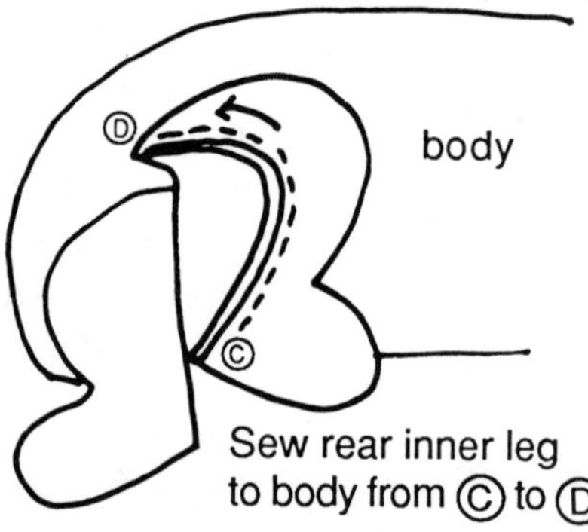

Sew rear inner leg to body from Ⓒ to Ⓓ.

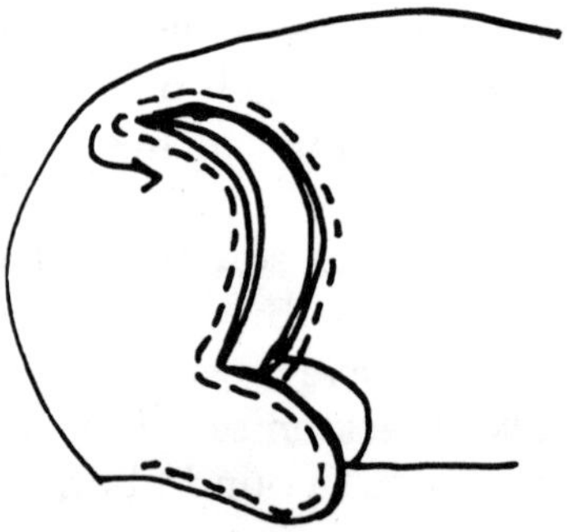

Pivot fabric on needle to continue seam to join rear inner leg.

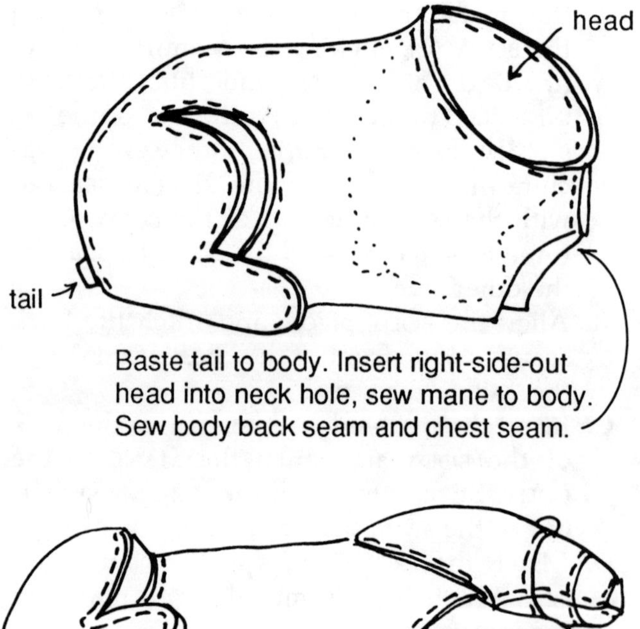

Baste tail to body. Insert right-side-out head into neck hole, sew mane to body. Sew body back seam and chest seam.

Join front paws at center; sew paws to body front.

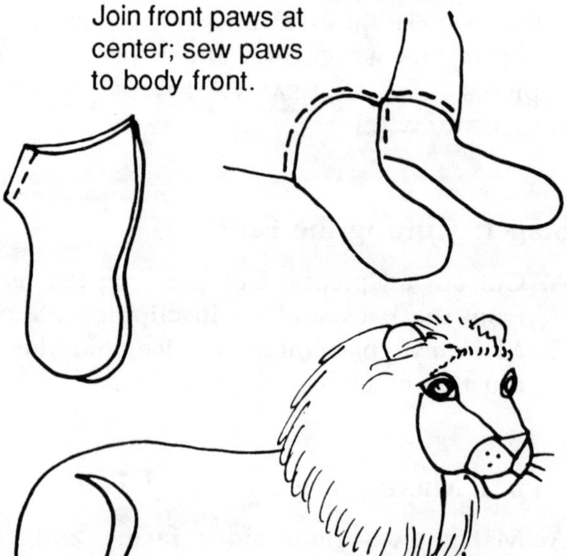

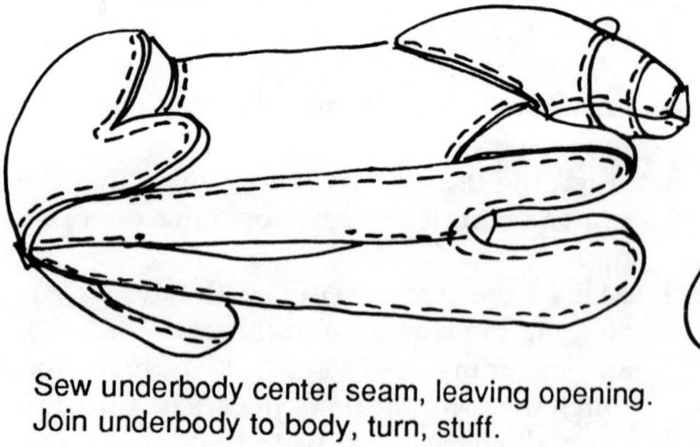

Sew underbody center seam, leaving opening. Join underbody to body, turn, stuff.

Sew opening closed. Embroider mouth, nose, paws; paint eye liners.

Step 4: Finishing the Lion

A. Turn the figure right side out. Begin stuffing with the LEGS. Next stuff the HEAD. Then fill the body firmly, and sew the opening closed.

B. Embroider the MOUTH as marked and shown.

C. To sew WHISKERS, thread a needle with black thread and tie a knot 1 inch from the end. Sew from one side of the MUZZLE to the other. Knot the thread firmly at the emerging point on the MUZZLE. Clip off at 1 inch. Repeat for each set of whiskers.

D. To make the TOES, knot the floss and insert the needle on the bottom of the PAW. Emerge ¾ inch back from the seam line on top, bring the floss over the seam line, and insert the needle ¾ inch back from the seam line. Pull firmly on the thread to shape the TOE and continue on to the next one. Repeat for about four TOES and knot the thread.

E. Use marker or dye paint to outline the EYES.

MONKEYS have long tails, apes do not. Even among monkeys big differences abound. Like the spider monkey shown, many of the 100 species of the New World monkeys have prehensile tails, useful for gripping trees and reaching for fruit. The highly developed tails have "fingerprints" at the tips, as sensitive as our fingertips for touching. Spider monkeys' tails are longer than their bodies, making it easy to hang from a branch and still use all hands and feet to eat!

The capuchin or "organ grinder's monkey" is the most familiar New World monkey. The most familiar Old World monkey is the baboon, noted for its mane, red rump, and close family groups. The long-armed gibbon looks like a monkey, but the missing tail identifies him as an ape. Other favorite apes include the whimsical orangutan called "old man of the forest," the imposing gorilla, who's much shyer than he looks, and the adorable chimpanzee, star of many zoo monkey shows.

NOTE: Wooden and wire armatures help this toy spider monkey perform some of the feats a real monkey can do—grip with his wire hands and tail, and bend at the knees and elbows. For a young child's toy, eliminate the wire and the bamboo plant stake rods so the toy will be safe and washable. For additional safety, hand- or machine-embroider the eyes in place of the plastic eyes. Sew Velcro fasteners on the hands and feet to give them a grip.

PATTERN

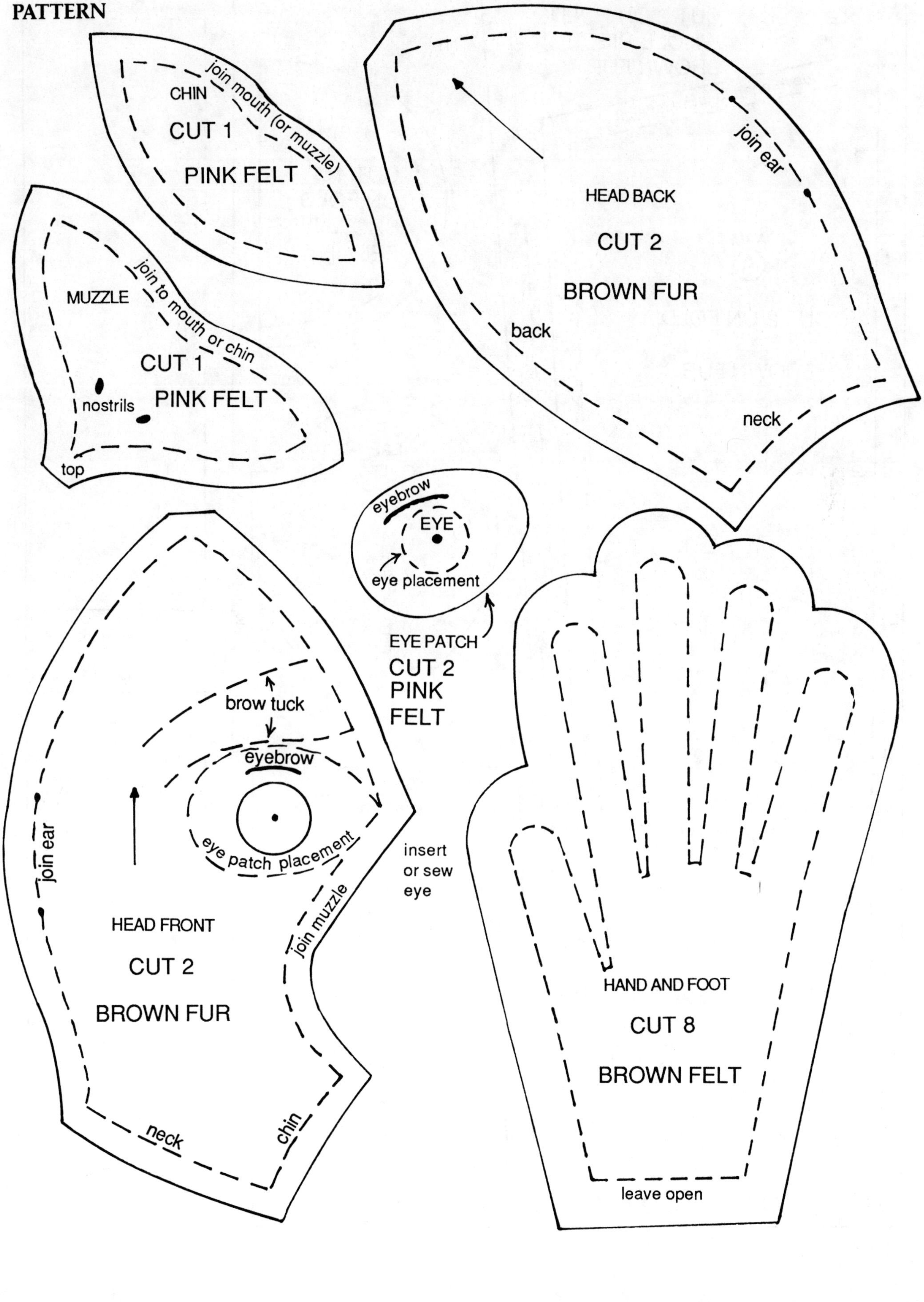
CHIN
join mouth (or muzzle)
CUT 1
PINK FELT
MUZZLE
join to mouth or chin
CUT 1
PINK FELT
nostrils
top
HEAD BACK
CUT 2
BROWN FUR
join ear
back
neck
eyebrow
EYE
eye placement
EYE PATCH
CUT 2
PINK
FELT
brow tuck
eyebrow
eye patch placement
insert
or sew
eye
join ear
HEAD FRONT
CUT 2
BROWN FUR
join muzzle
neck
chin
HAND AND FOOT
CUT 8
BROWN FELT
leave open

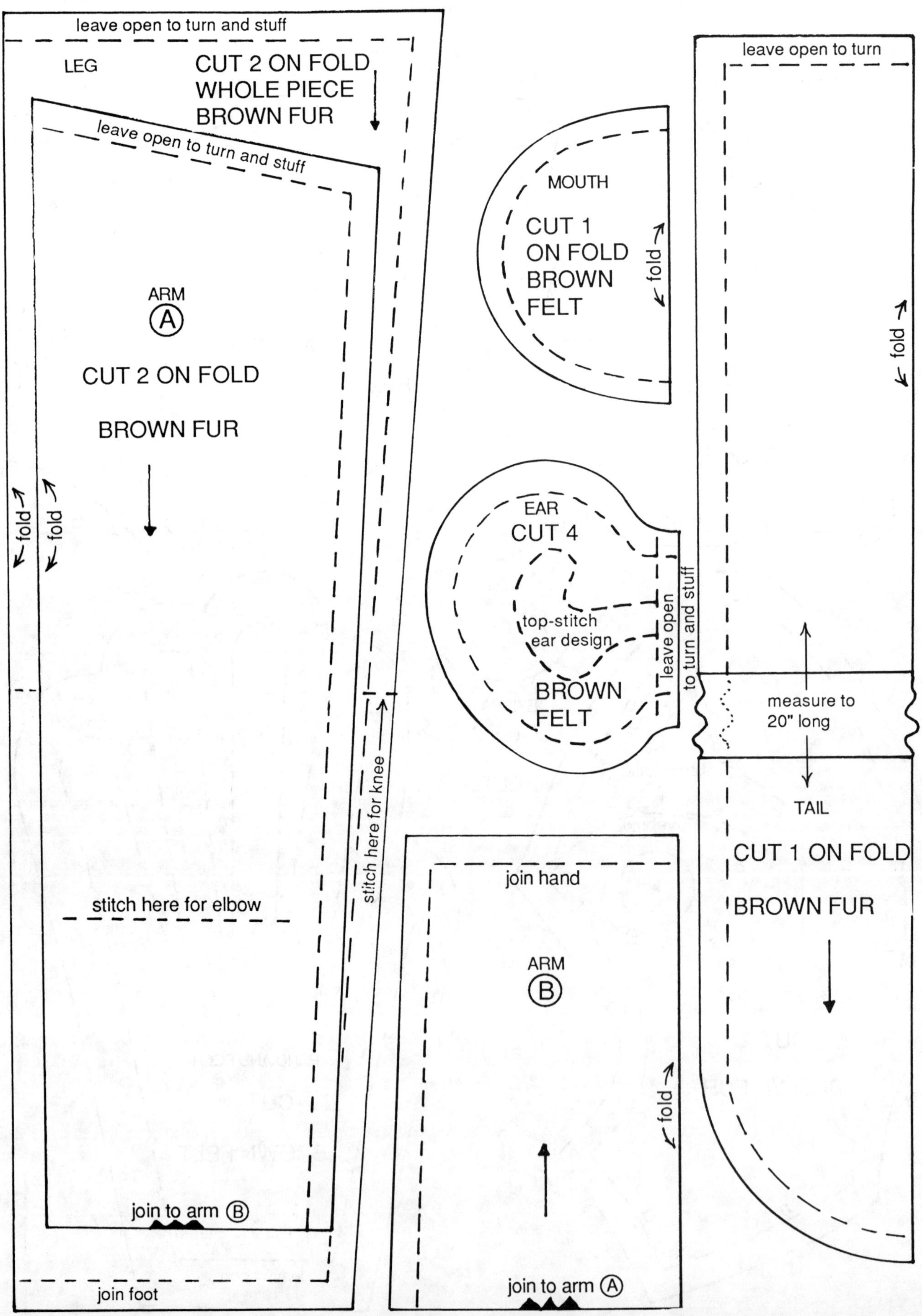
leave open to turn and stuff
LEG
CUT 2 ON FOLD
WHOLE PIECE
BROWN FUR
leave open to turn and stuff
ARM
A
CUT 2 ON FOLD
BROWN FUR
fold
fold
stitch here for elbow
stitch here for knee
join to arm B
join foot
MOUTH
CUT 1
ON FOLD
BROWN
FELT
fold
EAR
CUT 4
top-stitch
ear design
BROWN
FELT
leave open
to turn and stuff
join hand
ARM
B
fold
join to arm A
leave open to turn
fold
measure to
20" long
TAIL
CUT 1 ON FOLD
BROWN FUR

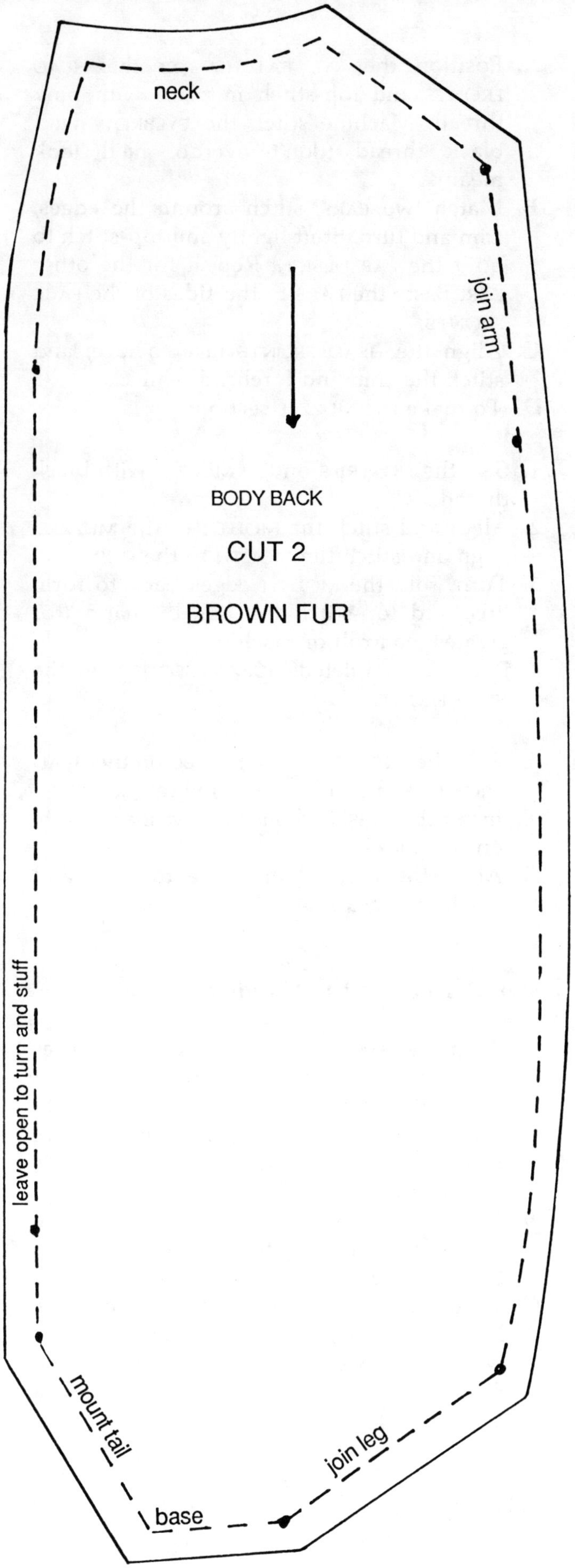
neck
join arm
BODY BACK
CUT 2
BROWN FUR
leave open to turn and stuff
mount tail
base
join leg

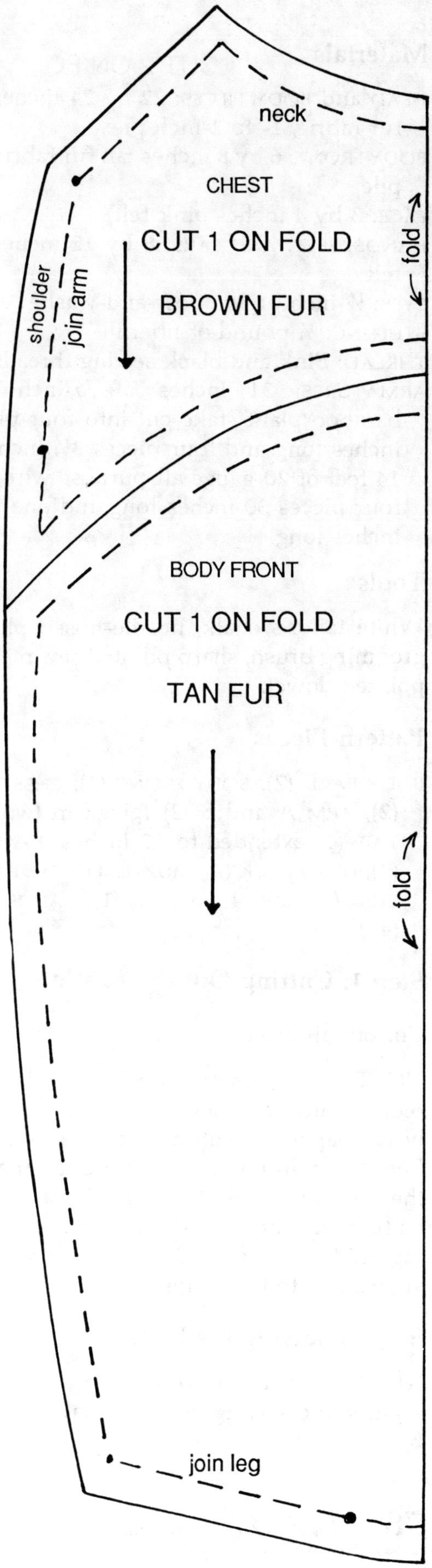
neck
CHEST
CUT 1 ON FOLD
BROWN FUR
fold
shoulder
join arm
BODY FRONT
CUT 1 ON FOLD
TAN FUR
fold
join leg

Materials

HEAD and BODY PIECES: 22 by 24 inches brown fur fabric, 1- to 2-inch pile
BODY FRONT: 6 by 8 inches tan fur fabric, 2-inch pile
FACE: 3 by 4 inches pink felt
HANDS, FEET, AND EARS: 8 by 12 inches brown felt
EYES: ½-inch brown post-and-washer eyes
STUFFING: ¼ pound of fiberfill
THREAD: Pink and black sewing threads
ARMATURES: 31 inches of ½-inch-diameter bamboo plant stake cut into four pieces 4½ inches long and four pieces 3¼ inches long, 14 feet of 20-gauge all-purpose wire cut into four pieces 30 inches long and one piece 48 inches long.

Tools

White tailor's chalk, needle-nosed pliers, dog grooming brush, sharp pointed sewing scissors, pointed dowel.

Pattern Pieces

BODY BACK (2), BODY FRONT (1), CHEST (1), LEG (2), ARM A and B (2) (given in two pieces), TAIL (1) extended to 20 inches, HEAD FRONT (2), HEAD BACK (2), MUZZLE (1), EYE PATCH (2), CHIN (1), EAR (4), MOUTH (1), HANDS (4), FEET (4)

Step 1: Cutting Out the Fabric

Cut out all pieces.

NOTE: For easier working, make pattern pieces into templates by tracing each onto heavy paper and cutting them out on the seam line. Trace around the templates on the back of the fur fabric. Add seam allowances before cutting out, then use the traced line for a sewing guide to stitch. Add ½ inch or wider seam allowances to the hands and feet.

Step 2: Sewing the Head

NOTE: Be sure to brush the pile out of the seam while sewing, to avoid having to pull or brush it out later.

A. Position the EYE PATCHES on the HEAD FRONTS and top-stitch in place with pink thread. Machine stitch the EYEBROW with black thread (don't overdo, he'll look mean).
B. Match two EARS, stitch around the edges, trim and turn. Stuff lightly and top-stitch to quilt the EAR DESIGN. Repeat for the other EAR. Baste the EARS to the sides of the FACE FRONTS.
C. Align the HEAD FRONTS face to face, and stitch the chin and forehead seams.
D. To make the MUZZLE section:

1. Sew the NOSTRILS on the MUZZLE with black thread.
2. Align and stitch the MOUTH to the MUZZLE, align and stitch the MOUTH to the CHIN.
3. Turn, fold the MOUTH edges back to form lips, and top-stitch the lips by hand (for greatest control) or machine.
4. Join the completed MUZZLE SECTION to the HEAD FRONT.

E. Fold the BROW TUCK as marked on the HEAD FRONTS and hand or machine top-stitch.
F. Insert the EYES, and push the washers firmly on the backs.
G. Align the HEAD BACKS face to face, and stitch the back seam.

Step 3: Making the Hands and Feet

A. Align two HAND pieces. These small pieces may shift while stitching, thus the wider seam allowances. Use a very short stitch to sew around the FINGERS, making a square inside corner one or two stitches wide at the base of the FINGERS.
B. Use sharp sewing scissors to trim the HANDS. Cut carefully to the stitch line at the base between each finger (or toe).
C. Turn the HAND. To do this pull the fabric layers apart. Begin to turn at the FINGERTIPS with the scissors tip, but do not pierce the fabric. Once started use a narrow rod (a chopstick) to turn each FINGER.

DIRECTIONS

Sew ear, turn, stuff; top-stitch design, join to head.

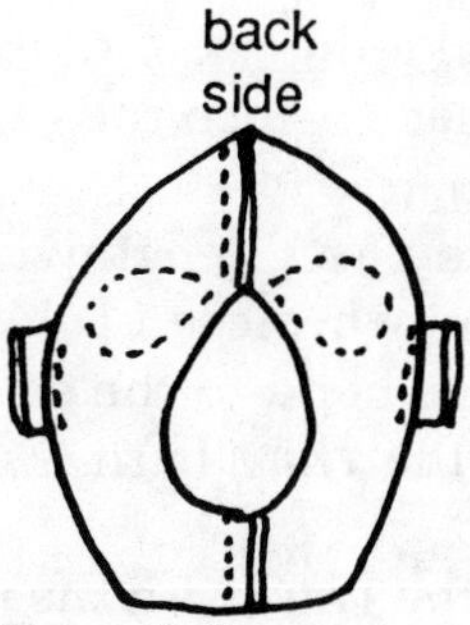

Top-stitch eye patches to face side. Sew head seams.

Sew mouth to muzzle and to chin, top-stitch lips, join to head.

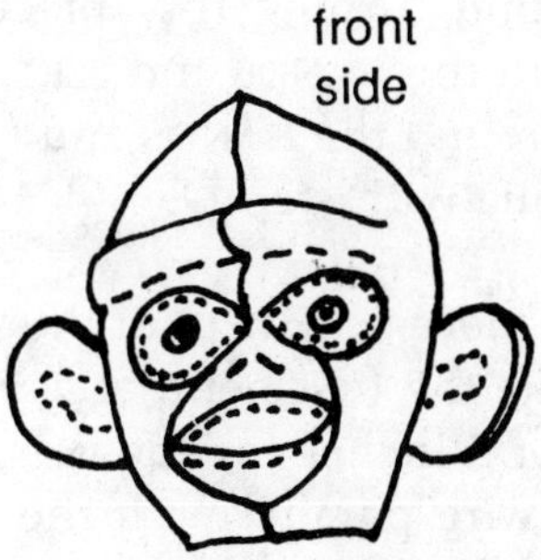

Fold brow tuck and hand sew; insert eyes, sew nose.

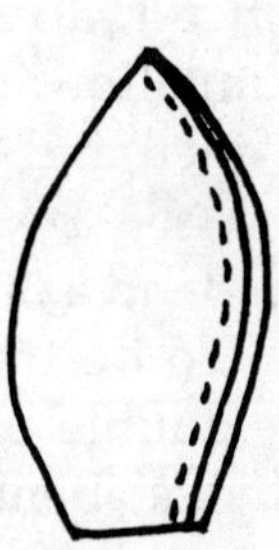

Sew head back seam.

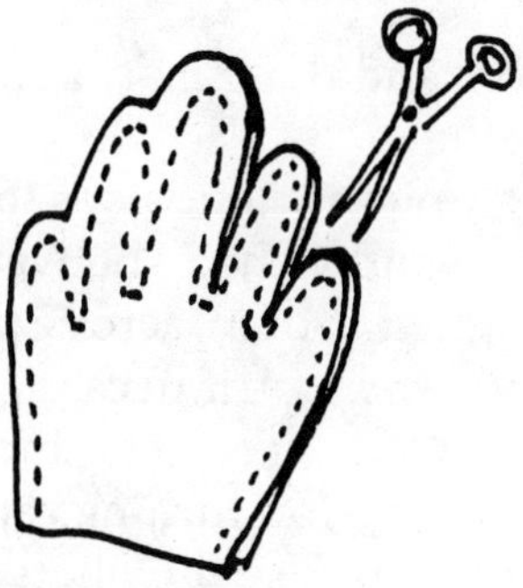

Sew hands (and feet), trim seam allowances, turn; repeat.

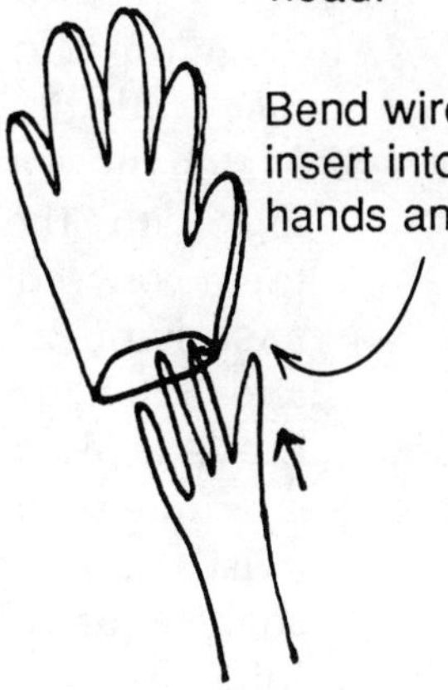

Bend wires, insert into hands and feet

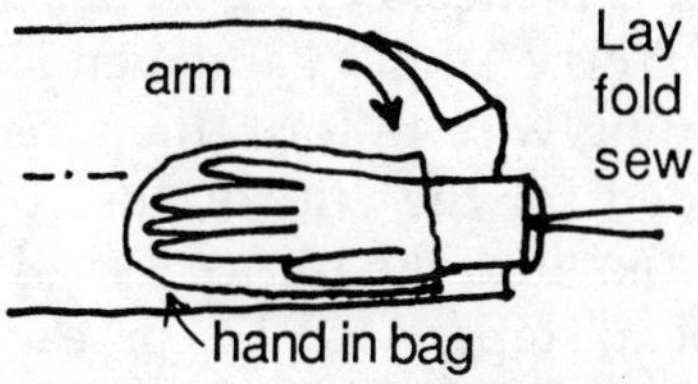

Lay hand on arm, fold arm over hand; sew.

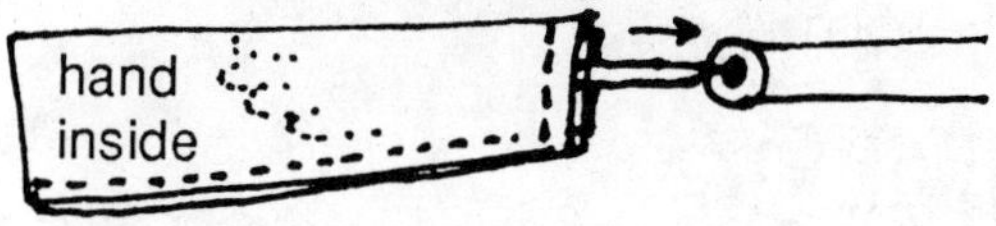

Stitch arm, insert hand wires into rod, turn

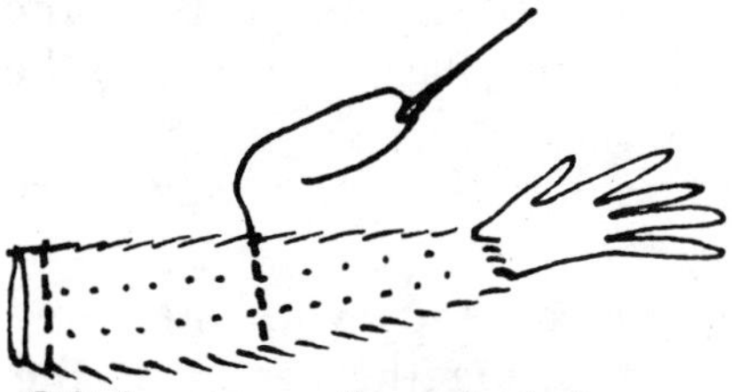

Stitch across elbow (knee), insert upper rod wrapped in stuffing, baste top.

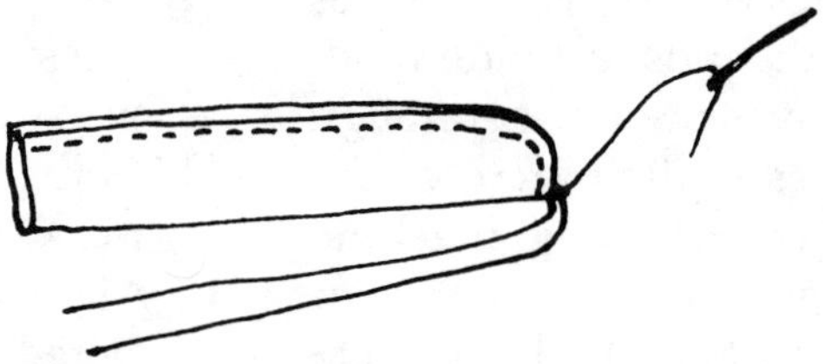

Sew tail, sew tail wire to seam allowance, turn.

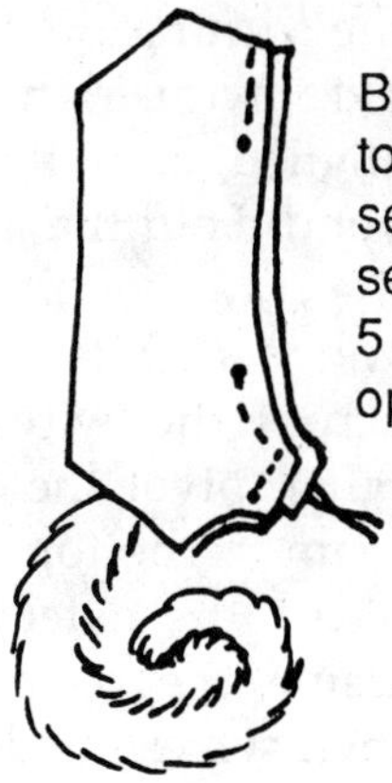

Baste tail to back, sew back seam, leave 5 1/2-inch opening.

Sew chest to body front, sew head to chest.

Baste arms and legs to body front.

Sew front to back with arms, legs, tail out of opening. Turn and stuff; sew closed.

Optional: If you find turning tiny pieces too difficult, do not turn the HANDS and FEET. Trim seam allowances around the HANDS and FEET to 1⁄16-inch and continue with step D.

D. Bend a 30-inch piece of wire to fit the HAND. To do this make the first bend at 7 inches, double back for 3 inches for the INDEX FINGER. Bend the wire parallel with the INDEX FINGER for 3¼ inches or to fit the MIDDLE FINGER, double back 3¼ inches. Bend parallel for the NEXT FINGER 3 inches, then double back 3 inches, bend parallel 2¾ inches for the LITTLE FINGER, and bend back the remaining wire to form the wrist. No wire is needed for the THUMB. Insert the WIRE ARMATURE into the HAND.

E. Repeat steps A to D for each HAND and FOOT.

Step 4: Making the Arms and Tail

A. Wrap the FINGERS in a small plastic bag so they won't tangle with the fur pile during the turning process. Place the HAND on the ARM with right sides facing, raw edges aligned, and the wire ends extended beyond. Fold the ARM over the HAND to align the raw WRIST edges. Stitch across the WRIST (hand-wheel your sewing machine across the wires if it does not sew over pins), pivot the corner, and stitch the ARM seam to the top.

B. Twist the extended HAND WIRES together. Using the pliers, bend the ends back on themselves, and push the wires into the hole in the 4½-inch bamboo armature rod. wrap a thin layer of stuffing around the rod, and push the rod into the ARM to begin turning it.

C. Turn the entire ARM and remove the plastic bag from the HAND. Hand- or machine-stitch across the ARM at the ELBOW, using a long stitch. Pull the threads to gather the ELBOW narrower. Insert the 4½-inch rod wrapped in a small amount of stuffing into the UPPER ARM. Baste across the top of the ARM. Repeat steps A to C for the other ARM.

D. To make the LEGS, repeat steps A to C except that 3¼-inch rods are used for each LEG section.

E. Fold the TAIL lengthwise and stitch. Bend the 48-inch piece of wire in half, and sew the wire bend to the seam allowance at the tip of the TAIL. Turn the TAIL including the WIRE.

F. Baste the TAIL (with the wire ends extended) to the BODY BACK as marked, hand-wheeling the machine if necessary.

Step 5: Assembling the Monkey

A. Align the BODY FRONT and the CHEST face to face, and stitch together.

B. Match the BODY BACK pieces right sides facing with the TAIL sandwiched between them, raw edges aligned. Stitch across the BASE, hand-wheel over the TAIL if necessary, and stitch up the BACK SEAM for 1 inch. Leave a 5½-inch opening for turning, and continue sewing at the top. Use the pliers to twist the TAIL WIRE ENDS into a loop so no sharp ends will protrude.

C. Join the assembled HEAD FRONT to the CHEST at the NECK. Baste the ARMS to the CHEST at the shoulder. Baste the LEGS to the BODY FRONT as marked.

D. Sew the HEAD BACK to the BODY BACK at the neck.

E. Align the completed BACK with the completed FRONT, matching the seams at the neck and the top of the HEAD. Pull the ARMS, LEGS, and TAIL partly out the back seam opening before stitching around the BODY, since they will not fit inside it. Sew around the HEAD and BODY.

F. Pull the ARMS, LEGS, and TAIL completely through the opening to turn the BODY. Turn the HEAD.

G. To stuff, first fill the top of the HEAD. Roll a wad of stuffing to fit the top of the MUZZLE, and stuff in place. Roll another for the lower MUZZLE, and stuff. Add more stuffing to the HEAD to hold the MUZZLE wads in place. Stuff the NECK and BODY firmly. Sew the opening closed. Brush any fur out of the seams with a dog-grooming brush.

NUTHATCHES get their name from the way they eat: they wedge a nut into a crack or the bark of a tree, then "hatch" it open with sharp blows of their bill. This small bird, about 6 inches long, lives in the southeastern United States. There are several varieties of nuthatch that differ in color and size. The bird shown is life size. Nuthatches' favorite food in the winter is sunflower seeds and suet, so you have a good chance of seeing them near your bird feeder if you put these foods out. In summer they use their sharp claws to cling upside-down to tree bark in search for insects, an activity that aids in insect control.

PATTERN

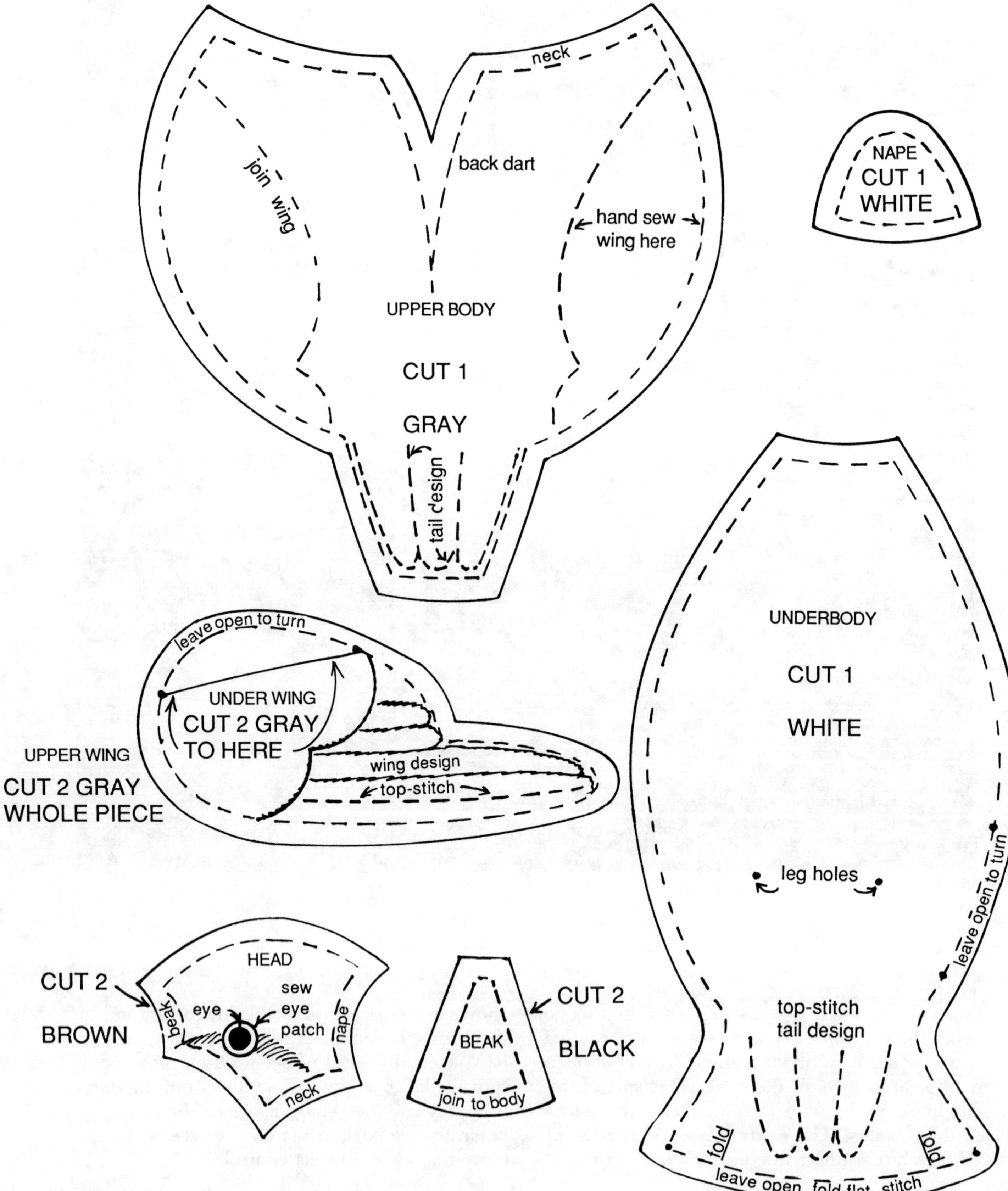

neck
back dart
join wing
hand sew wing here
UPPER BODY
CUT 1
GRAY
tail design
NAPE
CUT 1
WHITE
UNDERBODY
CUT 1
WHITE
leg holes
leave open to turn
top-stitch tail design
fold
fold
leave open, fold flat, stitch
leave open to turn
UNDER WING
CUT 2 GRAY
TO HERE
UPPER WING
CUT 2 GRAY
WHOLE PIECE
wing design
top-stitch
HEAD
CUT 2
BROWN
beak
eye
sew eye patch
nape
neck
CUT 2
BLACK
BEAK
join to body

Because most birds are active in the daytime, the same as most humans, people's associations with birds have been long and close, from the geese whose cries saved Rome to the canaries that warn miners about gas and those (like the nuthatch) that help control insects and distribute seeds. But man's greatest fascination and the object of his intense study has always been the bird's ability to fly.

NOTE: This life-size nuthatch measures 5½ inches long and 4 inches high. The bird is designed so that seams generally occur along color change demarcations. Even so, the pattern could make a yellow canary, by adding a slightly longer tail, or a bluebird with a white breast and appliquéd orange bib. Check the bird guide or encyclopedia for bird shapes and markings.

Materials

UPPER BODY and WINGS: 7 by 9 inches of gray felt or similar flat fabric
HEAD: 3 by 4 inches brown felt or closely woven wool
UNDERBODY and NAPE: 4 by 6 inches white felt
BEAK: 2 by 3 inches black felt
EYES: 2 post-and-washer eyes, ¼ inch across
LEGS: 36 inches of 22-gauge copper wire (other wires will do)
STUFFING: Small amount of fiberfill
THREAD: Black sewing thread

Tools

Sharpened ¼-inch dowel, wire clippers, C-clamp

Pattern Pieces

UPPER BODY (1), UNDER BODY (1), NAPE (1), HEAD (2), BEAK (2), UPPER WING (2) UNDER WING (2)

Step 1: Cutting the Fabric

A. Cut out all pieces.

B. Mark eye placement, eye patch, and wing and tail feathers with tailor's pencil.

Step 2: Making the Bird Body

A. Fold the UPPER BODY lengthwise to align the edges of the BACK DART. Stitch, tapering the end smoothly.

B. Machine or hand embroider the EYE PATCH on the HEAD pieces. Add pellon backing if the stitching puckers the felt. Lay the HEAD pieces facing, and stitch the TOP seam.

C. Open the HEAD pieces flat, align one BEAK, and stitch.

D. Align the NAPE with the HEAD pieces and stitch.

E. Align the HEAD NECK with the UPPER BODY NECK and stitch.

F. Attach the second BEAK to the UNDER BODY.

G. Match the edges of the UPPER BODY and the UNDER BODY from the TAIL to the BEAK. Begin stitching the seam line from the corner of the TAIL toward the BEAK. Make two short stitches across the tip of the BEAK to facilitate turning. On the second side leave a 1½-inch opening for turning, stopping at the other corner of the TAIL. Leave the TAIL end open.

H. Fold the TAIL flat. Two white triangles will appear on the top side since the underside is wider. Stitch across the TAIL.

I. Clip seam allowances around the BEAK closely, to avoid too much fabric inside the turned BEAK. Trim any other places necessary. Turn the bird. Insert the EYES.

J. Begin to stuff the bird, starting with tiny wads in the BEAK. Fill the HEAD firmly. Insert a small amount of stuffing in the TAIL and top-stitch the TAIL design to quilt the TAIL flat. Don't complete the stuffing yet, since the LEGS will be inserted in the next step.

Step 2: Making the Legs

A. Bend the LEG WIRE into four equal sections 9 inches long. Twist these wires together 1¼ inches from one end. Use the C-clamp to

DIRECTIONS

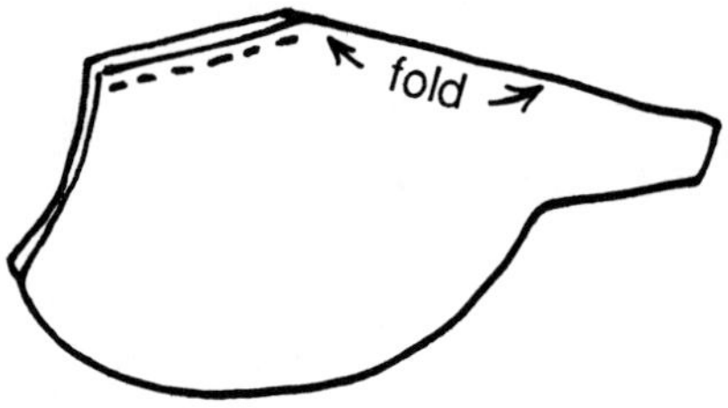

Taper body back dart.

Satin-stitch eye patch trim, stitch head seam.

Join beak to head.
Join nape to head.
Join head to upper body.

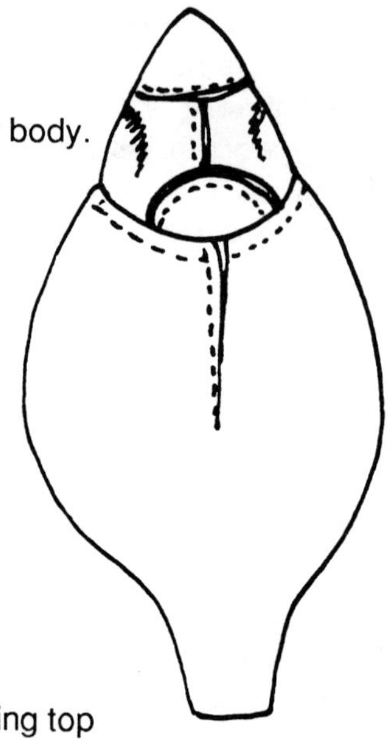

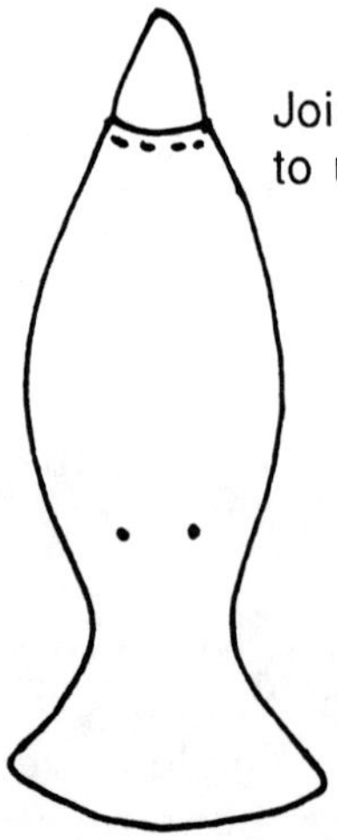

Join beak to underbody.

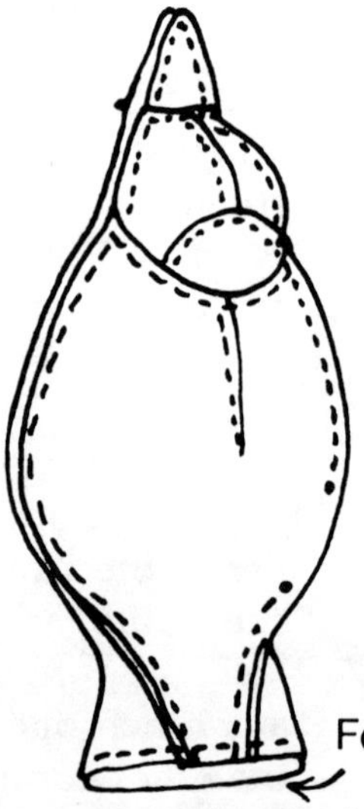

Join upper and under body, fold tail flat and stitch across. Partly stuff body; insert eyes.

Stitch wings, leaving top open, turn.

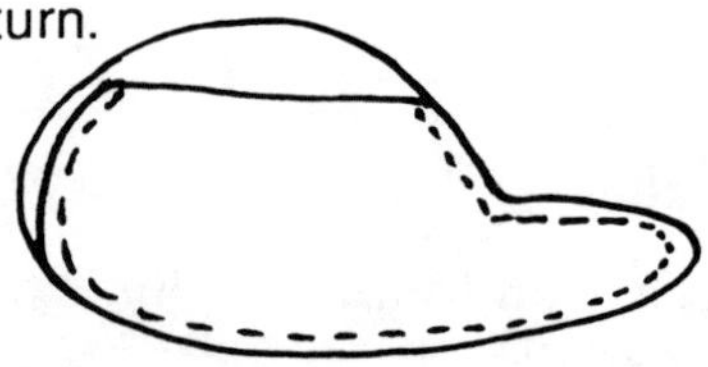

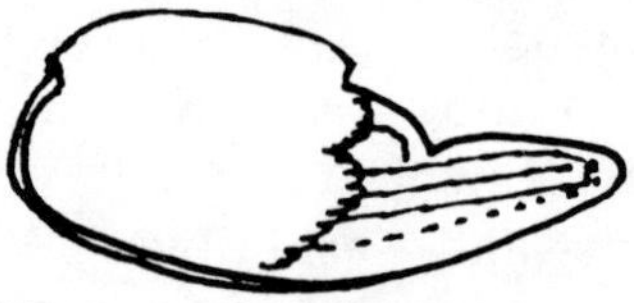

Top-stitch wing designs.

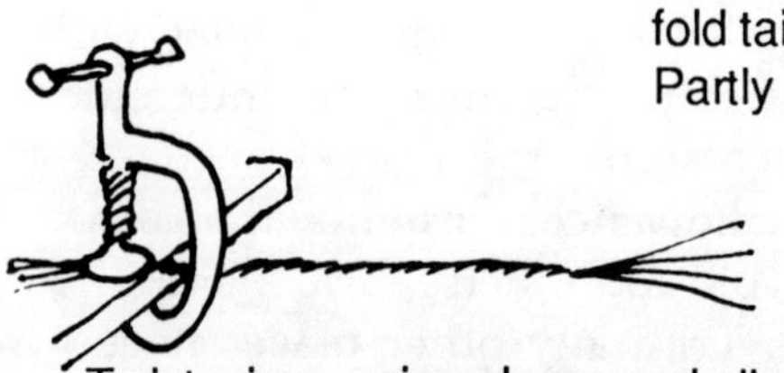

Twist wires, using clamp and pliers.

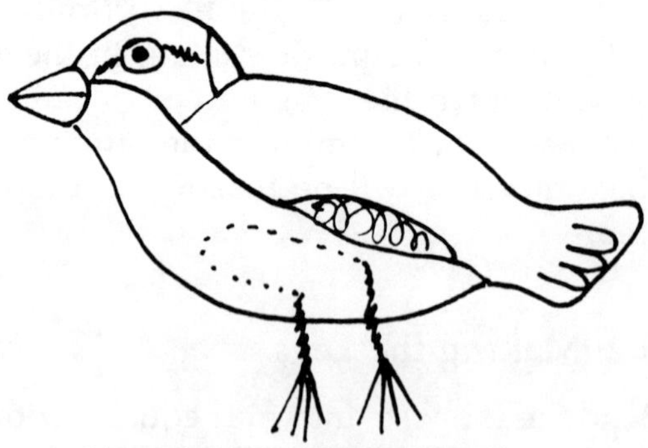

Insert leg wires in body and bend wire loop to fit breast.

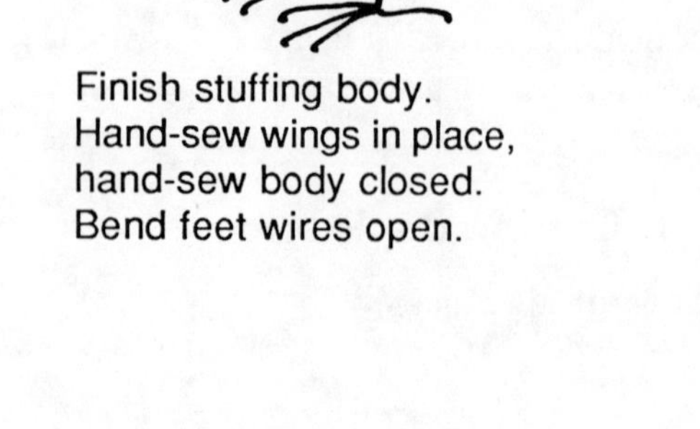

Finish stuffing body.
Hand-sew wings in place,
hand-sew body closed.
Bend feet wires open.

affix this end firmly to a table edge, since clamping the end of the wire helps to twist it tighter. Twist the wires firmly together into one 4-ply strand ending 1¼ inches from the other end. Use pliers if necessary.

B. Insert the end of the wires into one LEG HOLE and loop it out the other. Bend the wire in the center (inside the bird) so the wire makes a large "U." Next bend each WIRE LEG forward 2¼ inches from each end. Push the loop into the bird to the bends in the LEGS, and shape the loop inside so it fits snugly into the BREAST.

C. Continue to stuff the bird. Place a layer of fiberfill between the LEG WIRE LOOP and the BREAST. Fill the bird firmly. Hand-sew the opening closed.

Step 3: Making the Wings

A. Align the UPPER WING with the UNDER WING and stitch the seam line. Turn and press flat. Repeat for the other WING.

B. Top-stitch the completed WINGS, using a narrow satin-stitch to stitch the WING DESIGNS.

C. Position the WINGS on the bird's sides as marked. Tuck the seam allowance under on the top of the WING and hand-stitch the WING in place with hidden stitching.

D. On each leg, angle the twisted LEG WIRES to the proper angle, then bend three wires forward and one wire back to make the FEET. Curve the ends of the wires downward to make CLAWS. Adjust the angle of the LEGS so the bird balances.

OSTRICHES are the largest living birds, surpassed only by the extinct moa who grew 12 feet tall. Fully grown, an ostrich can stand nearly 8 feet tall and weigh as much as 300 pounds. Contrary to legend the ostrich does not bury its head in the sand; he merely lowers it to avoid the gritty desert winds of its habitat. Ostriches have only two toes on each foot, but this doesn't slow them any: they've been clocked running at 40 miles an hour. No horseman could catch them except for the fact that they run in wide circles. When the ostrich is caught, the hunters snatch out the beautiful plumes that grow on the ostrich tail and let it go until next year.

The male ostrich has glossy black feathers on his body and white plumes on his tail and wings, highly valued in the fashion industry. The female's gray-brown plumes may end up as feather dusters. Ostriches have no feathers on their legs and thighs, and only sparse down on their long necks and heads.

NOTE: In the same manner that early teddy bears and dolls were made, this pattern specifies disk and cotter-pin leg joints. This gives the leg complete mobility, so the toy bird can stand, sit, or run with its owner's help. For a simpler bird, sew the completed leg to the body.

Furry animals are appealing, but the ostrich will look more realistic if the neck, head, and legs are made from felt or a flat fabric, the body of fur fabric, and the wing tips and tail of feathers. As with most of the other patterns it is easier to make an enlarged version because of some of the small details. Making the disk

Monkey
The tip of the spider monkey's tail is as sensitive to touch as are our fingertips.

Zebra and Unicorn
Now almost extinct, the zebra can still be seen at the zoo. The beloved unicorn, on the other hand, never really did exist.

Sea Animals
Three representatives of the sea world—the starfish, scallop, and sea horse.

Ostrich
Ostriches are the largest birds in existence today.

Lion
The lion's regal presence, not to mention his potential ferocity and strength, are what give him his reputation as "King of Beasts."

Yak
Yaks are the largest members of the oxen family.

Dogs and Cats
Our favorite pets.

Penguins
Penguins cannot fly, but they can move through the water at surprising speeds.

Quail
Quail make a clear, sharp whistle that sounds as though they are saying "Bob White . . . Bob White."

Hogs

Contrary to popular opinion, hogs are actually smarter than cows, horses, and sheep.

Rabbit and Vole

Two representatives of the rodent world. The vole is the European name for several kinds of field mice.

Turtle

Turtles range in size from tiny ones that fit in terrariums to large ones up to 1500 pounds in weight.

PATTERN

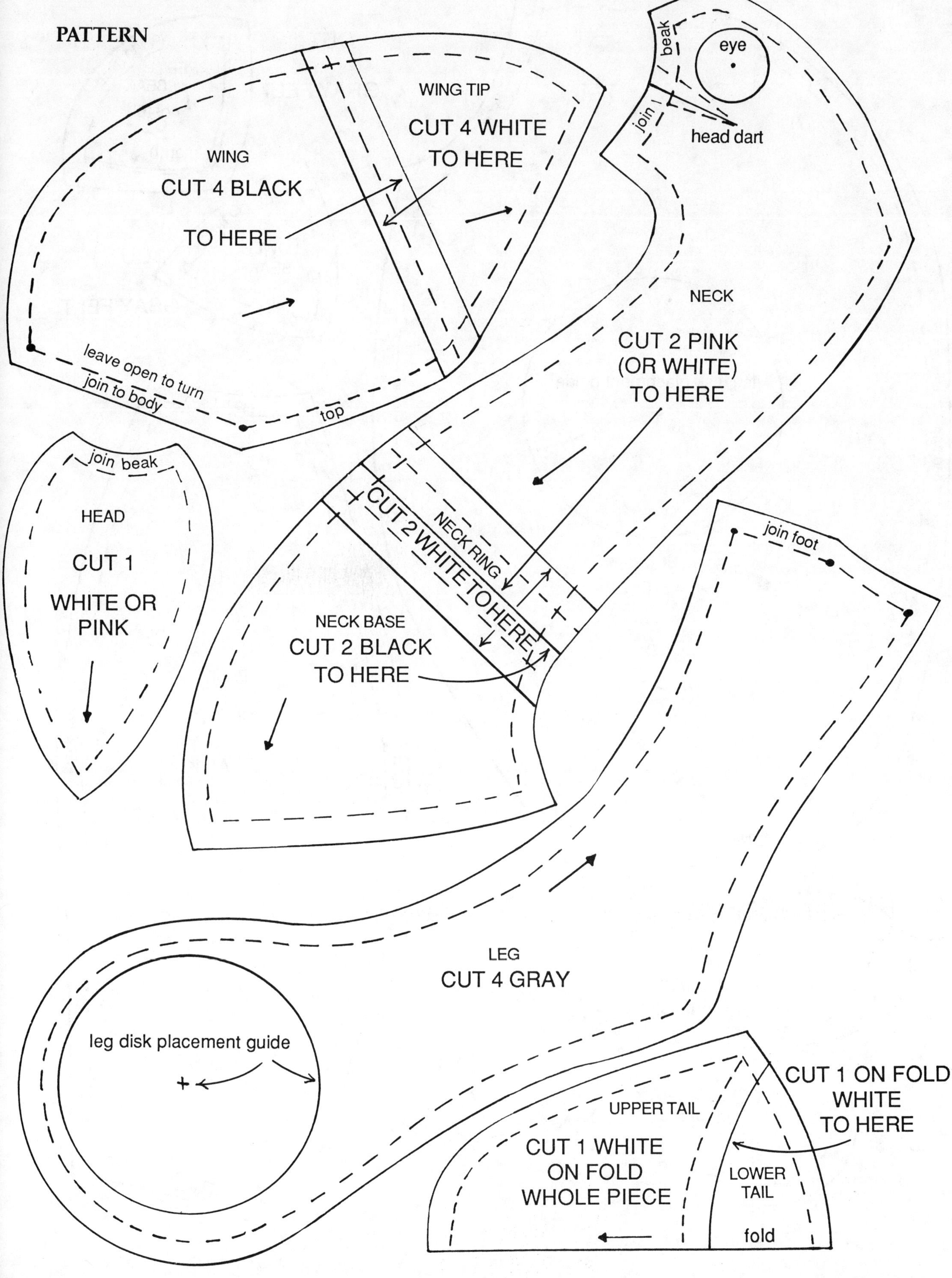
WING
CUT 4 BLACK
TO HERE
leave open to turn
join to body
top
WING TIP
CUT 4 WHITE
TO HERE
beak
eye
join
head dart
NECK
CUT 2 PINK
(OR WHITE)
TO HERE
join beak
HEAD
CUT 1
WHITE OR
PINK
NECK RING
CUT 2 WHITE TO HERE
NECK BASE
CUT 2 BLACK
TO HERE
join foot
LEG
CUT 4 GRAY
leg disk placement guide
UPPER TAIL
CUT 1 WHITE
ON FOLD
WHOLE PIECE
CUT 1 ON FOLD
WHITE
TO HERE
LOWER
TAIL
fold

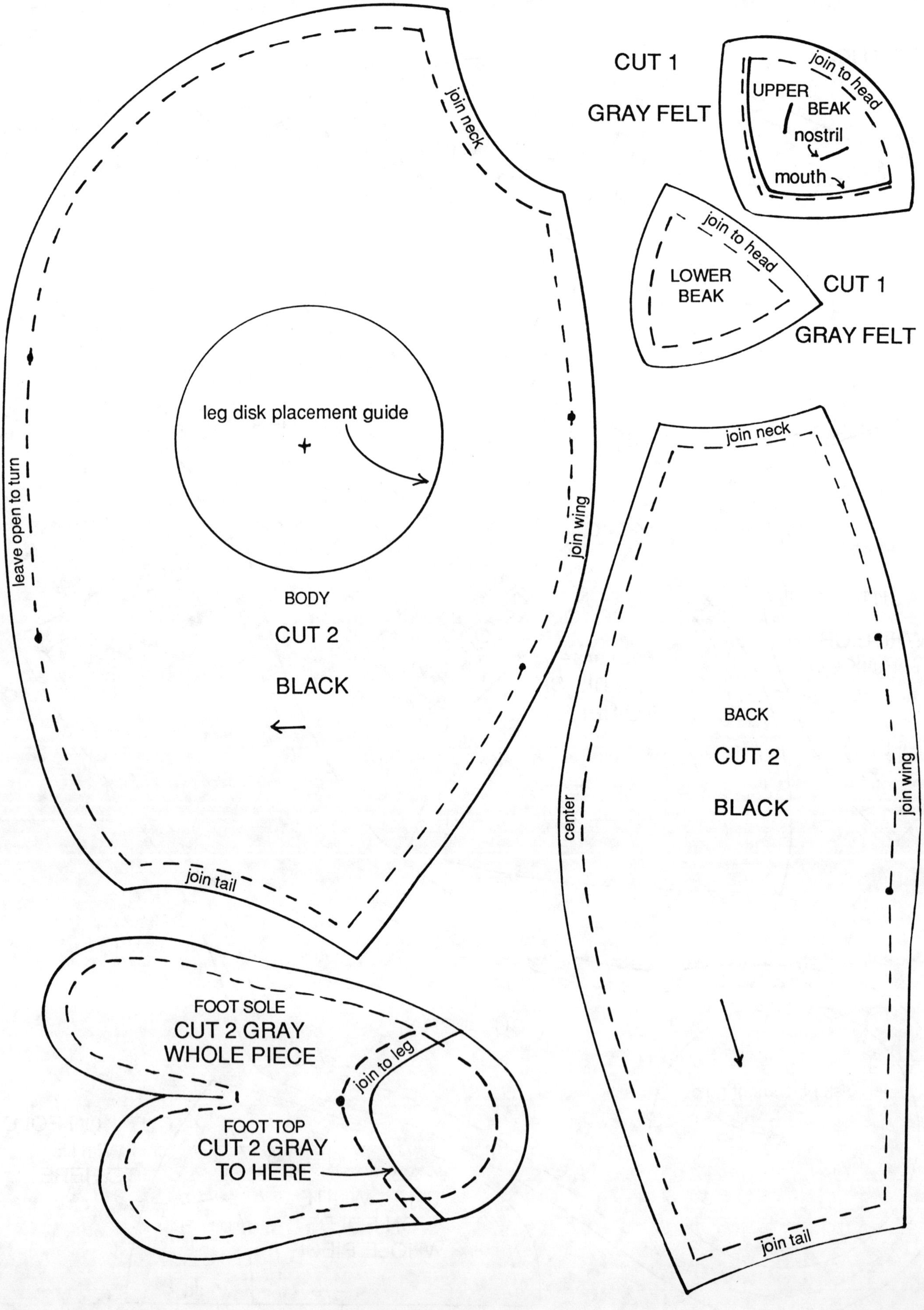
CUT 1
GRAY FELT
join to head
UPPER
BEAK
nostril
mouth
join to head
LOWER
BEAK
CUT 1
GRAY FELT
join neck
leave open to turn
leg disk placement guide
join wing
BODY
CUT 2
BLACK
join tail
join neck
BACK
CUT 2
BLACK
center
join wing
join tail
FOOT SOLE
CUT 2 GRAY
WHOLE PIECE
join to leg
FOOT TOP
CUT 2 GRAY
TO HERE

joints may seem unfamiliar, but just follow the directions for best results.

Materials

BODY, NECK BASE, WINGS: 8 by 23 inches black fur fabric, ¼-inch pile
TAIL, WING TIPS: 8 by 10 inches white fur fabric, ¼-inch pile
NECK: 5 by 6 inches pink fur fabric, or velveteen
LEGS: 8 by 16 inches gray fur fabric, or velveteen
BEAK: 2 by 3 inches gray felt
STUFFING: 8 ounces fiberfill
EYES: 16 mm (⅝-inch) brown post-and-washer eyes
ARMATURE: 40 inches coathanger wire (2 hangers) or stiff ⅛-inch wire
JOINT: Four 2-inch disks (wood, masonite, or plastic), two cotter pins ⅛ inch by 2½ inches, two 1-inch washers with ⅛-inch holes.

NOTE: These disk sets are available from doll-supply houses such as Build-A-Bear, 20730 Kennoway, Birmingham, Michigan 48010. (Send a self-addressed stamped envelope for information.)

THREAD: Black sewing thread, white sewing thread, black embroidery floss

Tools

Stuffing rod, needle-nosed pliers

Pattern Pieces

BODY (2), BACK (2), UPPER BEAK (1) LOWER BEAK (1), FOOT TOP (2), FOOT SOLE (2), WING (4), WING TIP (4), HEAD (1), NECK (2), NECK RING (2), NECK BASE (2), LEG (4), UPPER TAIL (2), LOWER TAIL (2)

Step 1: Cutting the Fabric

A. Draw or pin the pattern pieces on the reverse side of the fur fabric. Mark the EYE placement hole and the leg placement hole and clip a ⅛-inch slit.
B. Cut out all pieces.

Step 2: Sewing the Body

A. Thread the sewing machine with black thread, top and bottom. Align the WING TIP with the WING and stitch. Repeat for all four WINGS. Match two WINGS face to face and stitch, leaving the top open for turning. Repeat for the other wing. Turn both right side out.
B. Pin or baste the WING to the BODY. Align the BODY with the BACK and stitch, including the WING in this seam. Repeat for the other side. Match the center BACK seams and stitch.
C. Match the NECK BASE seams and stitch the back seam only. Align the NECK BASE with the BODY at the seams and stitch.
D. Change the sewing machine to white thread. Pin the HEAD to the NECK and stitch. Align this assembled piece with the other NECK and stitch along the back from the HEAD to the base of the NECK.
E. Align the NECK RINGS and stitch the back seam. Match the NECK RING with the NECK and stitch.
F. Stitch the UPPER BEAK to the HEAD.
G. Align the assembled HEAD AND NECK with the BODY and stitch from the front of the NECK to the TAIL opening.
H. Stitch the LOWER BEAK to the NECK opening. Align the UPPER AND LOWER BEAKS and the HEAD DARTS. Begin to stitch by tapering the HEAD DART, continue around the BEAK, and complete with the HEAD DART taper on the other side. Insert the EYES. To do this, work the EYE up inside the NECK into the (wrong side out) HEAD and push the post out the clipped eye placement hole. Force-fit the washer onto the eye post, pushing it down firmly. Repeat for the other EYE.
I. Align the UPPER AND LOWER TAILS and stitch. Fit the TAIL to the BODY, and stitch to join. Clip any inside seam allowances that might pull, especially at the neck and turn.

Step 3: Making the Legs

A. Match two LEGS face to face, and stitch the front and back seams, leaving the bottom and top open. Repeat for the other LEG.

DIRECTIONS

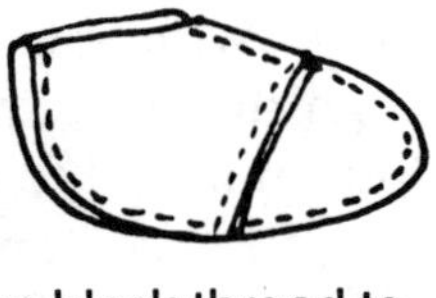

Use black thread to sew wing tips to wings, wing to wing; turn.

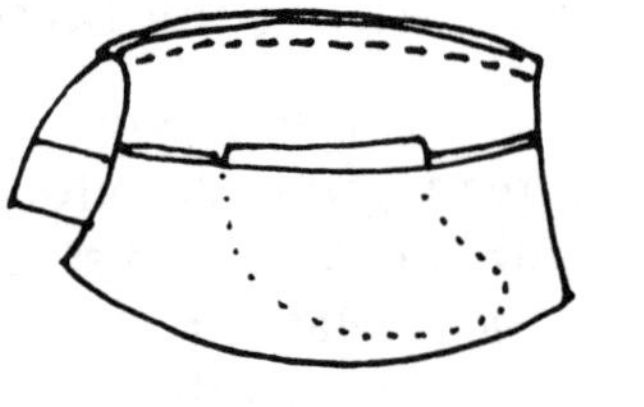

Sew back to body including wing inseam. Sew back seam.

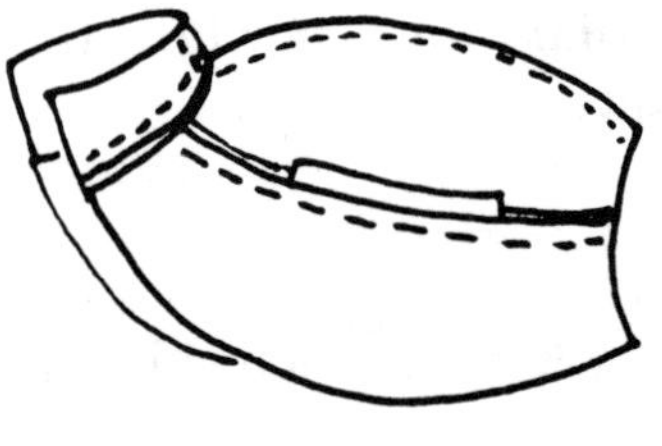

Sew neck base back seam. Join neck base to body.

Change to white thread to sew head to neck. Sew head and neck back seam.

Sew neck ring back seam; sew to neck.

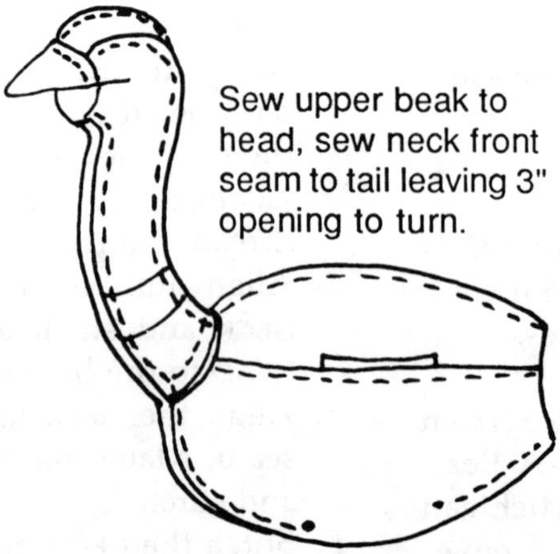

Sew upper beak to head, sew neck front seam to tail leaving 3" opening to turn.

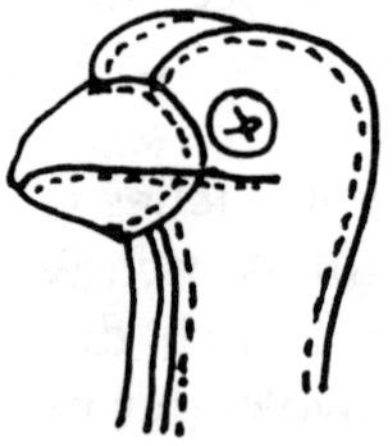

Join lower beak to neck; align beaks, dart and stitch. Insert eyes.

Join tails.

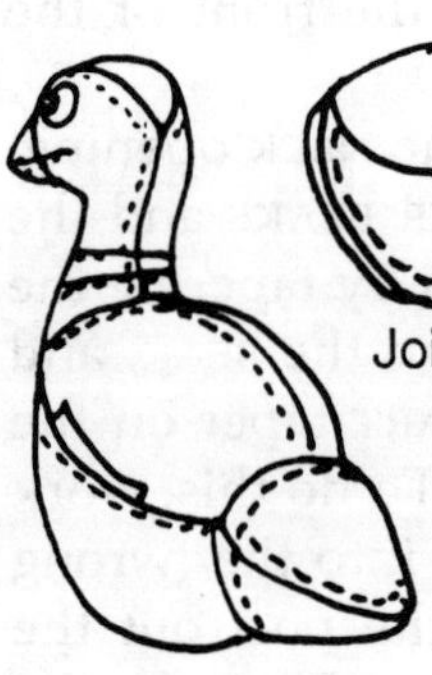

Join tail to body.

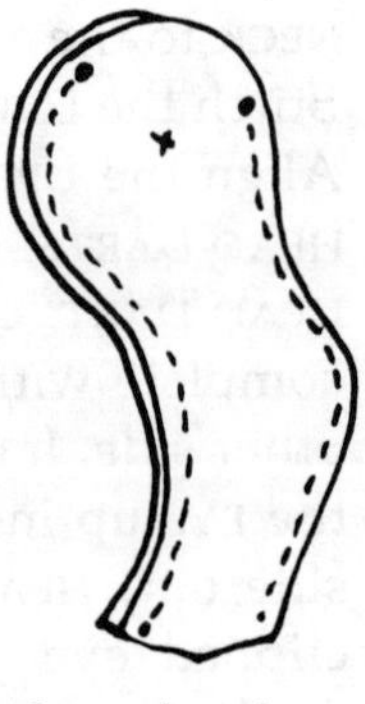

Sew legs, leaving top and bottom open.

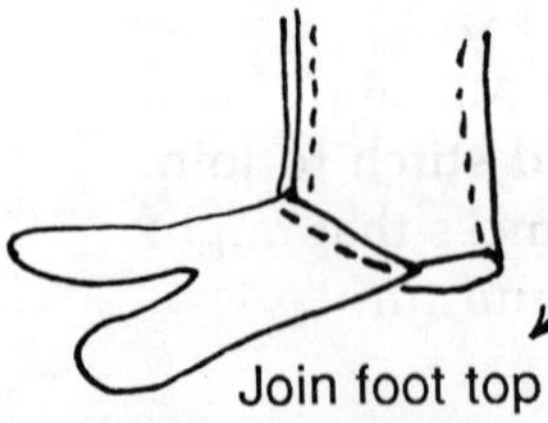

Join foot top to leg front.

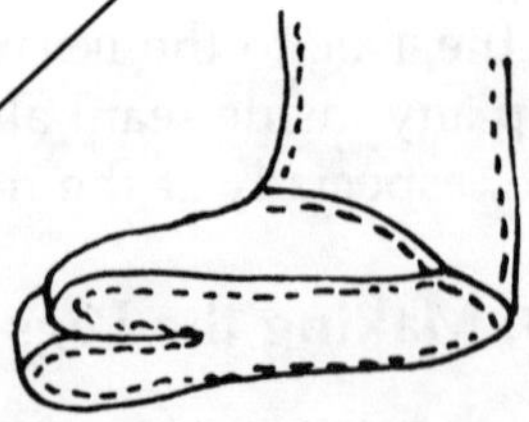

Join foot sole to foot top and leg.

Cross-section of stuffed leg

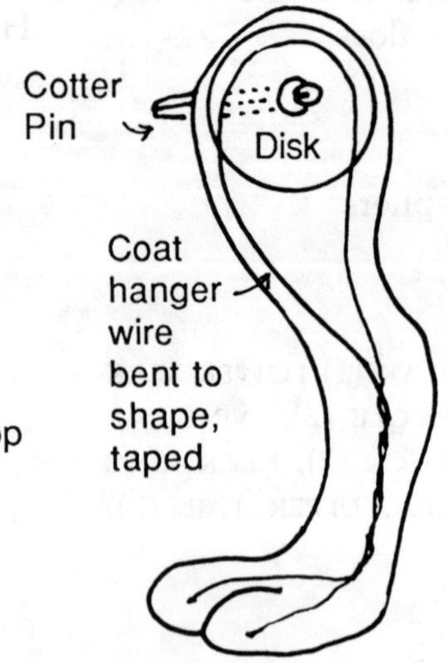

Insert wire; insert disk and cotter pin. Finish stuffing, sew closed.

Cross-section of body

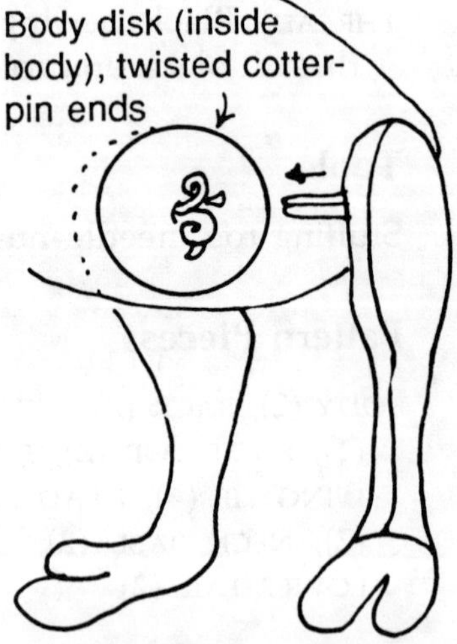

Push leg cotter pin into body and body disk, twist ends of pin firmly to disk; stuff body, sew closed.

B. Align the FOOT TOP with the LEG FRONT and stitch. Repeat.

C. Match the FOOT SOLE with the FOOT TOP and the LEG BACK and stitch. Clip the seam allowances between the toes to the stitch line. Turn. Repeat for the other LEG.

D. To make the WIRE ARMATURE to support the LEGS, straighten the coat hanger with the pliers. Using a 20-inch piece, measure 2½ inches from one end and make a right angle bend for the large TOE. Measure up 3 inches and bend slightly for the MIDWAY JOINT. Make a loop 4 inches long for the THIGH so the wire aligns with itself, and twist the wires together at the MIDWAY JOINT. Bend the second TOE wire forward 2 inches and clip off. Tuck the wire into the LEG to see if it fits. Adjust with the pliers. Repeat for the other LEG. Wrap the TOES and FEET with tape to pad the wires.

E. Stuff a small wad of stuffing into each TOE. Push the WIRE ARMATURE into the LEG, fitting the wires into the TOES. Using the stuffing rod, push stuffing into the LEG, packing it around the wires to fill the LEG. Before stuffing the last 2 inches, insert the 2-inch DISK. Push the cotter pin through the SMALL WASHER, through the DISK, and through the DISK PLACEMENT HOLE. Continue to stuff the LEG very firmly, and sew the top closed with hidden stitching. Repeat for the other LEG.

F. To join the LEGS to the BODY, push the tip of the LEG COTTER PIN into the BODY DISK PLACEMENT HOLE. Insert a DISK over the PIN. Twist the long PIN end into a loop that presses firmly against the DISK. Twist the other PIN end into a loop in the opposite direction to firmly join the LEG. Repeat for the other LEG.

G. Stuff the ostrich head and body firmly, beginning with small wads packed in the head around the EYE posts. When the body is stuffed very firmly, sew the opening closed.

H. Embroider the MOUTH AND NOSTRILS. Adjust the leg wires so the TOES turn outward and the FEET are flat.

PENGUINS are birds that have lost the ability to fly, but they can porpoise through the water at up to 30 miles an hour with a sea lion in pursuit. They appear only in the southern hemisphere from the Galapagos Islands to Antarctica. Only two of the eighteen kinds, the small agile Adelie (shown) and the three-foot-tall Emperor, live in Antarctica. These charming, compact little animals can withstand a 90-mile-an-hour blizzard and temperatures far below freezing. Both parents alternate tending their egg; each holds the egg cradled on its feet with its warm abdomen covering the egg or newly hatched chick.

Penguins always live in colonies, waddling or hopping on land like full-dress partygoers, or sliding along on their chests like children sledding. They leave land in groups to feed in the

PATTERN

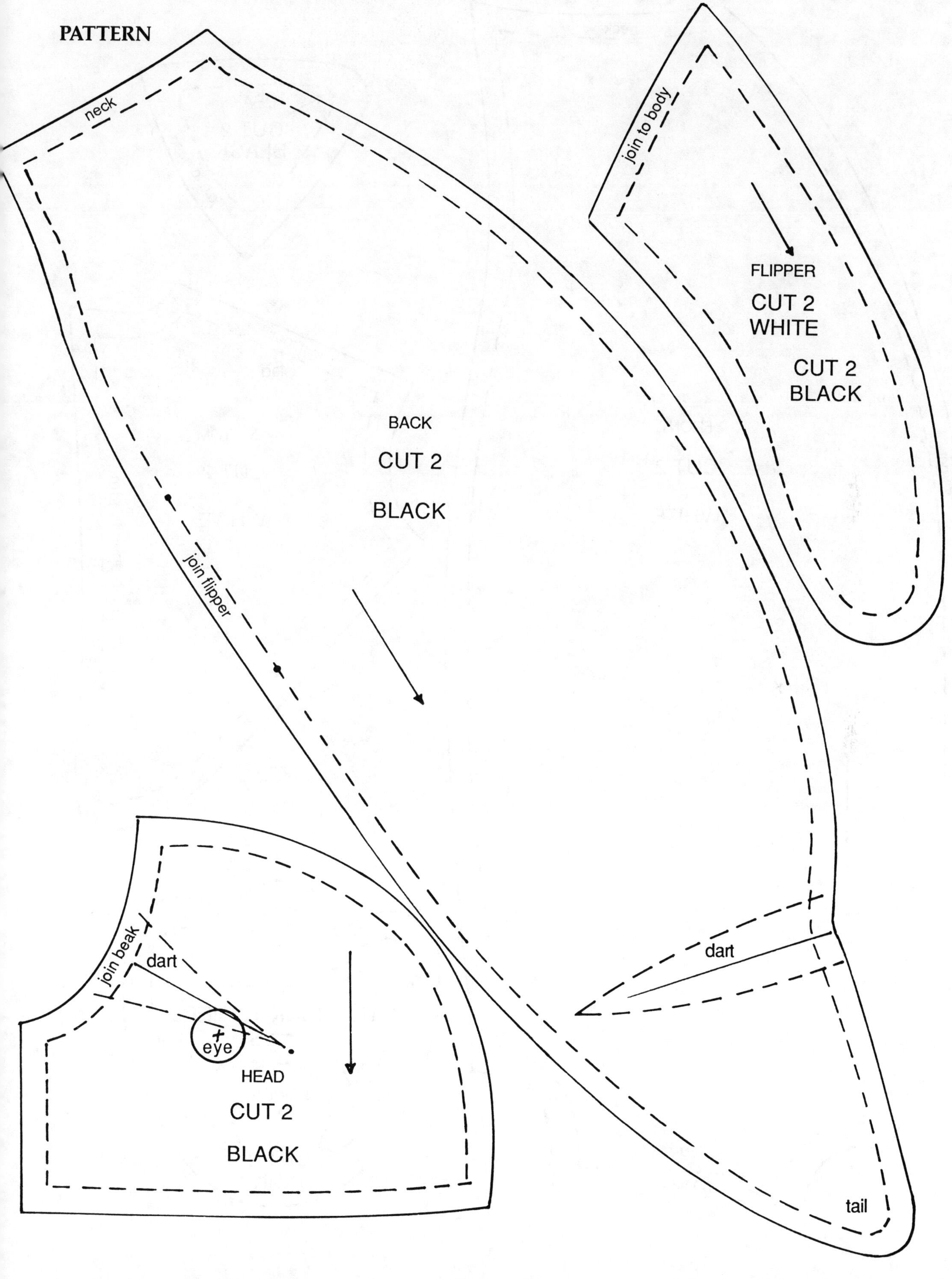

neck
join flipper
BACK
CUT 2
BLACK
dart
tail
join to body
FLIPPER
CUT 2
WHITE
CUT 2
BLACK
join beak
dart
eye
HEAD
CUT 2
BLACK

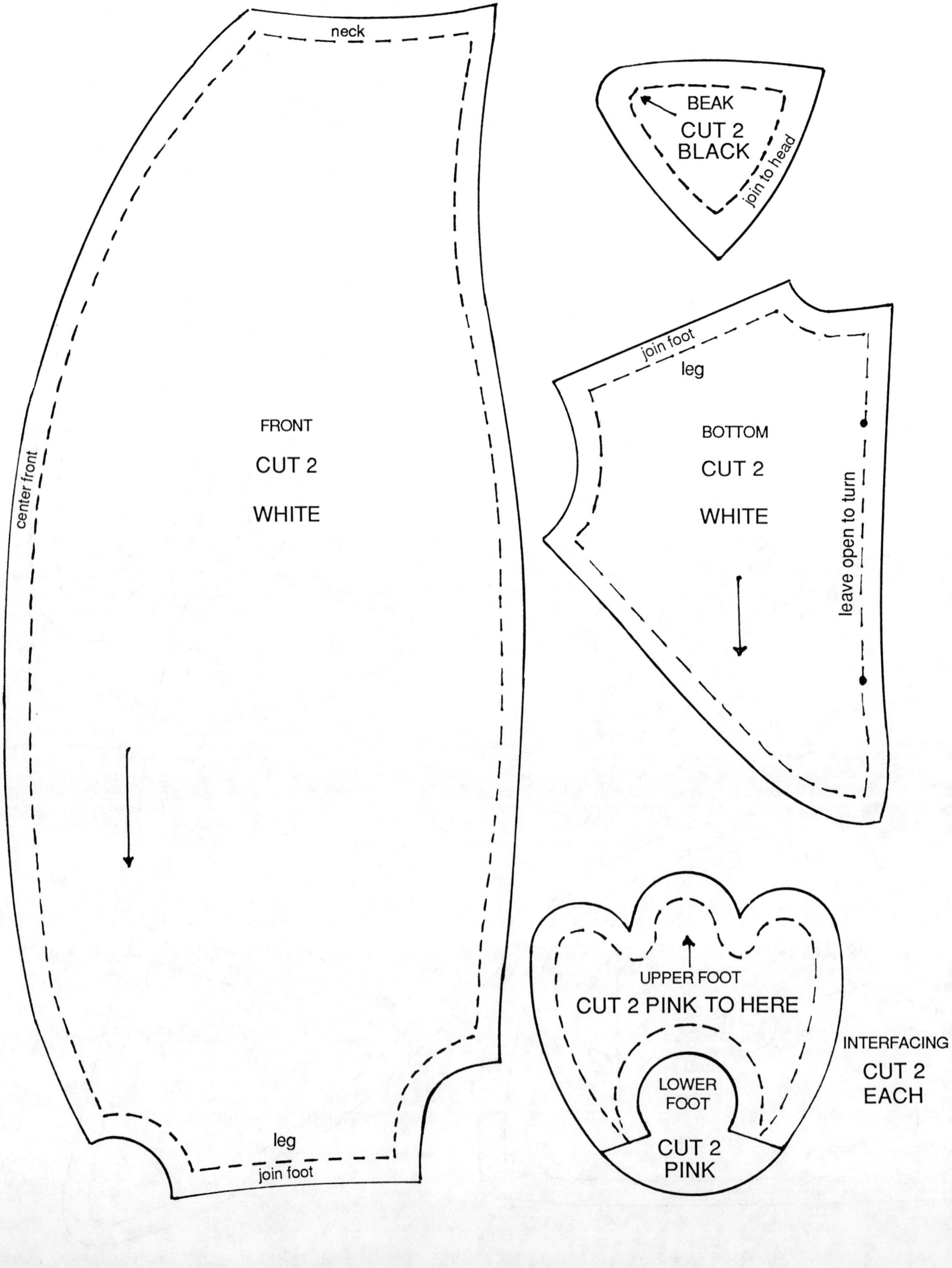
neck
center front
FRONT
CUT 2
WHITE
leg
join foot
BEAK
CUT 2
BLACK
join to head
join foot
leg
BOTTOM
CUT 2
WHITE
leave open to turn
UPPER FOOT
CUT 2 PINK TO HERE
LOWER
FOOT
CUT 2
PINK
INTERFACING
CUT 2
EACH

DIRECTIONS

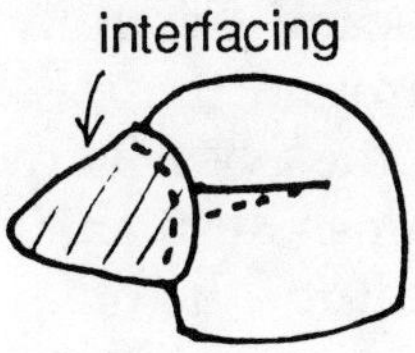

Sew head dart, join head to beak; repeat.

Sew flippers, turn and press.

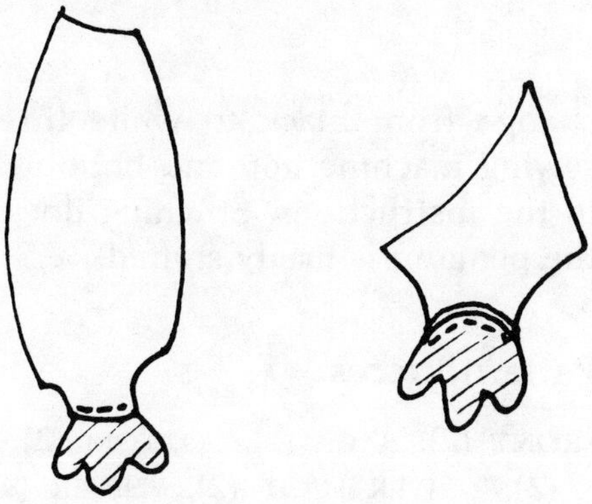

Sew interfaced upper foot to front leg. Sew interfaced lower foot to bottom leg.

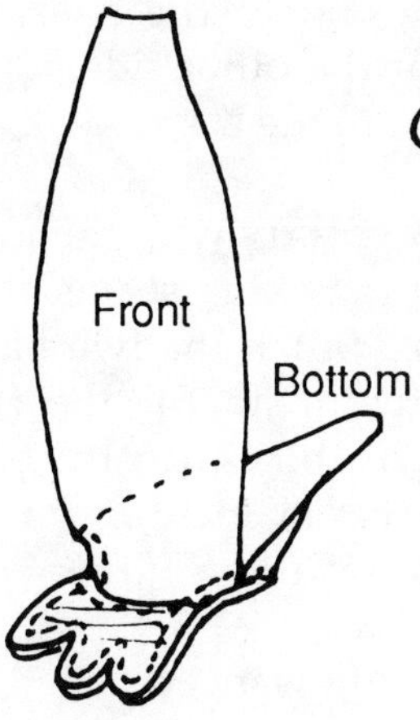

Align feet and legs. Sew foot and leg seams.

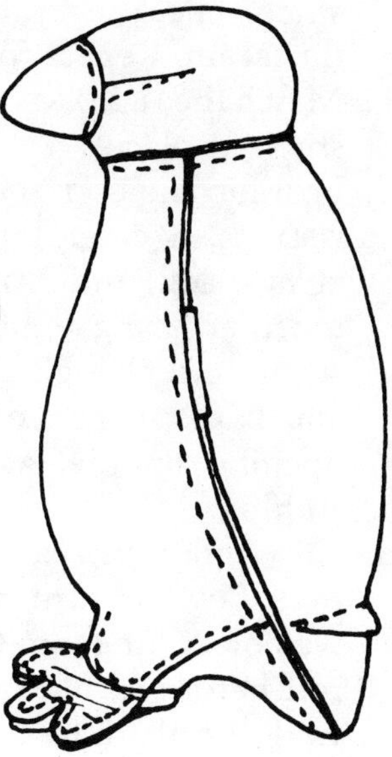

Baste flipper to back. Join back and front at side seam, flipper in seam. Sew tail dart. Join head to body, insert eye, repeat.

Sew left and right sides together, leaving opening on bottom.

Trim, turn, and stuff.

cold sea, and can shoot out of the water up to 7 feet in the air to scale the rocky shore or escape a predator.

NOTE: This 12-inch-tall penguin is nearly life size. The satin bird looks like an adult penguin. The fur one resembles a full-grown youngster moulting its baby feathers. All penguins are black and white, but head markings and size vary. Consult your encyclopedia for other markings.

Materials

HEAD, FLIPPERS, and BACK: 12 by 14 inches black fur or satin

FRONT and FLIPPERS: 11 by 15 inches white fur or satin

FEET: 6 by 6 inches pink fur or doubleknit fabric

BEAK: 2 by 4 inches black satin (for fur animal)

INTERFACING: 8 by 8 inches medium to heavyweight

EYES: Two ⅜-inch post-and-washer plastic eyes (Many penguins have red eyes. These are now available commercially.)

STUFFING: About ¼ pound fiberfill

THREAD: Black and white sewing thread, black and white bobbins

NOTE: To do the best job, use clear synthetic thread, or if this is difficult to find or use, change from black to white thread on your sewing machine, top and bobbin, as indicated in the instructions. Stitching does show when the penguin is firmly stuffed.

Pattern Pieces

FRONT (2), BACK (2), BOTTOM (2), UPPER FOOT (2), LOWER FOOT (2), FLIPPER (4), HEAD (2), BEAK (2), UPPER FOOT INTERFACING (2), LOWER FOOT INTERFACING (2), BEAK INTERFACING (2)

Step 1: Cutting the Fabric

Cut out all pieces.

Step 2: Assembling the Penguin

A. Using black thread on top and on the bobbin, fold and stitch the HEAD DARTS. Fit and stitch the BEAK to the HEAD.

B. Match a black and a white FLIPPER (white in front and black in back), seam, turn, and press flat. Repeat for the other FLIPPER. Use the pointed dowel to turn.

C. Switch to white thread on the machine, top and bobbin. Pin the INTERFACINGS to each FOOT. Align the UPPER FOOT with the FRONT LEG and stitch. Align the LOWER FOOT with the BOTTOM LEG and stitch. Match the FEET and LEG seams and join the FEET, FRONT and BOTTOM, by stitching this seam. Carefully trim the seam allowances around the LEGS and TOES, and clip between the TOES. Turn the FOOT to check the seams. Restitch if necessary to reinforce. Repeat for the other FOOT.

D. Using black thread, sew the BACK DARTS. Position and baste the FLIPPERS on the BACK as marked on the pattern, black to black, raw edges aligned.

E. Align the FRONT and BACK SIDE SEAMS and stitch, enclosing the end of the FLIPPER in this seam. Repeat for the other side.

F. Match the HEAD NECK to the BODY NECK, and stitch in place.

G. Position the LEFT BODY HALF with the RIGHT BODY HALF carefully matching seams at the BEAK, NECK, and TAIL. Stitch the two halves together using white thread for the front seam, and changing to black for the HEAD and BACK seam. Leave an inch and a half opening on the BOTTOM for turning and stuffing.

H. Clip and trim seam allowances. Insert the EYES. Begin to turn at the BEAK. Push a small wad of stuffing into the BEAK with the dowel rod before turning completely. Push small wads firmly into the TOES. Stuff the bird firmly. Hand sew the bottom opening closed.

QUAIL are small rotund birds about the size of a meadowlark. These sturdy ground birds have bills shaped for grubbing, and stout toes for scratching. They eat insects, seeds, buds, and berries. The two most memorable characteristics of these birds are their call and their parenting. The quail's clear sharp whistle seems to say "Bob White" and has given the common variety the name bobwhite. These birds live in fields and hedges, nesting on the ground. When they hatch, the little round nestlings follow their mother in single file as they dart in and out through the grass.

The bobwhite quail ranges throughout central and eastern United States and as far south as Guatemala and Cuba. The scaled quail appears in southwestern United States. Both are members of the partridge family (family *Phasianidae*) and belong to the larger grouping called fowl. This includes domestic fowl:

PATTERN

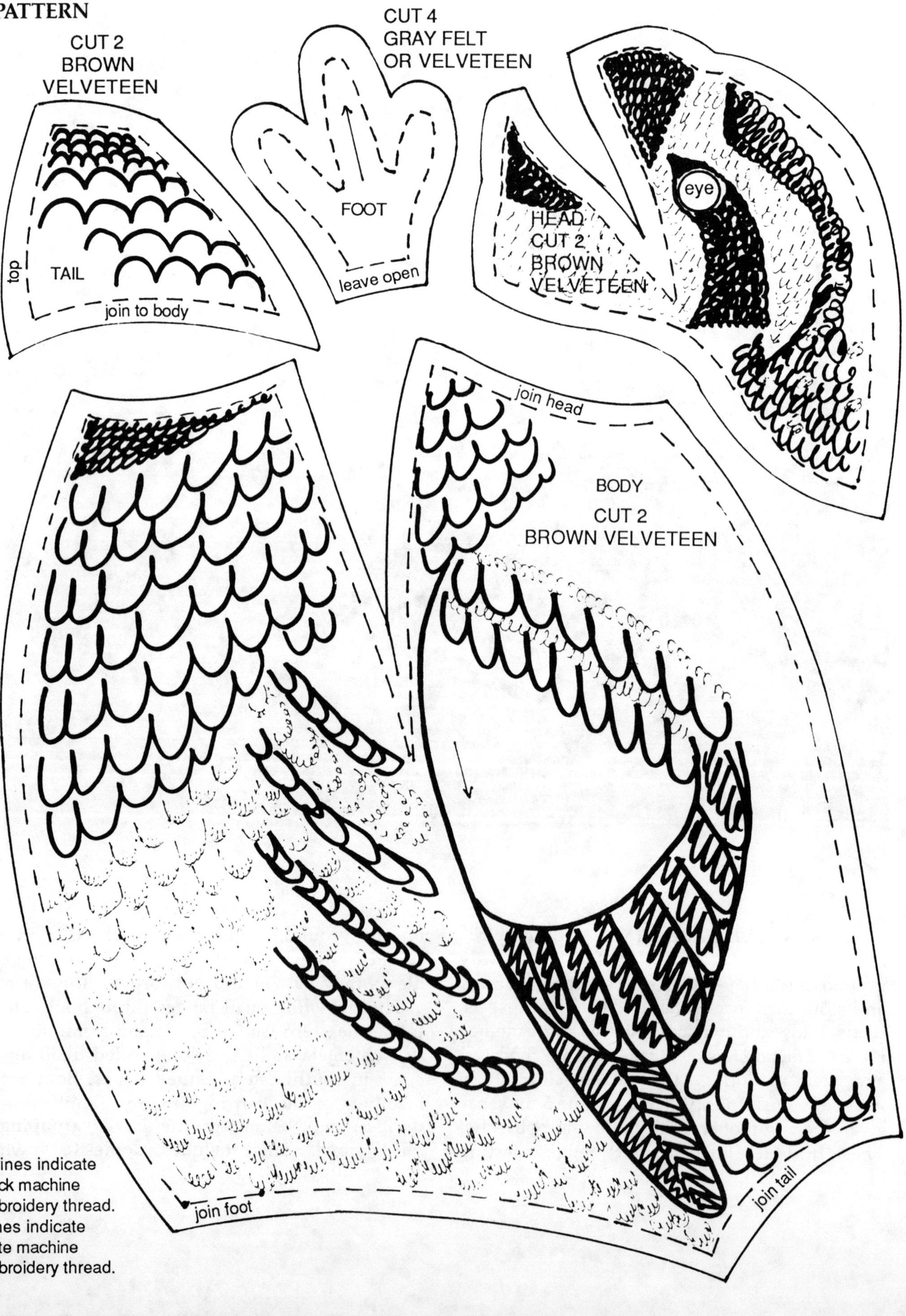

KEY:
Heavy lines indicate black machine embroidery thread.
Light lines indicate white machine embroidery thread.

chickens, geese, ducks, and turkeys, and wild fowl: geese, ducks, swans, and wild turkeys.

NOTE: This quail is approximately life size. Since the charm of the bird is in the elaborate feather patterns, directions tell how to machine-embroider these designs before sewing the bird. Designs can also be applied with hand embroidery or textile paints before or after sewing the bird.

Materials

BODY, HEAD, TAIL, and BASE: 8 by 22 inches light-brown velveteen

BODY, HEAD, TAIL, and BASE: 8 by 22 inches Pellon interfacing (for machine embroidery only)

FEET: 6 by 8 inches gray velveteen, felt, or velour

CHEST: 1 by 1½ inches black felt, or a black feather

FOOT WIRES: Two 4-inch pieces stovepipe wire

EYES: 7 mm (¼-inch) post-and-washer plastic eyes, yellow with black center

THREADS: Regular sewing thread or machine embroidery thread in black and white, matching brown sewing thread

STUFFING: 8 ounce fiberfill

Tools

Wooden chopstick or dowel to turn and stuff, embroidery foot for sewing machine if needed, machine-embroidery hoop

Pattern Pieces

TAIL (2), FOOT (4), HEAD (2), BODY (2), BASE (1), CREST (1)

Step 1: Decorating the Quail

NOTE: Do not cut the pattern pieces until Step 2.

A. To machine embroider:

1. Trace the pattern on the velveteen with tailor's chalk or pencil. To avoid confusion, mark only major design lines within each piece, such as the outline of the wings, the head line, and the neck line. For the smaller details within these areas, consult the pattern while you machine-embroider. For help in tracing the design details, use dressmaker's tracing carbon or an artist's light box.
2. Pin the velveteen fabric to the interfacing.
3. Machine-embroider the designs using a medium zig-zag setting and free-motion sewing guided by hand. Heavy design lines indicate black embroidery stitching. Lighter lines mean white embroidery. Use a machine embroidery hoop to hold the fabric taut as you stitch. Sew all the lines as indicated within the hoop, then move it for the next section. Complete all machine embroidery before cutting out the pieces.

NOTE: Each sewing machine embroiders a little differently. On some the machine is set for medium width zig-zag stitching and the pressure on the presser foot is released to allow free movement of the fabric. On others an embroidery-foot attachment allows the fabric to move freely. In either case the person sewing guides the fabric instead of the feed dogs pulling it through. For more specific information about machine embroidery, consult your sewing machine manual or see my *Sewing Machine Craft Book*, Van Nostrand Reinhold, 1981.

B. To hand-embroider: Eliminate the interfacing backing. Use a hand-sewing embroidery hoop to keep the fabric taut while stitching. Use whatever stitches give the desired effect, for example, a combination of chain stitch, feather stitch, and satin stitch. It is also possible to hand-embroider the quail after assembly if a fine needle and thread that will not catch in the stuffing is used.

C. To paint the surface: Eliminate the interfacing backing. If you have a light box or bright window, tape the fabric over the design, and use acrylic or textile paint to trace over the lines. (See the Instructions for making the Butterfly for more detail on this

DIRECTIONS

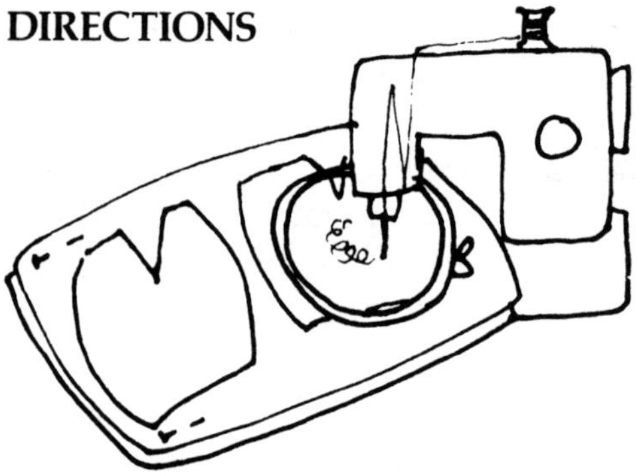

Pin velveteen to Pellon backing, use hoop to machine-embroider designs on head, body, and tail (or hand-embroider).

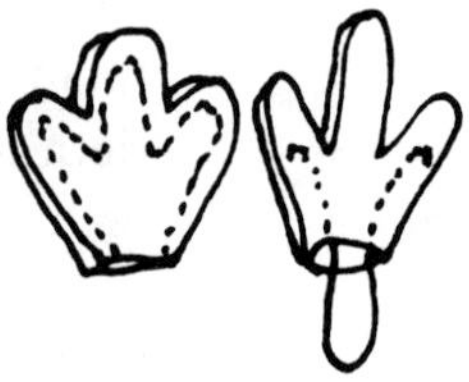

Sew feet; turn and stuff lightly. Bend wire points back, wrap with stuffing, insert into toes.

Sew body dart.

Sew head dart.

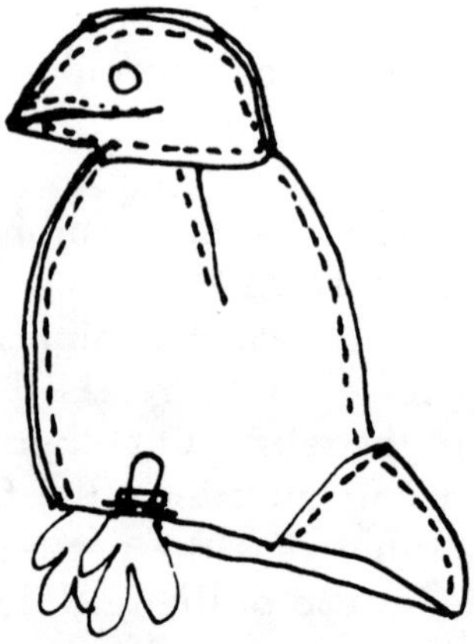

Baste crest to head, insert eyes. Sew head, tail, and feet to body. Sew assembled bodies together.

Sew base to body, sewing over leg wires.

Turn, stuff, and sew opening closed. Bend foot wires to support body.

CUT 1
BLACK FELT

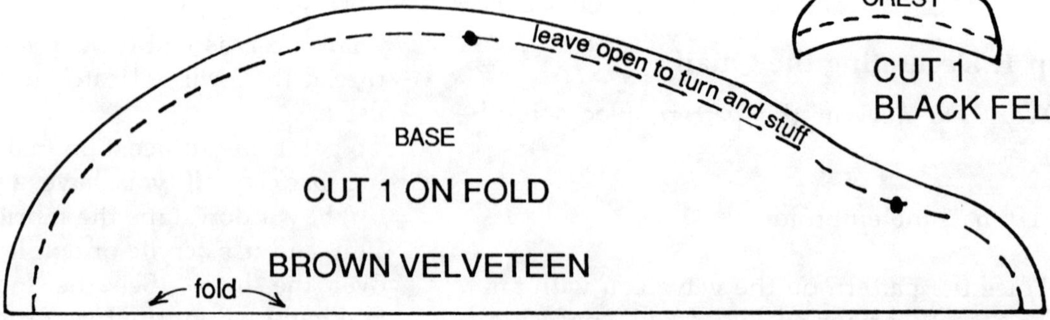

technique.) Otherwise, trace the lines as in Step 1, and paint over them.

Step 2: Cutting Out the Quail

Cut out all pieces.

Step 3: Sewing the Quail

A. Match two FEET and stitch around the TOES with very short stitches, making squared or rounded corners at the base of the TOES to provide enough seam allowance to keep from fraying. Leave the end open for turning. Repeat for the other FOOT. Turn the FOOT right side out, using the chopstick to push the TOES out carefully.

B. Push small wads of stuffing into the TOES. Bend small loops in each end of the two 4-inch FOOT WIRES to keep the ends from poking through the fabric. Wrap thin wads of stuffing around the wires, bend the wire into a "V," and stuff the wire ends into the center TOE and one outside TOE. Stuff the remaining TOE. Baste across the open end of the TOE, hand-wheeling the machine if necessary to sew over the protruding wires. Repeat for the other FOOT.

C. Align the edges of the BODY DART and stitch, beginning at the center end of the dart. Taper the end smoothly. Repeat for the other side.

D. Sew the HEAD DART, tapering the end smoothly. Repeat for the other side.

E. Baste the CREST to one side of the HEAD (unless a feather is used). Insert a post-and-washer EYE in each side of the HEAD.

F. Join the HEAD to the BODY. Sew the TAIL to the BODY. Repeat for the other side.

G. Align the two BODY pieces and sew from the front to the tail. Baste the FEET in place on the BODY.

H. Pin the BASE in place and sew, leaving a 3-inch opening for turning. Machine-stitch over the FEET WIRES with care, or hand-wheel over them.

I. Clip inside seam allowances at the BEAK, NECK and TAIL to avoid pulls. Turn, using the chopstick to push the BEAK out and to push a small wad of stuffing into it. Continue to stuff with small wads. Pack the bird very firmly to create the rounded shape. Sew the opening closed with hidden stitching.

J. For a FEATHERED CREST sew or glue the FEATHER in place and trim to the right shape. To complete the bird, hand-sew to complete any machine embroidery areas needed, for example, where seams join.

RABBITS, as rodents, are among the most common animals in the world. They breed rapidly and grow up fast to keep ahead of the predators. At the sight of an enemy the rabbit may freeze in its tracks hoping to escape detection. Failing that, the rabbit dashes off zig-zagging for cover. As a last effort the rabbit may turn to face an aggressor, puffing itself up defiantly. The timid, cuddly cottontail rabbit has been known to kick a bobcat in the face with its strong back legs. Jack rabbits have the strongest back legs of all rabbits, useful for bouncing over the Western prairies.

Rabbits dig burrows to raise their young, and

PATTERN

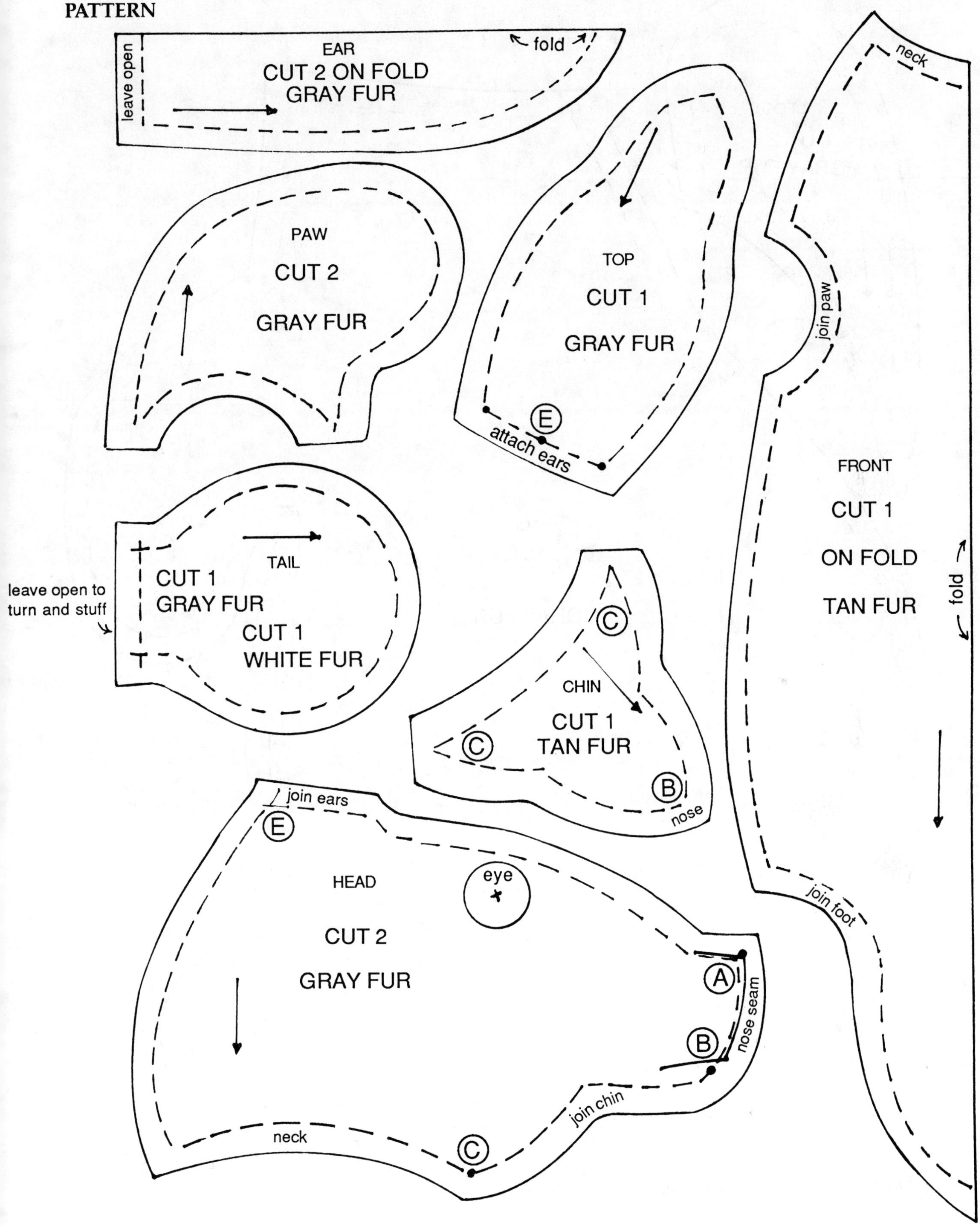
EAR
CUT 2 ON FOLD
GRAY FUR
leave open
fold
PAW
CUT 2
GRAY FUR
TOP
CUT 1
GRAY FUR
E
attach ears
neck
join paw
FRONT
CUT 1
ON FOLD
TAN FUR
fold
join foot
TAIL
CUT 1
GRAY FUR
CUT 1
WHITE FUR
leave open to
turn and stuff
CHIN
CUT 1
TAN FUR
C
C
B
nose
join ears
E
HEAD
eye
CUT 2
GRAY FUR
A
B
nose seam
join chin
neck
C

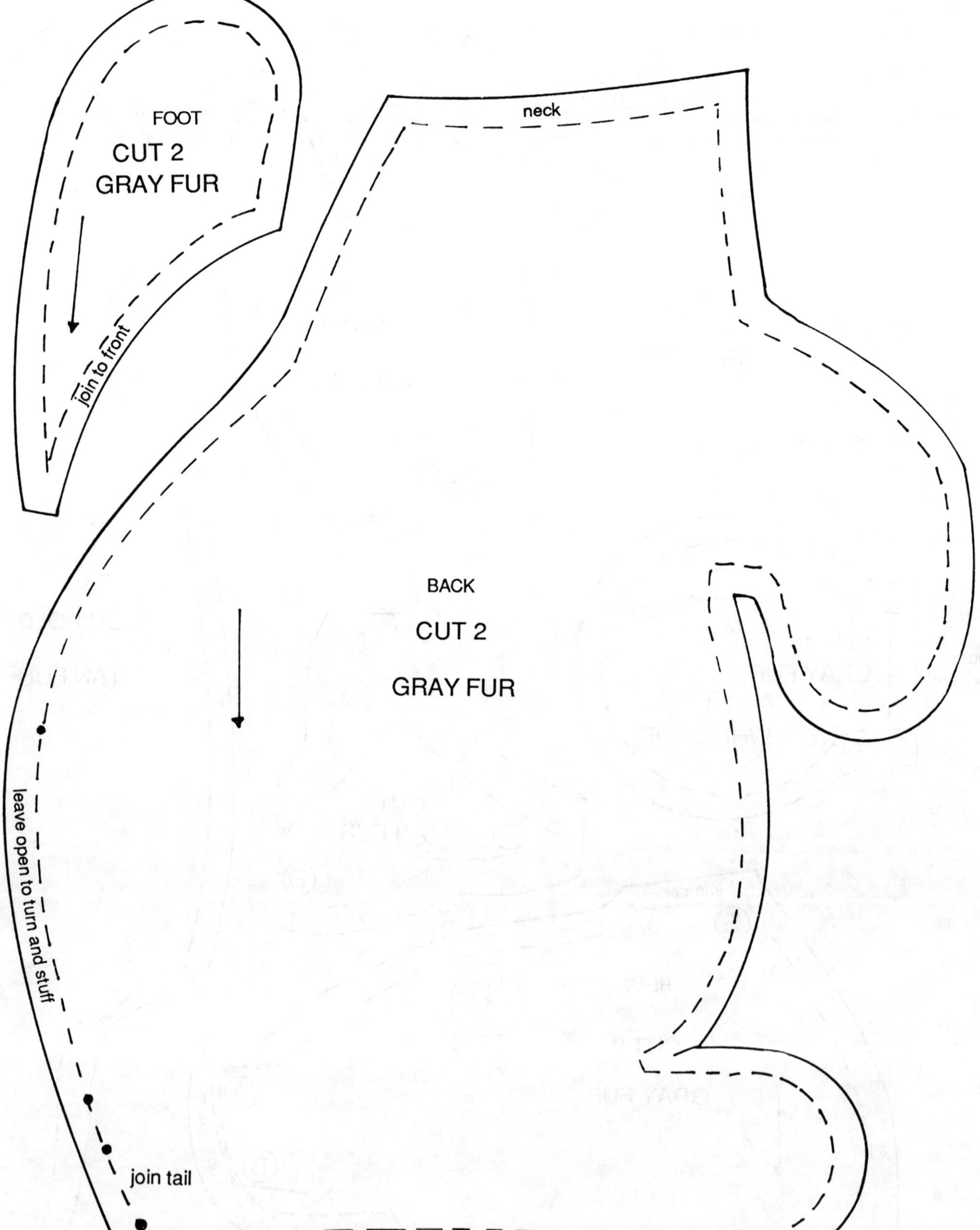
FOOT
CUT 2
GRAY FUR
join to front
neck
BACK
CUT 2
GRAY FUR
leave open to turn and stuff
join tail

adapt easily to living in suburban neighborhoods. In ours, visiting wild rabbits know that our dog can't blast through the picture window even though she's bouncing up and down barking, so they keep on munching. Go to the state fair animal exhibit to see the remarkable range of domestic rabbit breeds from tiny to giant, silky to angora.

NOTE: This rabbit measures 12 inches tall. Fur fabric makes the same pattern appear much plumper than the woven wool fabric. Choose any number of fabrics from plush to velveteen, calico, felt, or velour to make this toy.

Materials

BACK, FOOT, PAW, TOP, EARS, and TAIL: 15 by 15 inches gray fur fabric, ½-inch pile
FRONT, TAIL, CHIN: 7 by 10 inches tan fur fabric
EARS: 4 by 3 inches tan felt
TAIL: Optional 3 by 3 inches white fur fabric, 1-inch pile, and 3 by 3 inches tan fur fabric, 1-inch pile
EYES: Two ½-inch brown plastic post-and-washer eyes
STUFFING: About ½ pound fiberfill
WHISKERS: Monofilament fish line
THREAD: Brown embroidery floss, matching sewing thread

Pattern Pieces

BACK (2), FOOT (2), EAR (4), PAW (2), TOP (1), FRONT (1), CHIN (1), HEAD (2), TAIL (2)

Step 1: Cutting the Fabric

Cut out all pieces. Take care not to cut fur fibers when cutting the backing.

Step 2: Making the Rabbit Head

A. Align the fur fabric EAR face to face with the felt EAR. Stitch, leaving the end open to turn. Turn and press. Top-stitch the EAR edges if the piece does not stay flat. Fold lengthwise and baste. Repeat for the other EAR.
B. Fit the folded EARS to the TOP and baste in place.
C. Align the TOP to the HEAD and stitch. Join the TOP to the other HEAD and stitch. Sew the NOSE seam on the HEAD for ¾-inch from A to B as indicated on the pattern.
D. Align the CHIN with the HEAD from C to B and stitch.
E. Fold the HEAD flat, aligning the back seams and stitch to D, which will leave an opening at the top. Fold the back seam D to align with E at the center of the EARS. Stitch across the seam including the ends of the EARS.
F. Turn the HEAD right side out. Insert the EYES.

Step 3: Making the Body

A. Align the PAW face to face with the FRONT and stitch. Repeat for the other PAW. Align the FOOT face to face with the FRONT and stitch. Repeat for the other FOOT.
B. Fit the FRONT, FEET, and PAWS to the BODY and stitch from the neck to the tip of the FRONT. Repeat for the other BODY. Clip the seam allowances on the inside corners around the PAWS and FEET to avoid pulls when turned.
C. Lay the TAIL pieces face to face, and stitch, leaving the end open to turn. Turn. Stuff lightly. Fold to align the seams and stitch.
D. Join the TAIL to the BODY and baste, angling the TAIL upward.
E. Stitch the BACK seam from base to top, including the TAIL in this seam, and leaving a 2½-inch opening above the TAIL for turning.

Step 3: Finishing the Rabbit

A. Insert the HEAD (right side out) into the BODY, aligning the back seams. Stitch around the neck to join.
B. Trim seam allowances if necessary. Turn the rabbit right side out. Stuff the rabbit, beginning with the PAWS, FEET, and HEAD. When the shape is plump and firm, sew the opening closed with hidden stitching.

DIRECTIONS

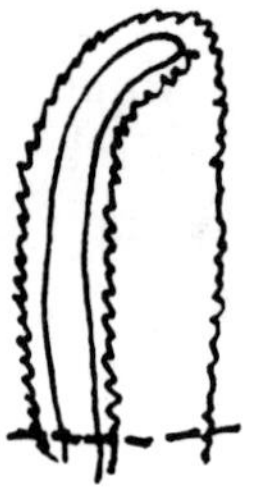

Sew ear, turn, fold. Sew across bottom of ear.

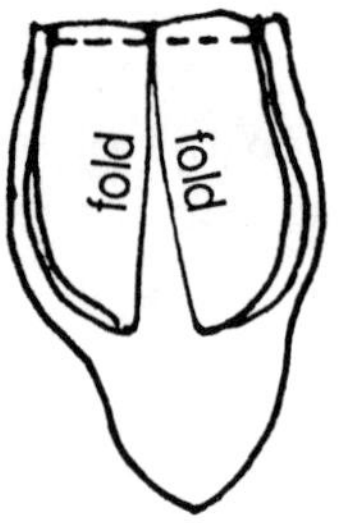

Sew ears to top; leave seam allowance on sides.

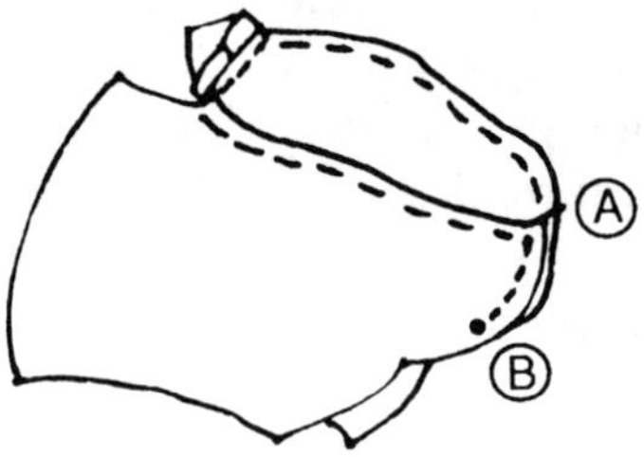

Join top to head. Join nose seam Ⓐ to Ⓑ.

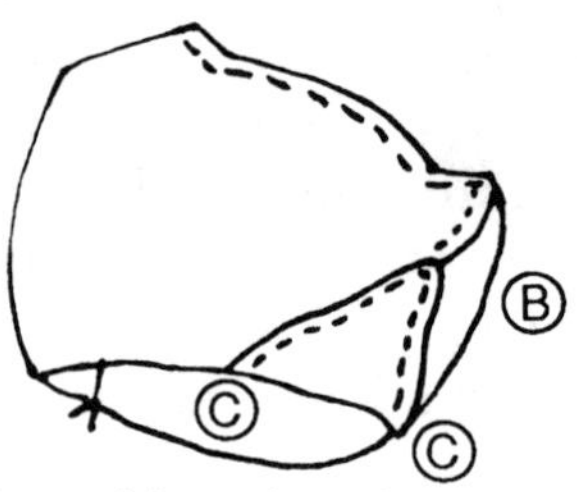

Sew chin to head, Ⓑ to Ⓒ. Sew back seam.

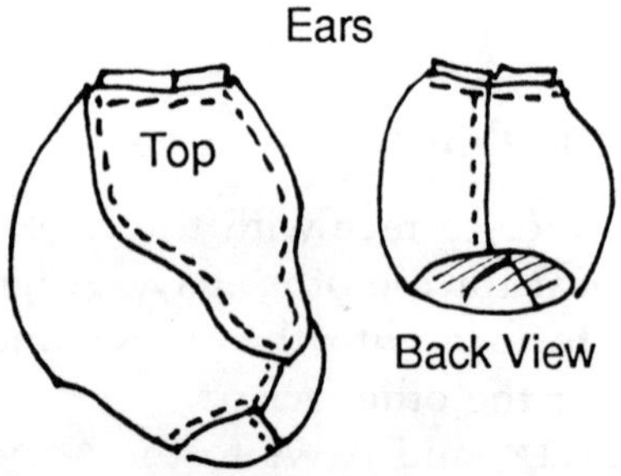

Fold top to head and sew ears into this seam.

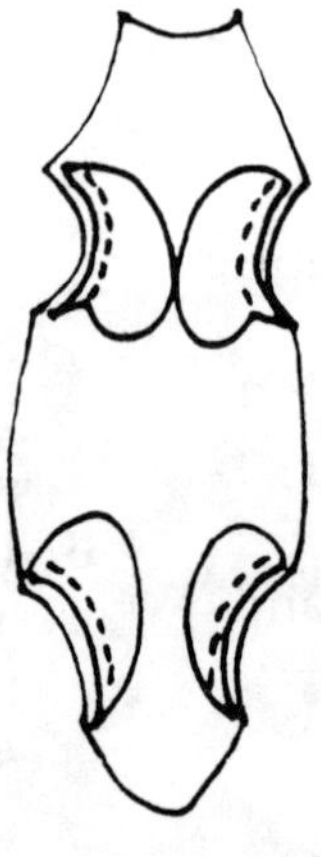

Sew paws and feet to front.

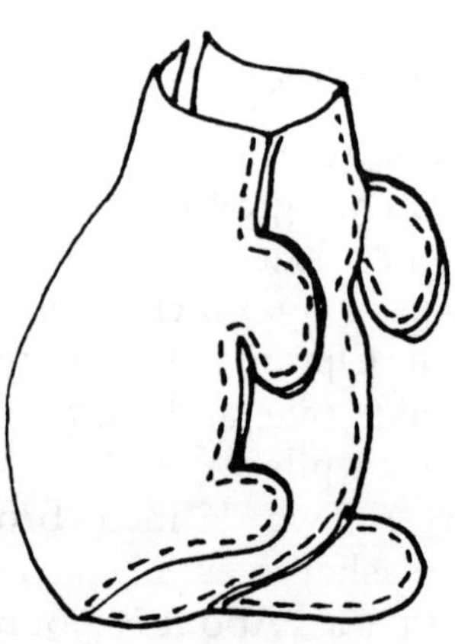

Sew front to body.

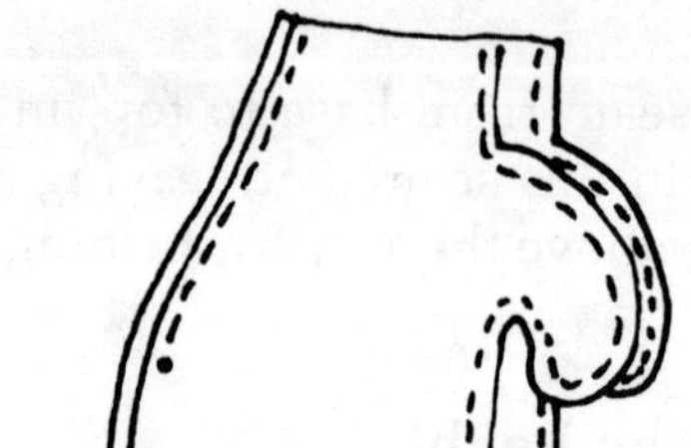

Insert tail. Sew back seam, leaving opening to turn.

Insert right-side-out head into body, sew neck, turn.

Sew eye to eye, nose and mouth, whiskers.

C. Use brown embroidery floss to sew the NOSE and MOUTH along the seam lines. Pull the stitching for the MOUTH tightly to indent it.

D. Knot the thread and sew from the front of one EYE to the other. Pull the thread to indent the EYES and secure the end.

E. To make the WHISKERS, thread the monofilament line on a needle. Tie a knot 3 inches from the end. Sew into the cheek 1 inch from the NOSE, coming out on the opposite cheek. Tie a knot tight against the fur and clip off at 3 inches. Repeat for three or four WHISKERS on each side.

F. With sharp sewing scissors trim the fur where necessary around the EYES and along the jowl to help shape the rabbit's head.

SEA ANIMALS come in as many wondrous assorted shapes, sizes and colors as those on land. Starfish come in two thousand varieties, each with five or more "arms"—always an odd number. Their pebbled skin has skeleton spines protruding, thus their category *echinoderm* or hedgehog skin. Some grow to 3 feet across.

The scallop, one of the brighter bivalves, has a shell ringed with thirty to forty blue eyes that can see danger. He jets quickly away. The scallop's colorful shell is so beautiful that people scour the beaches to collect them.

Ancients named the sea horse, since his long head perched on an arched neck looked so much like a horse. This small odd fish rarely grows more than 10 inches tall, swims upright, and clings to sea plants with his tail.

Many sea animals have "S" names: sailfish, salmon, sand dollar, sardine, sawfish, swordfish, sea urchin, shad, shark, shrimp, smelt, sponge, squid, sunfish, sea bass and more.

NOTE: Since the sea horse and the scallop are decorated with machine designs, and trapunto-stuffed, a lining fabric is required. Be sure to choose firmly woven light-weight material for all fabrics to facilitate turning the sewn animal.

Materials

STARFISH BODY: 7 by 14 inches peach-colored doubleknit fabric with silver thread interwoven (available at holiday season). Other nonfraying fabrics such as felt, calico, jersey, or similar light-weight materials may be used.

TRIM: Orange and pink glass beads

SCALLOP SHELL: OUTER TOP and BOTTOM SHELLS and SCALLOP: 6 by 16 inches of dark peach-colored knit, or similar light-weight material, cotton, felt, satin, and many others may be used.

INNER TOP AND BOTTOM SHELLS: 6 by 14 light peach-colored fabric

BACKING: 6 by 7 inches cotton fabric

EYES: 32 blue beads

SEA HORSE BODY: 10 by 12 inches metallic coated knit fabric.

EYE: One or two ½-inch post-and-washer eye(s) in green or a color related to the fabric.

NOTE: Decorative fabrics are available at holiday time. Many other closely woven, light-weight fabrics will do, but the fabric must be light-weight and flexible in order to turn this complex pattern. To avoid this problem, use felt with exposed unturned seam allowances or, if you choose a heavier weight fabric, increase the size of the pattern.

STUFFING FOR ALL ANIMALS: A few ounces of fiberfill stuffing for each thread: Machine sewing thread in related or harmonizing colors (orange, pink, moss green, etc.), yarn

Tools

Blunt tapestry needle, ¼-inch sharpened dowel, tracing paper, backing paper, double sewing-machine needle

Pattern Pieces:

STARFISH: BODY (2)

SEA SCALLOP: OUTER SHELL (2) INNER SHELL (2), SCALLOP (2), BACKING (1 or 2)

SEA HORSE: BODY (2)

PATTERN

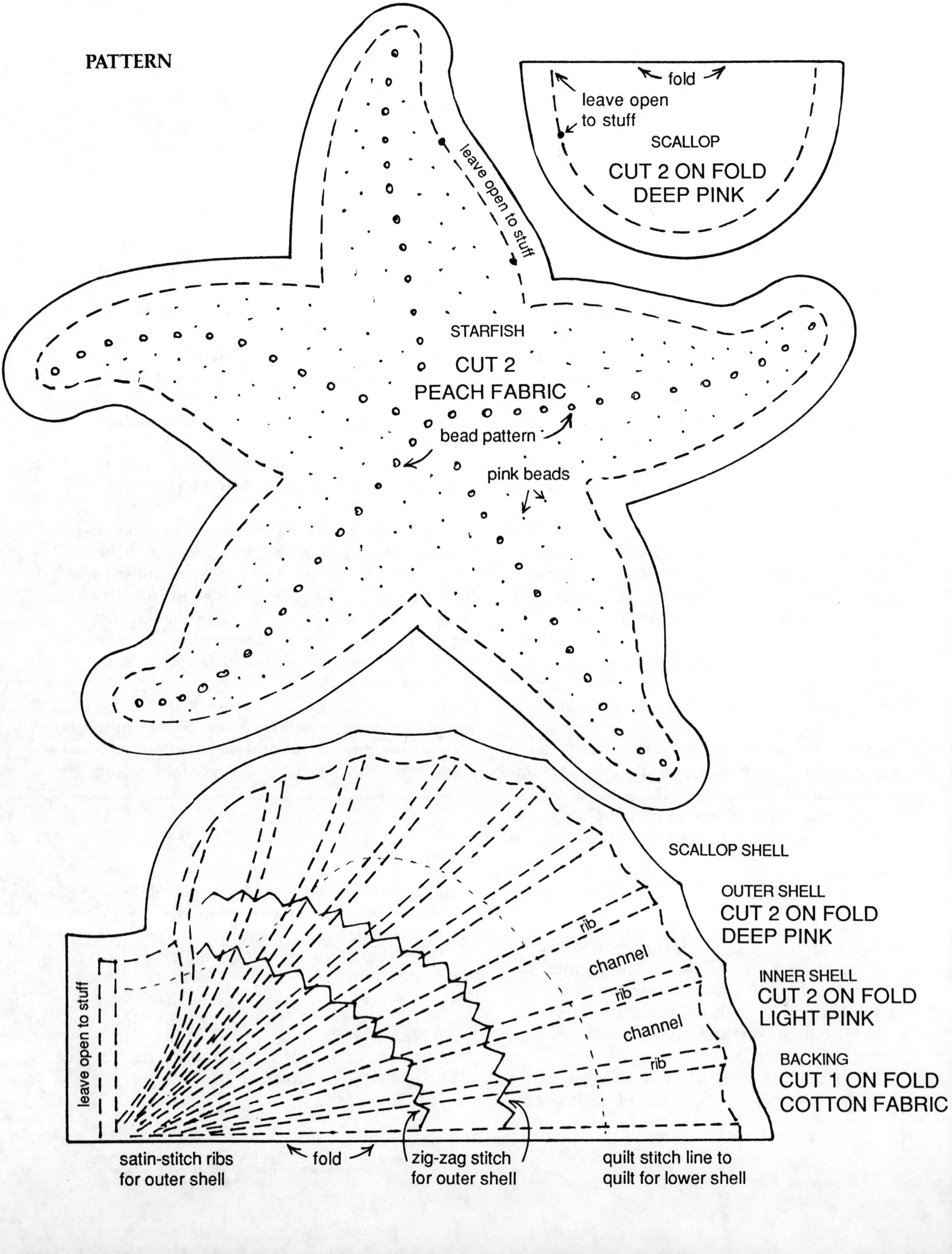
fold
leave open to stuff
SCALLOP
CUT 2 ON FOLD
DEEP PINK
leave open to stuff
STARFISH
CUT 2
PEACH FABRIC
bead pattern
pink beads
SCALLOP SHELL
OUTER SHELL
CUT 2 ON FOLD
DEEP PINK
INNER SHELL
CUT 2 ON FOLD
LIGHT PINK
BACKING
CUT 1 ON FOLD
COTTON FABRIC
rib
channel
rib
channel
rib
leave open to stuff
satin-stitch ribs
for outer shell
fold
zig-zag stitch
for outer shell
quilt stitch line to
quilt for lower shell

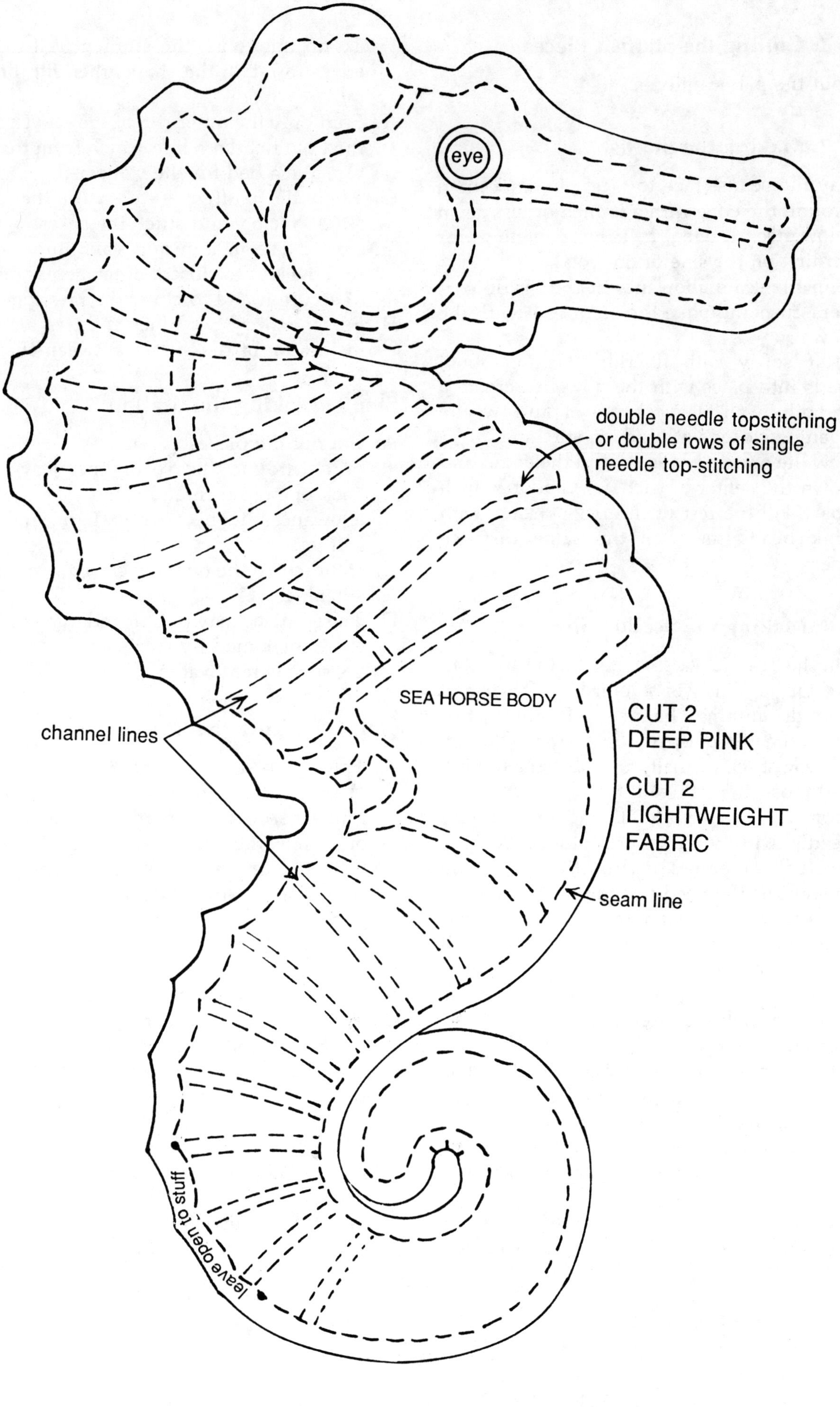
eye
double needle topstitching
or double rows of single
needle top-stitching
SEA HORSE BODY
CUT 2
DEEP PINK
CUT 2
LIGHTWEIGHT
FABRIC
channel lines
seam line
leave open to stuff

Step 1: Cutting the Starfish Pieces

Cut out the pattern pieces.

Step 2: Making the Starfish

A. Lay the BODIES face to face, pin, and stitch around the edge with a ¼-inch or less seam allowance, leaving a 1-inch opening for turning on the side of one ARM.

B. Clip the seam allowance at the inside corners, turn and poke the points out with the dowel.

C. Stuff softly with fiberfill, pushing small wads into place with the dowel to create a smooth, well-filled shape. Hand-sew the opening closed with hidden stitching.

D. Sew the orange beads around the edges and down the center of each ARM about ¼ inch apart. Fill the rest of the TOP SURFACE with pink beads sewn on the same distance apart.

Step 3: Making the Scallop Shell

A. Pin the TOP OUTER SHELL fabric to the BACKING fabric. This will stabilize the fabric and provide quilting channels. Machine satin-stitch the RIBS of the SHELL in orange thread. Zig-zag stitch the half-circle designs in pink and moss green thread.

B. From the reverse side, thread the tapestry needle with yarn to stuff the CHANNELS created by the rows of satin stitching. To do this, insert the needle at the narrow end of the CHANNEL through the BACKING fabric. Follow the CHANNEL to the outer edge, pull the needle out, smooth the yarn and fabric in place, and clip off the yarn. Continue until the shell is stuffed to suit.

C. Cut out all pieces.

D. Align the TOP OUTER SHELL with the TOP INNER SHELL and stitch around on the seam line, leaving the end open for turning. Clip the inside corner seam allowance to avoid pulls, and turn. Repeat for the BOTTOM SHELL.

E. Stuff the TOP SHELL so it is flat on the underside and about 1 inch thick in the center. To do this, push the stuffing well into the edges to retain the shape, then fill the center.

F. Stuff only the outer rim of the LOWER SHELL, then quilt stitch a line 1 inch from the edge to make a bed for the SCALLOP.

G. Align the stuffed SHELLS with the OUTER SHELLS facing, and stitch the bases together. Trim the seam allowances and threads, then fold the SHELLS closed. Stitch across the fold to secure it and to cover the raw edges.

H. Sew the thirty-two blue EYE BEADS along the inside rim of the SHELLS between channels.

Step 4: Making the Scallop

A. Cut out the pieces.

B. Stitch around the seam line, leaving the back open to turn and stuff. Trim the seam allowances if necessary. Turn and stuff softly.

C. Hand-stitch the opening closed with hidden stitching.

D. The SCALLOP may be stitched in place in the SHELL, or joined by snaps or Velcro fasteners so it is removable.

Step 5: Making the Sea Horse

A. Trace a FIRST COPY of the SEA HORSE PATTERN on tracing paper or typing paper. Make a SECOND COPY reversed, which need only show the outside seam line. To do this, trace the reversed FIRST COPY over a light source (a window, for example), or turn the traced SECOND COPY over and trace the line again on the reverse side.

NOTE: Since trapunto quilting contracts the fabric, the paper remains in place during stitching to stabilize the fabric, and the sea horse is cut out after surface decoration is applied.

B. Pin the FIRST COPY to the FACE side of the fabric. Align the SECOND COPY with the first and pin it on the BACK side of the fabric, making a sandwich. Use a double needle in your sewing machine to stitch all the chan-

DIRECTIONS

SCALLOP SHELL

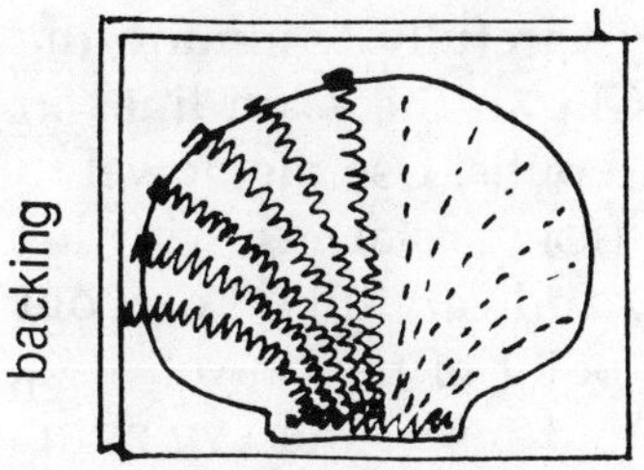

Trace design on fabric, machine satin-stitch shell top.

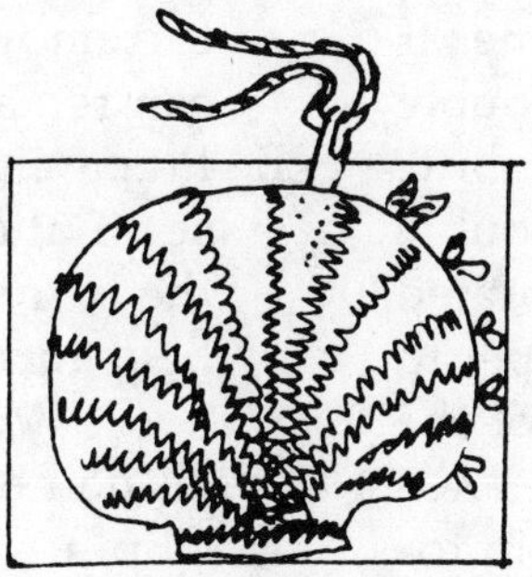

Fill channels with yarn, using tapestry needle.

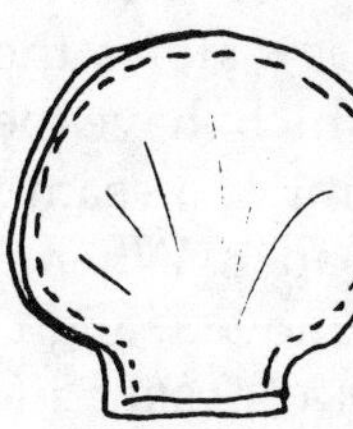

Stitch seam to join shell to lining, turn and stuff. Repeat.

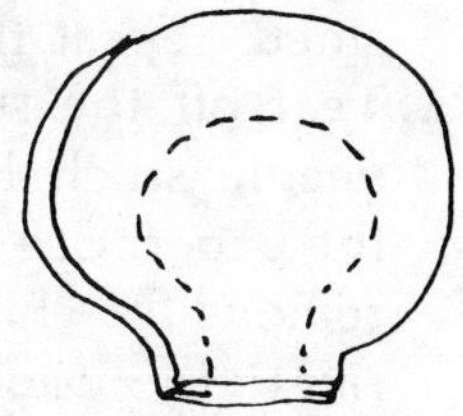

Top-stitch nest on stuffed lower shell.

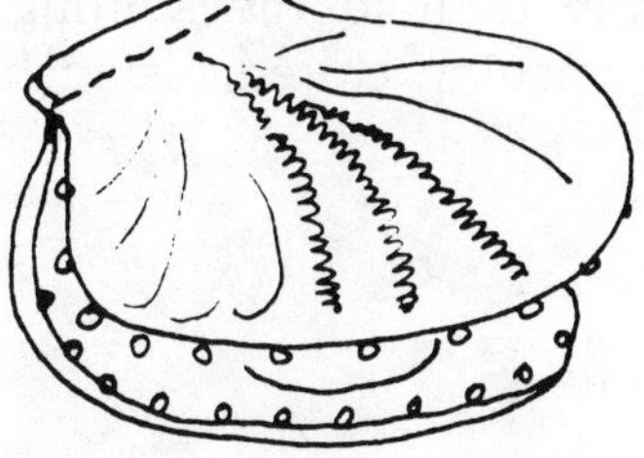

Stitch across base. Fold and stitch across base again. Attach scallop. Sew 32 eyes in place on rim.

STARFISH

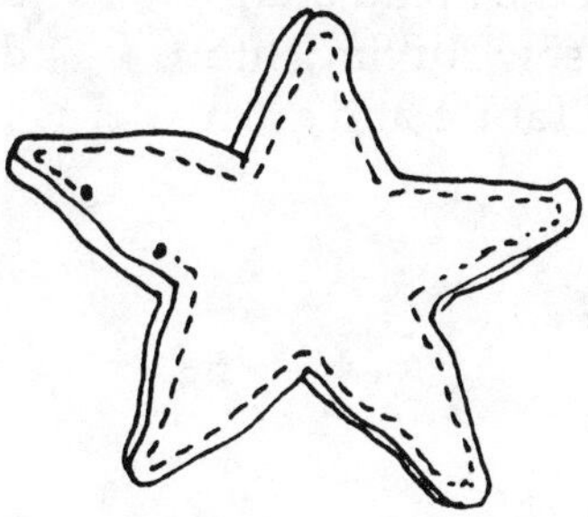

Stitch seam lines, turn, stuff.

Sew opening closed; bead the surface.

SEA HORSE

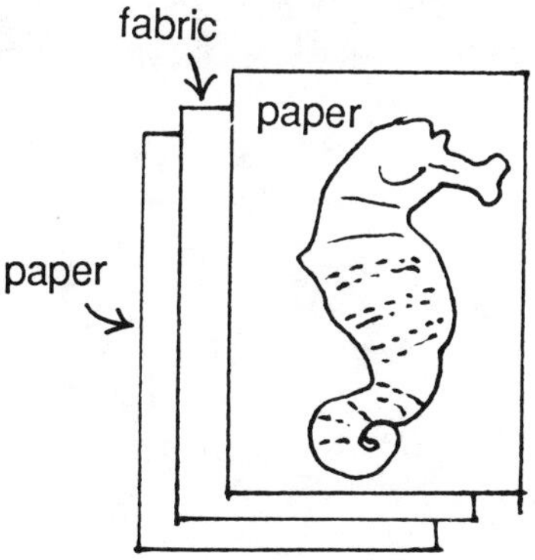

Double-needle stitch channel lines, remove top paper (first copy).

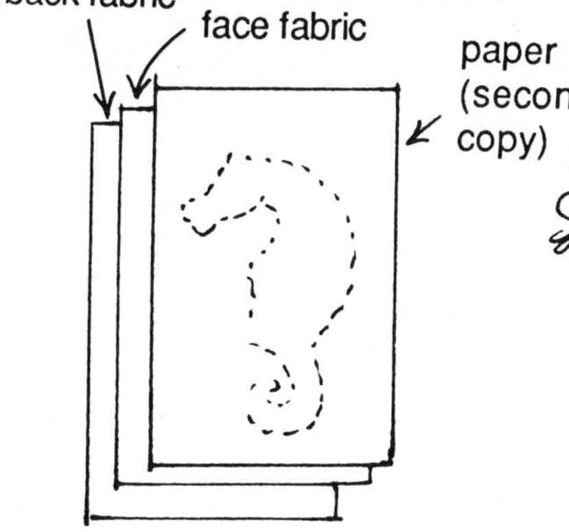

Sew around seam line, cut out sea horse.

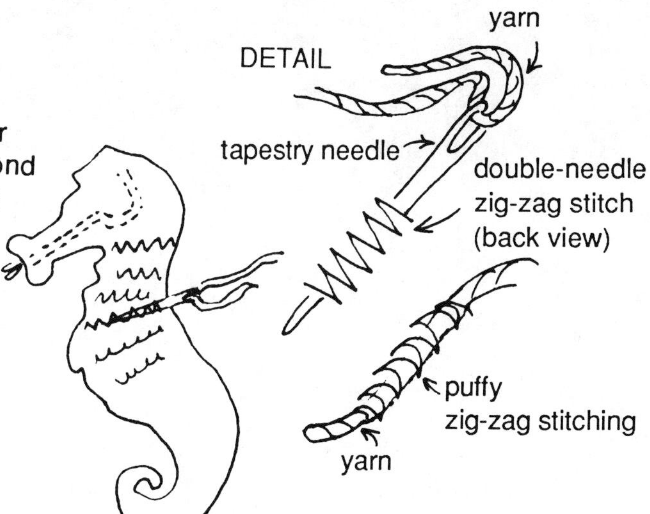

Sew yarn stuffing into zig-zag channels on reverse side of front, turn. Insert eyes, stuff, and sew closed.

nel lines on the pattern continuing past the seam line. Do not stitch the seam line. If you plan to make the SEA HORSE double sided, repeat this step for the back fabric.

C. Tear off the FIRST COPY along the double needle stitch lines which have perforated the paper. Use the point of a seam ripper to remove the channel paper. When all of the FIRST COPY paper is removed, align the FACE FABRIC with the BACKING FABRIC and pin together. Stitch the seam line, using the SECOND COPY still in place for a guideline. Leave a 1-inch opening at the tail for turning and stuffing. Remove the backing paper, leaving the paper under the zig-zag stitching. Don't turn yet.

D. On the reverse side, the bobbin thread has zig-zagged from one top stitch row to the other and formed a CHANNEL. Thread a tapestry needle with yarn and sew stuffing into the CHANNELS. Smooth the fabric and yarn and clip off the ends of the yarn. Don't try to remove the paper from the channels. It can remain in place.

E. Prepare to turn by carefully trimming the seam allowances. Clip to the seam lines in the corners to avoid pulls. Use the dowel to help turn the SEA HORSE, starting with his nose. Work slowly and carefully. Poke out all points with the point of the dowel.

F. Clip a small hole and insert the EYE POST. Insert the washer into the turning hole and work it up into place in the HEAD behind the EYE POST. Push the EYE firmly in place. If you use two EYES, clip off the posts to shorten.

G. Stuff the SEA HORSE, using small wads of fiberfill pushed carefully into place with the dowel. Fill firmly to hold the stuffing in place. Sew the opening closed, using hidden stitching.

TURTLES are reptiles noted mainly for an architectural specialty: their domed shells. Most turtles have grown these hard, heavy shells since dinosaur days, with only a few seagoing turtles having lighter shells. The turtle shown looks most like the small American "red-eared" turtle, although nearly all turtles have similar shell plate patterns. Turtles come as small as the baby "painted turtles" people keep in terrariums, or can grow to the enormous size of more than 1,500 pounds. Turtles don't actually live forever, as popularly stated, but can reach 100 years old.

As handy as shells look to live in, the turtle has had to make a lot of accommodations to manage. The backbone is fused to the shell, and the shoulder and hip girdles fit into the chest. Unable to expand his chest to breath, the turtle moves muscles inside to draw in and expel air. The necks of most turtles retracts into a long "S" curve, but a type of turtle living only in the Southern Hemisphere tucks its neck under the shell.

NOTE: The turtle shown measures 15 inches across and 20 inches from nose to tail. The top shell is assembled like a pieced patchwork quilt. Directions given tell how to sew the legs and shell in one final seam, but you may opt to make the shells, legs, tail, and head separately and sew them all together by hand later.

Materials

NOTE: A one-color turtle takes ½-yard of velveteen. For the turtle shown, five or six different printed velveteen fabrics in harmonizing browns were used, so dimensions are given for each pattern piece.

PATTERN

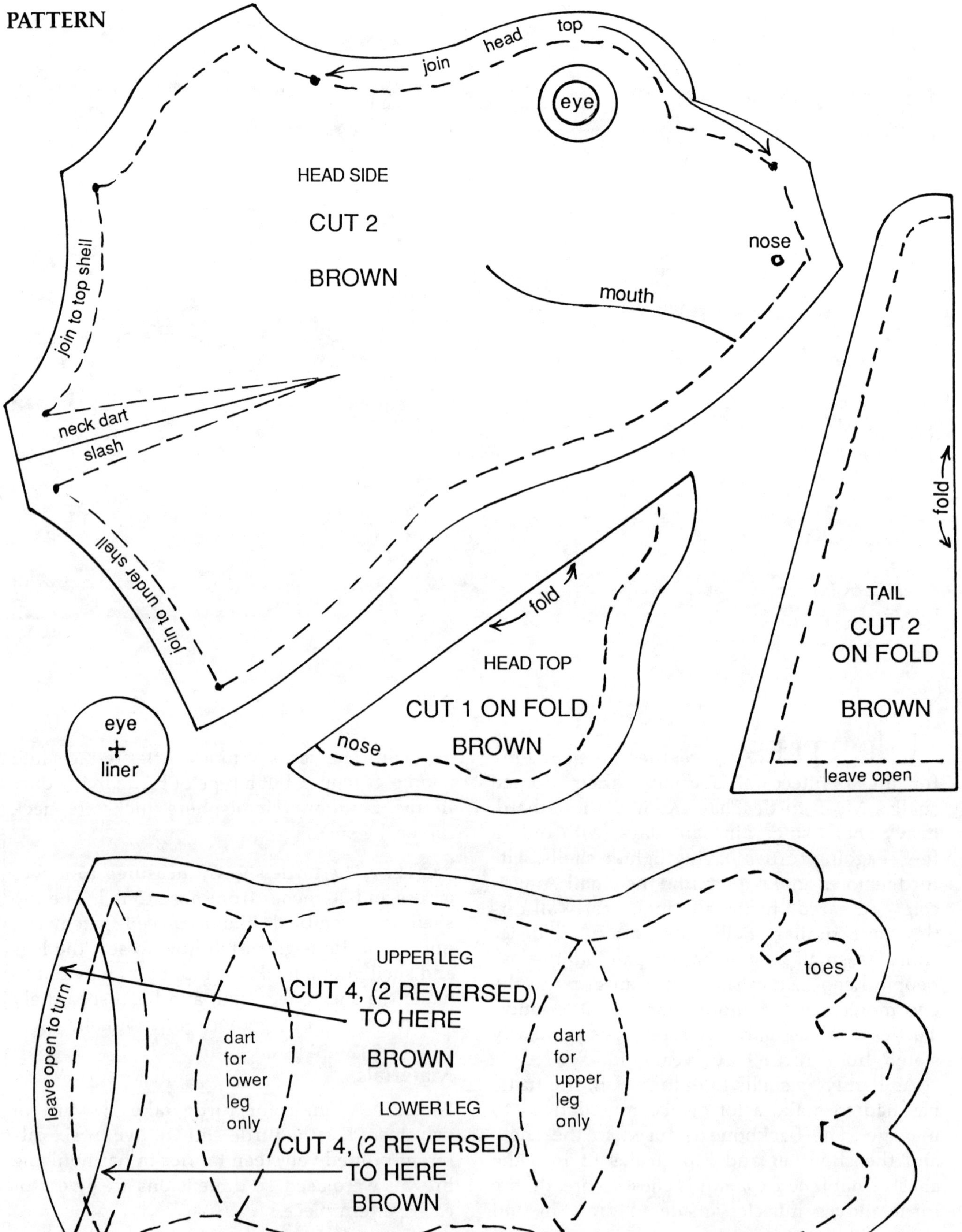
join head top
eye
HEAD SIDE
CUT 2
BROWN
nose
mouth
join to top shell
neck dart
slash
join to under shell
fold
HEAD TOP
CUT 1 ON FOLD
BROWN
nose
eye
+
liner
fold
TAIL
CUT 2
ON FOLD
BROWN
leave open
UPPER LEG
CUT 4, (2 REVERSED)
TO HERE
BROWN
toes
leave open to turn
dart
for
lower
leg
only
LOWER LEG
CUT 4, (2 REVERSED)
TO HERE
BROWN
dart
for
upper
leg
only

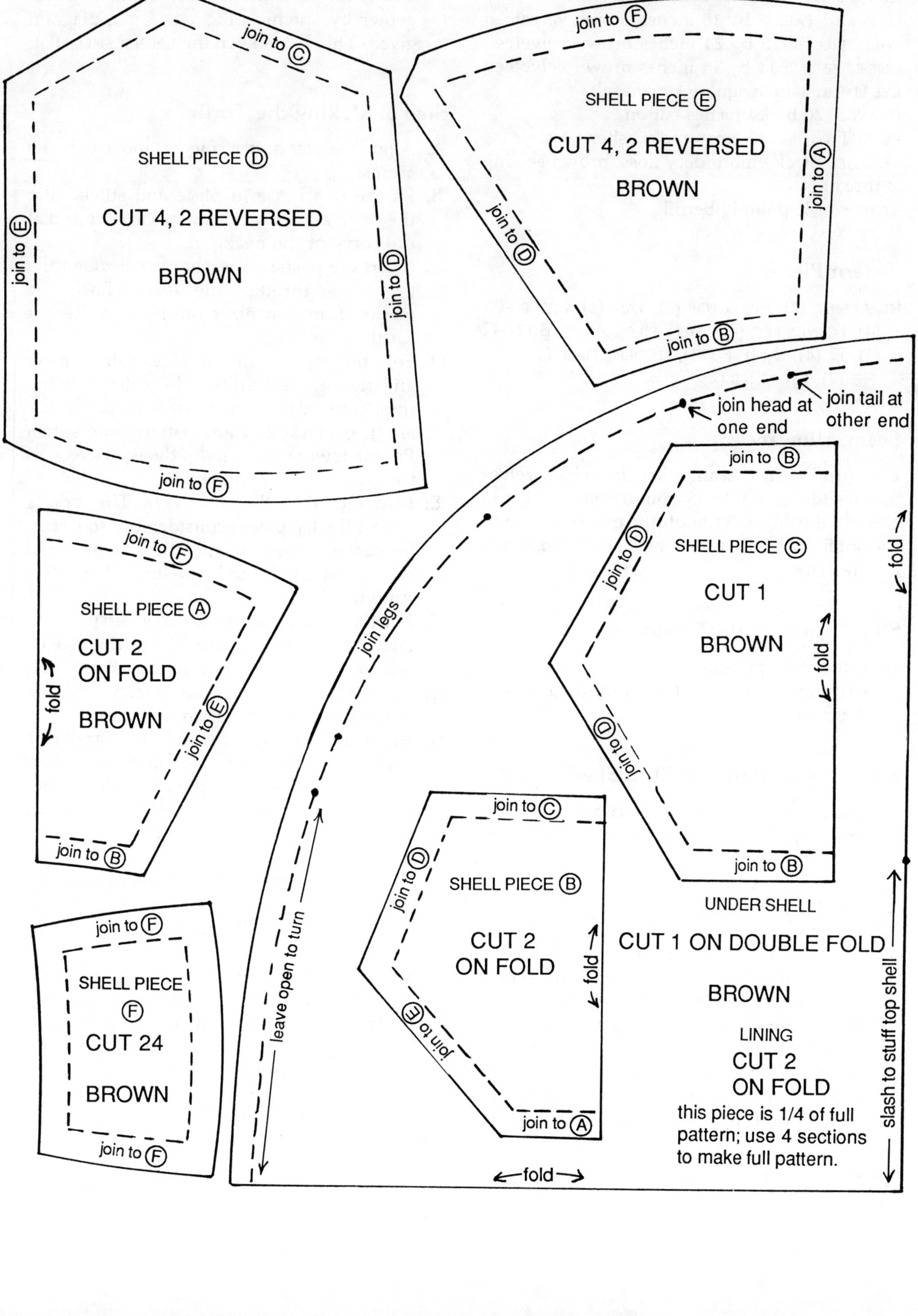

SHELL PIECE D
CUT 4, 2 REVERSED
BROWN
join to C
join to E
join to D
join to F
SHELL PIECE E
CUT 4, 2 REVERSED
BROWN
join to F
join to A
join to D
join to B
join head at one end
join tail at other end
SHELL PIECE A
CUT 2 ON FOLD
BROWN
join to F
fold
join to E
join to B
SHELL PIECE C
CUT 1
BROWN
join to B
join to D
fold
join to D
join to B
join legs
SHELL PIECE F
CUT 24
BROWN
join to F
join to F
leave open to turn
SHELL PIECE B
CUT 2 ON FOLD
join to C
join to D
fold
join to E
join to A
UNDER SHELL
CUT 1 ON DOUBLE FOLD
BROWN
LINING
CUT 2 ON FOLD
this piece is 1/4 of full pattern; use 4 sections to make full pattern.
fold
fold
slash to stuff top shell

HEAD: 7 by 12 inches brown velveteen
LEGS and TAIL: 7 by 18 inches brown velveteen
SHELL PIECES: 15 by 24 inches brown velveteen
UNDER SHELL: 11 by 14 inches brown velveteen
EYE LINER: 1-inch square brown felt
LININGS: 20 by 14 inches cotton
EYES: Two ⅝-inch post-and-washer eyes
THREAD: Black embroidery floss, brown sewing thread
STUFFING: ½ pound fiberfill

Pattern Pieces

HEAD SIDE (2), HEAD TOP (1), TAIL (2), UPPER LEG (4), LOWER LEG (4), SHELL PIECE A (2), B (2), C (1), D (4), E (4), F (24), UNDER SHELL (1), LINING (2), EYE LINER (2)

Seam Allowances:

Use a full ¼-inch seam allowance since velveteens slide and fold if you try stitching too close to the edges. Trim off the excess or clip to the stitch line only where needed, for example on the TOES.

Step 1: Cutting the Fabric

A. Cut out all pieces.
B. Lay out the SHELL PIECES according to the diagram.

Step 2: Assembling the Top Shell

A. Join PIECES A and E face to face and stitch the seam. Stitch another E to the other side of A. Open flat.
B. Sew B to E, A, and E.
C. Sew the DS to B. Sew C to D, B, and D.
D. Continue piecing the shell until the PIECED TOP SHELL oval is complete.
E. Join all the F SHELL PIECES with the center facing inward to make a RING. Stitch this RING to the outside of the PIECED TOP SHELL.
F. Top-stitch the TOP SHELL to the LINING through the F RING seam line. Stuff the TOP SHELL later through the SLASH. Line the UNDER SHELL with a thin layer of stuffing and cover with the LINING. Quilt them together by stitching the TOP SHELL diagram given. This helps keep the UNDER SHELL flat.

Step 3: Making the Turtle

A. Align the HEAD SIDE pieces and stitch the seams.
B. Fit the HEAD TOP in place and stitch. Clip the seam allowances around the eyes and at the curve of the neck.
C. Insert the post-and-washer EYE through the EYE LINER through the HEAD. Push the washer firmly in place on the post. Repeat for the other EYE.
D. Fold the HEAD so the NECK seam lines meet and the SLASHES are on the sides. Pin the upper raw edge of the HEAD NECK to the TOP SHELL as marked on the pattern, and stitch. Pin the lower raw edges of the HEAD NECK to the LOWER SHELL, and stitch.
E. Fold and stitch the LEG DARTS. These darts distort the leg pieces considerably so it may be easier to sew them after stitching the outer seam line or to hand-stitch them after stuffing.
F. Pin the UPPER LEGS to the TOP SHELL, TOES facing forward, and stitch. Pin the LOWER LEGS to the UNDER SHELL and stitch in place.
G. Pin one TAIL piece to the TOP SHELL and one to the UNDER SHELL. Stitch in place.
H. Align the TOP SHELL, HEAD, LEGS, and TAIL with the same on the UNDER SHELL. Beginning on the side, stitch the seam all around. Sew the TOES carefully with two small stitches between each. Sew the SLASHES on the side of the HEAD closed.
I. Trim and clip the seam allowances carefully around the TOES. Use the pointed dowel to help turn. Carefully turn the turtle right side out.
J. Using the dowel, push stuffing firmly into the HEAD and FEET. Push small separate wads carefully into each TOE. Stuff the TAIL softly. Don't put too much stuffing in the SHELL or the turtle may look too puffy.
K. Sew the opening closed. Embroider the MOUTH and the NOSE.

DIRECTIONS

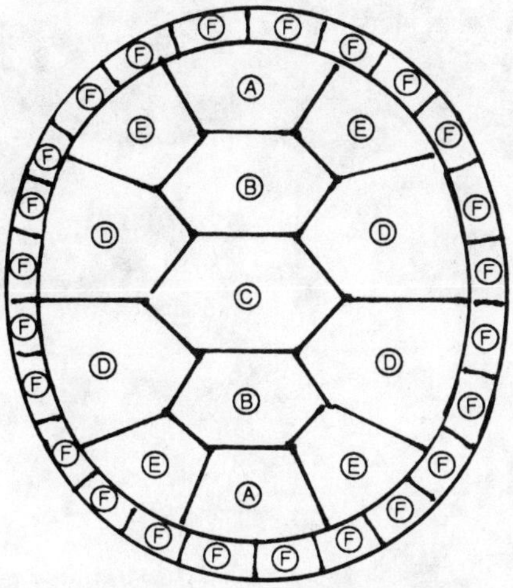

Piece top Ⓐ to Ⓔ as shown, join all Ⓕs to make ring. Join Ⓕ ring to shell.

Diagram for assembling top shell and as quilting guide for under shell.

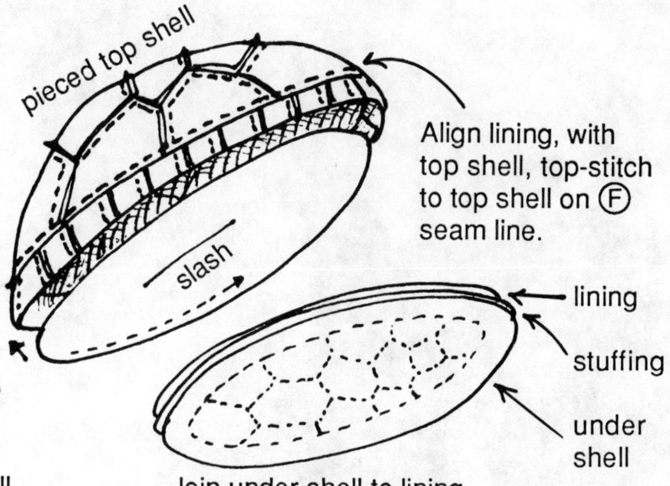

Align lining, with top shell, top-stitch to top shell on Ⓕ seam line.

Join under shell to lining, turn and stuff. Quilt together by top stitching shell design.

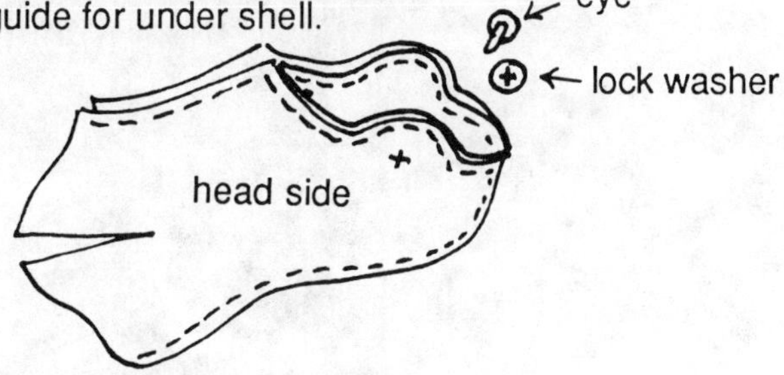

Sew head sides together, insert head top and stitch.

Sew upper and lower leg darts.

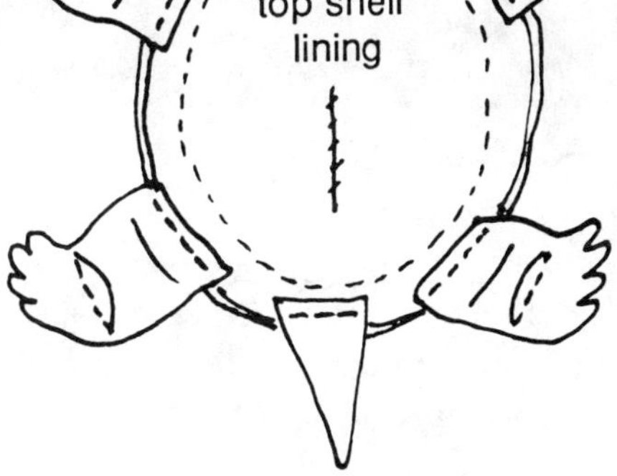

Join upper neck, legs, and tail to top shell. Join lower neck, legs, and tail to under shell.

Match assembled top to bottom and stitch, leaving opening.

side view of leg.

Turn, stuff, sew closed. Embroider nose and mouth.

UNICORNS, alas, are mythical animals, so it's not possible to get a baby one at the pet store and raise your own. The unicorn's name derives from the long, spirally twisted horn emerging from its forehead. Unicorns in ancient Greek and Roman myths had a multi-colored horn, a red head sporting a horse's mane, a goat's beard, a white body with the rear legs and cloven hooves of an antelope, and finally, a lion's tail. By the Middle Ages the unicorn began to look more like a bearded white horse with a long horn and cloven hooves, and stood for purity. The most familiar one appears in the Unicorn Tapestries surrounded by a little fence in a field full of flowers.

This idealized gentle white animal appears everywhere nowadays, as a motif for embroidery, on china cups and plates, as jewelry, as a character in stories, on clothing and, of course, as a stuffed toy. But the original probably was a one-horned billy goat!

NOTE: This unicorn measures about 8½ inches high and 12 inches long, the same size as the zebra. Both patterns are designed to use interchangeably to make different poses or animals. For example, to make an arched-neck straight-legged unicorn, trace the zebra's legs onto the unicorn pattern. For a merry-go-round horse, use the unicorn pattern without the horn, and use loose yarns for the tail. Appliqué, machine-embroider, or paint colorful designs on the horse.

PATTERN

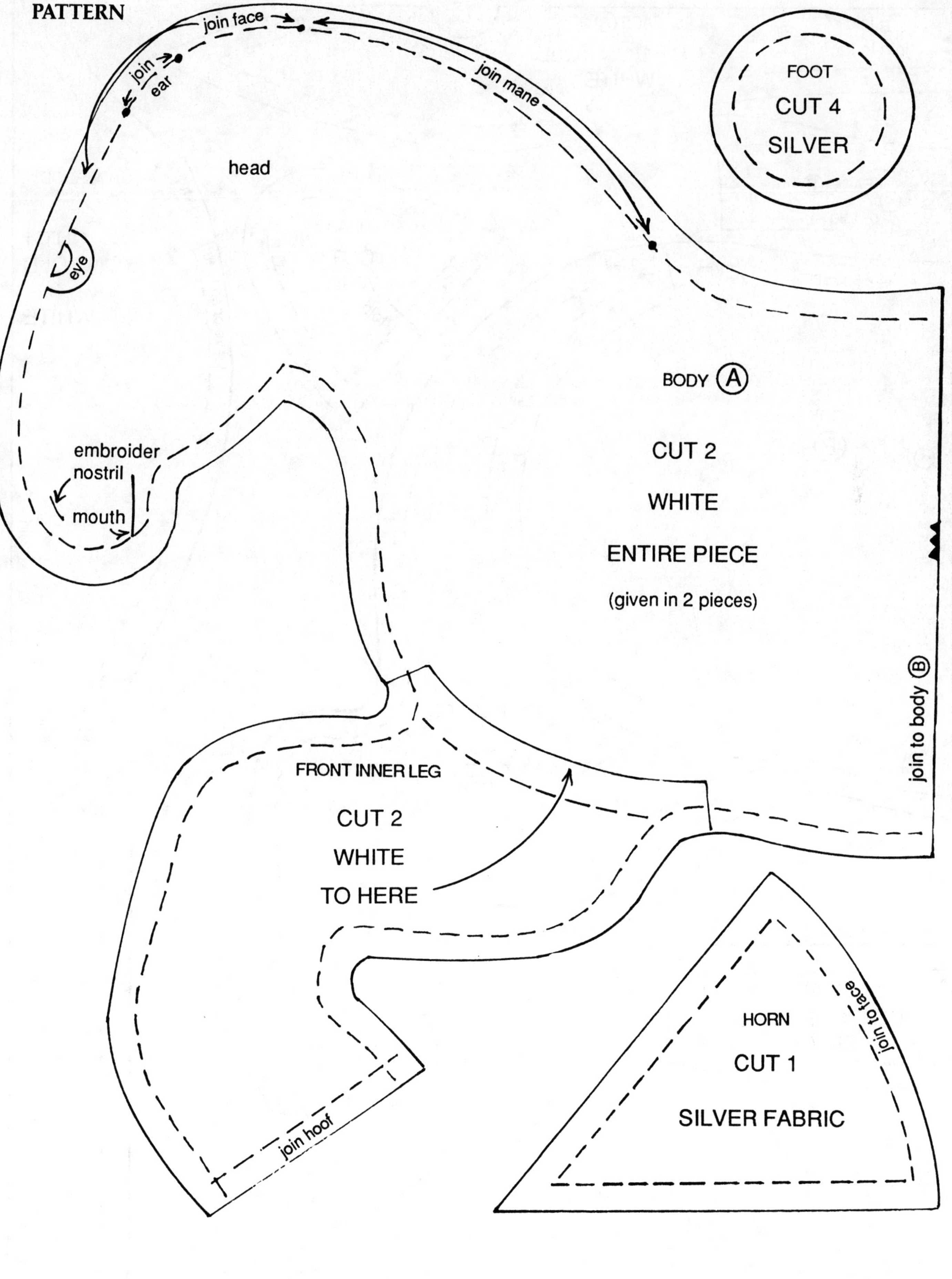
join face
join ear
join mane
head
eye
embroider nostril
mouth
FOOT
CUT 4
SILVER
BODY (A)
CUT 2
WHITE
ENTIRE PIECE
(given in 2 pieces)
join to body (B)
FRONT INNER LEG
CUT 2
WHITE
TO HERE
join hoof
HORN
CUT 1
SILVER FABRIC
join to face

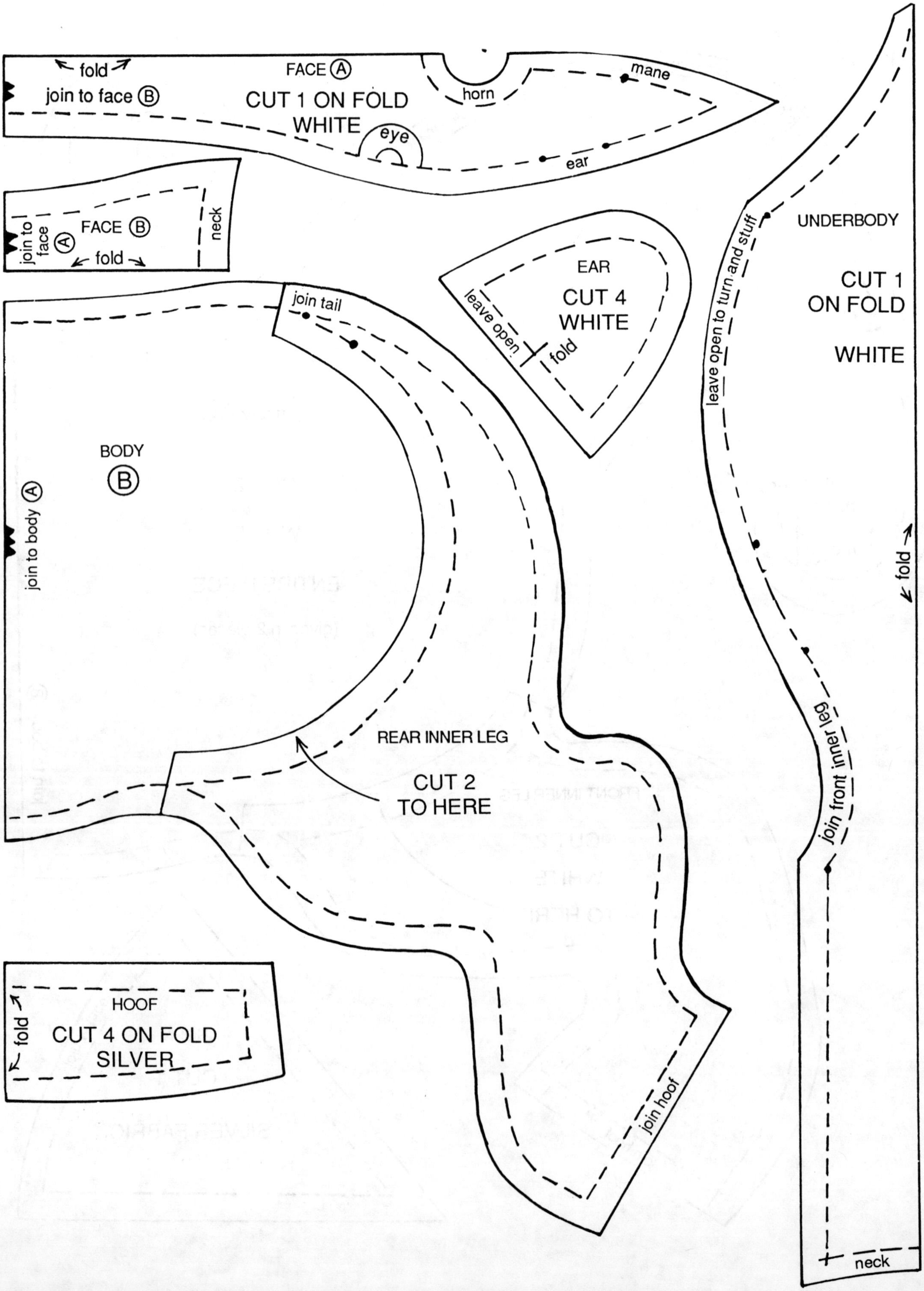

fold
FACE Ⓐ
join to face Ⓑ
CUT 1 ON FOLD
WHITE
horn
mane
eye
ear
FACE Ⓑ
join to face Ⓐ
fold
neck
UNDERBODY
CUT 1
ON FOLD
WHITE
leave open to turn and stuff
EAR
CUT 4
WHITE
leave open
fold
join tail
BODY
Ⓑ
join to body Ⓐ
fold
REAR INNER LEG
CUT 2
TO HERE
join front inner leg
HOOF
CUT 4 ON FOLD
SILVER
fold
join hoof
neck

Materials

BODY, UNDERBODY, LEGS, FACE, and EARS: 10 by 39 inches of firmly woven cotton/polyester embroidered fabric; other possible choices are velveteen, suede cloth, felt, or decorative fabrics

HORN, HOOVES, FEET: 8 by 8 inches silver-coated firmly woven fabric

MANE, TAIL, and BEARD: 32 inches of ½-inch-wide rayon braid, or a 1-ounce skein of white rayon or nylon yarn. Use 6 inches of braid or about 100 small strands of yarn for the tail, 6 4-inch-long pieces of braid or six hundred strands of yarn for the mane, one 2-inch-long piece of braid for the beard.

EYE DISKS: 1½ by 3 inch piece of white felt

EYES: Two ½-inch (12.5 mm) post-and-washer brown eyes

THREAD and TRIM: White sewing thread, tan embroidery floss

STUFFING: ½ pound fiberfill

BASE: 6-inch piece of ¼-inch dowel, 3 by 8 by 1 inch thick wooden base

Tools

Long narrow stuffing tool

Pattern Pieces

BODY A and B (2) (given in two pieces), FRONT INNER LEG (2), BACK INNER LEG (2), HOOF (4), FACE (1), UNDERBODY (1), EAR (4), FOOT (4), EYE DISK (2) and (2), HORN (1)

Step 1: Cutting the Fabric

A. Lay out pattern pieces to select the embroidery pattern desired for each piece.
B. Cut out all pattern pieces

Step 2: Assembling the Pieces

A. Match two EARS, right sides facing, and sew, using a short machine stitch. Leave the end open to turn. Clip seam allowances at the tip, turn, and press flat. Fold the EAR vertically, pin to the HEAD with the fold forward, and baste in place. Repeat.
B. For the HORN, use very fine pins or your fingers to join the HORN to the opening in the FACE, and carefully stitch. Hand-wheel the machine if necessary. Do not sew the length of the HORN yet.
C. Pin the FACE to the UNDERBODY, and stitch.
D. Join the FRONT INNER LEG to the UNDERBODY. Repeat for the other FRONT INNER LEG.
E. Pin the REAR INNER LEG to the UNDERBODY. Baste the TAIL BRAID to the REAR INNER LEG. Align the other REAR INNER LEG with the joined REAR INNER LEG and the UNDERBODY and stitch the crotch from the UNDERBODY to the TAIL, including the TAIL in this seam.

Step 3: Assembling the Body

A. To join the assembled UNDERBODY to the BODY, match and pin the FRONT LEGS, pin the UNDERBODY to the NECK with the CHIN seam aligned with the turn of the NECK, pin the FACE to the HEAD, including the basted EARS in the seam. Stitch from the front of the LEG to the end of the FACE. Repeat for the other side, being careful to align one side with the other.
B. Open the FRONT LEG flat and join the HOOF, right sides facing. Repeat for the other FRONT LEG and HOOF.
C. Fold the FRONT LEG AND HOOF to align the matching back edges of the LEG, and stitch from the HOOF to the REAR LEG HOOF. Repeat for the other side except to leave an opening to turn and stuff on the BODY.
D. Join the HOOF to the REAR LEG. Repeat for the other REAR LEG.
E. Fold the REAR LEG AND HOOF to match the back seams, and stitch from the HOOF to the end of the LEG at the tail. Repeat for the other side.
F. Pin the FOOT to the HOOF, and stitch. Repeat for all four HOOVES.
G. Insert the EYES in the HEAD as marked. Pad the washer with the WHITE FELT DISK, and push onto EYE POST. (The slightly larger EYE washer creates the bony eye socket ridge).
H. Pin the ends of one MANE BRAID piece to the FACE 1/2 inch above the horn and continue pinning the rest along the BODY to the

DIRECTIONS

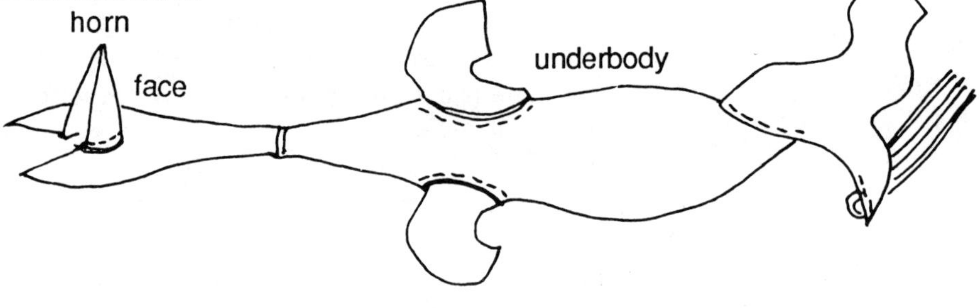

Join horn to face, join face to underbody, join front inner legs to underbody. Join rear inner leg to underbody, baste tail.

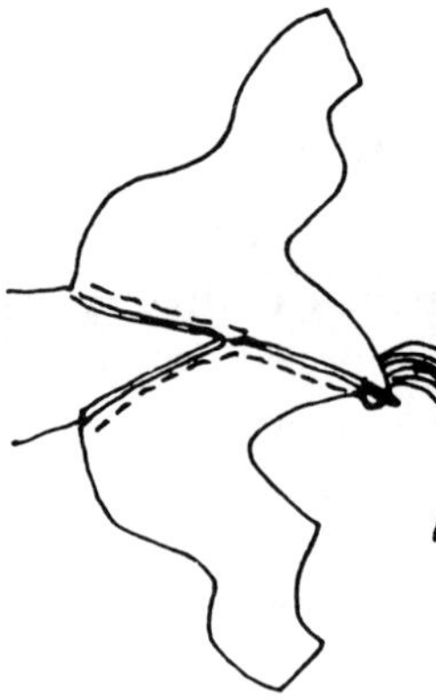

Join other rear leg to underbody and rear leg.

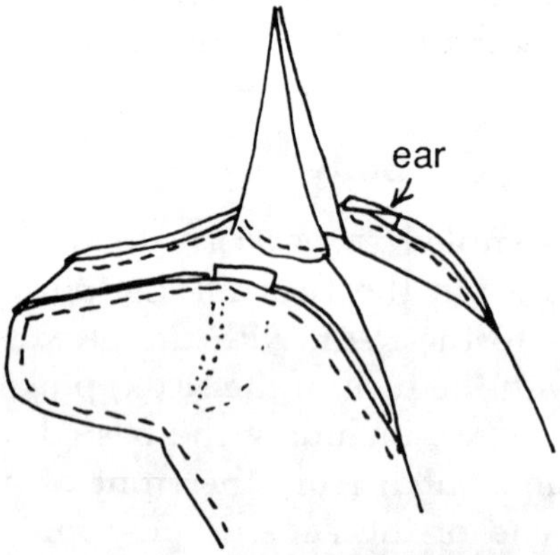

Fold and baste ears to head. Join face to head and continue seam to foot on front leg; repeat.

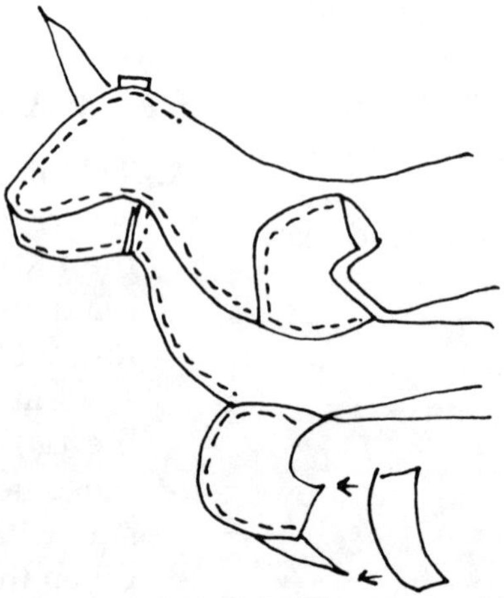

Join hoof to leg; repeat.

Sew foot to hoof; repeat.

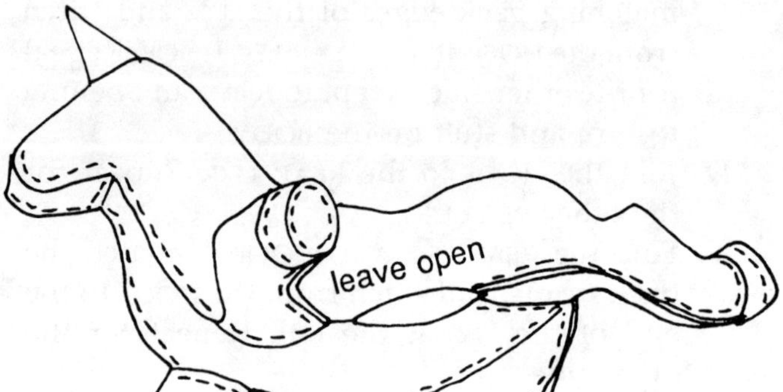

Sew back seam of front leg to the hoof on the back leg; join hoofs. Sew back seam of back leg up to tail, sew foot to hoof; repeat.

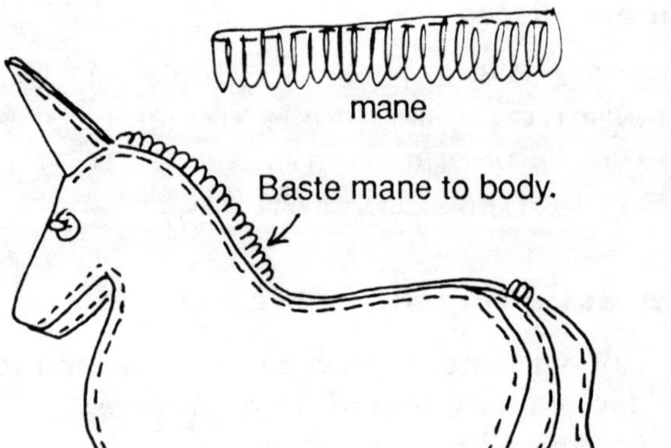

Insert eye, sew back seam from horn top to tail including mane, turn, stuff.

shoulder. Baste in place. If loose yarn is used, stitch it to a 4-inch piece of bias tape to make a fringe and baste this to the FACE and BODY as above. Baste in place.

I. Fold the HORN lengthwise to align the raw edges, and continue aligning the back seam. Stitch from the TAIL to the tip of the HORN, rounding the tip to 1/8 inch wide. This seam includes the MANE.

Step 4: Finishing the Unicorn

A. Clip inside seam allowances that might cause pulls or wrinkles. Make several short clips to the seam line on inside corners. Reinforce any stitching that looks as if it might pull out.

B. Turn, beginning at the HORN, using a pointed tool. Stuff the HORN firmly, then continue turning the animal. Use a long, narrow blunt tool to turn the LEGS and MUZZLE.

C. Stuff the HOOVES AND LEGS very firmly. Fill the HEAD with small wads to model the shape. Fill the unicorn very firmly and sew the opening closed.

D. To finish, unbraid the MANE. Unbraid the TAIL part of the way, or unbraid it all the way and wrap it half way. Hand-sew the BEARD in place if desired. Embroider the MOUTH and NOSTRILS with tan floss, using a chain stitch.

E. For the spiral HORN, use embroidery thread to sew a knot at the base of the HORN. Wind the thread in a spiral around the HORN pulling firmly to indent. Sew a knot at the tip and sew the thread end into the HORN before clipping off.

F. To make a CLOVEN HOOF, stitch front to back on the HOOF and pull tightly to indent. Knot the thread. Repeat for all four HOOVES.

G. Use the unicorn as a toy, or make a cluster of unicorns and merry-go-round horses to hang from a cord for a mobile. To make a stand, use the dowel stick and wooden base. Make a small slit in the UNDERBODY 1/2 inch behind the front legs, and push the dowel into the stuffing for 2 inches. Drill a hole in the base for the dowel and push it in. Paint or varnish the base to suit.

VOLE is the European name for several kinds of wild mice. Field voles, shown, have stumpy tails, thick bodies, and grayish tan fur similar to field mice. Gray water voles have small ears, short hairy tails, and swim with their hind feet only. Bank voles (they live on riverbanks) have reddish fur. Voles and mice, squirrels, rabbits, mink, and beaver are all rodents, a group representing more than a third of all land mammals and characterized by chisel-shaped incisors for gnawing.

Rodents are among the most clever of the animal architects. For example, mice build sturdy ball-shaped nests sometimes lined with soft milkweed puffs. Vole and mice babies, helpless at birth, are weaned by 3 weeks, independent a week later, and can bear litters at 6 weeks. Survival depends on growing up fast. Vegetarian voles can stuff seeds in their cheek pouches, dash home, and store them for later. These tiny animals can scamper up stems and down holes to escape, but will rear up, bite, and spar with their front feet when cornered.

NOTE: This vole measures 4½ inches tall, larger than actual size. By changing the fur color and the length of his tail, many varieties of vole or mouse can be made, including an albino (all white) mouse with pink feet, ears, eyes, and nose.

Materials

BODY: 5 by 6 inches gray brown fleece, felt, suede cloth, or similar non-raveling fabric
FRONT: 3 by 5 inches tan fabric, as above
EARS and TAIL: 2 by 5 inches brown felt

PATTERN

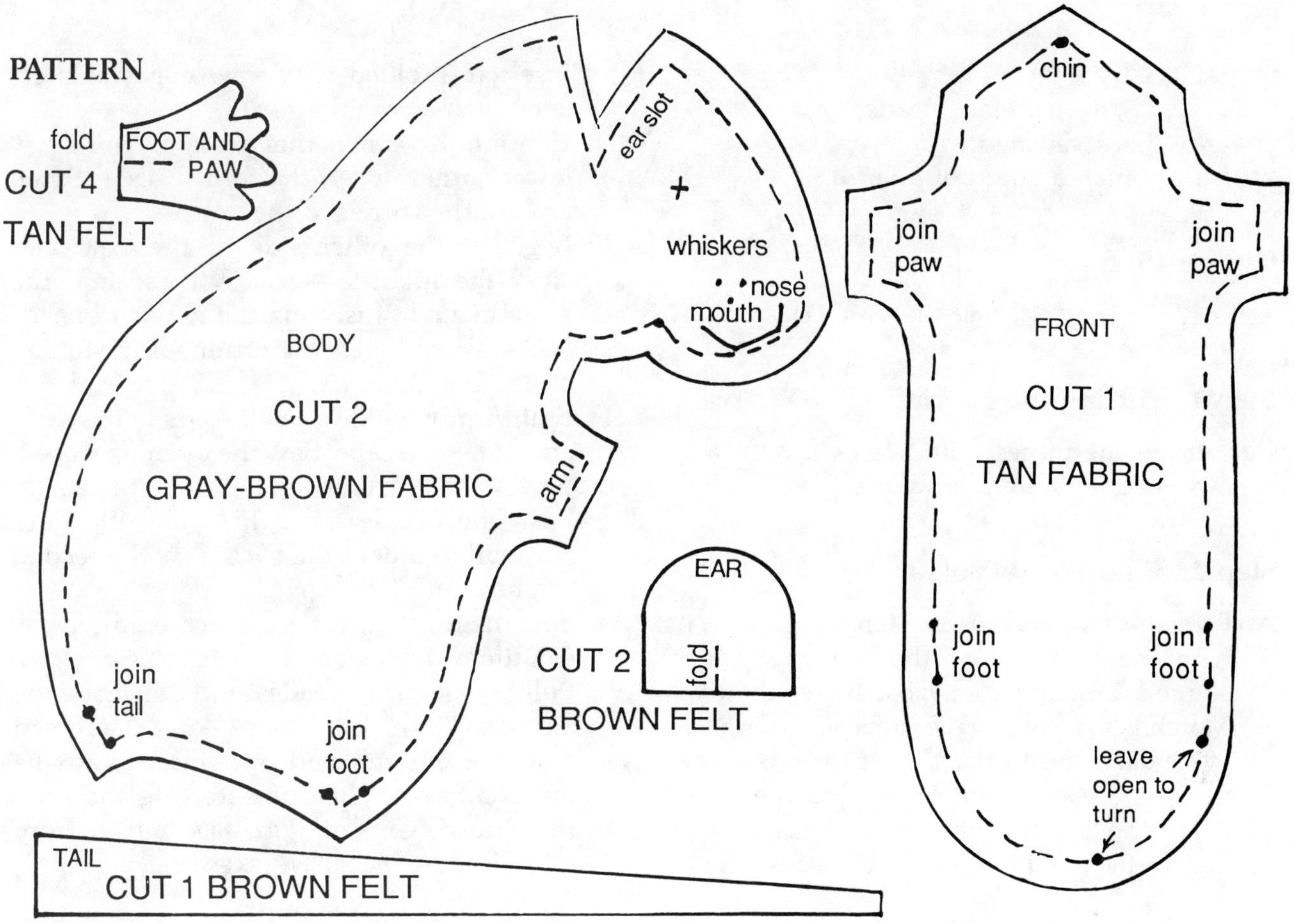

DIRECTIONS

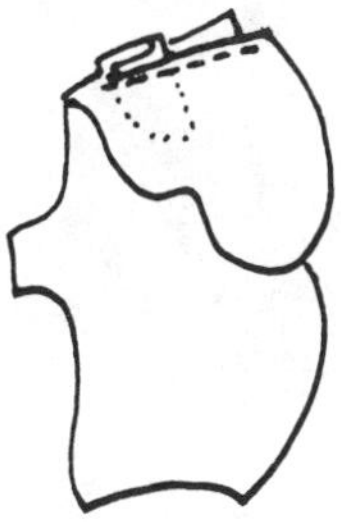

Insert folded ear in ear slot, stitch body.

Insert tail, sew body seam from tail to chin.

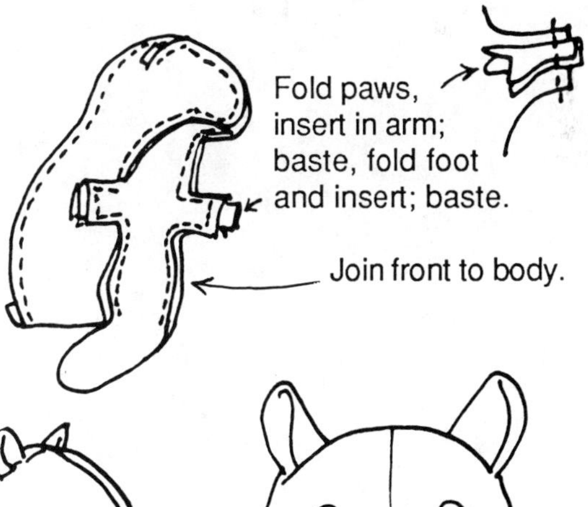

Fold paws, insert in arm; baste, fold foot and insert; baste.

Join front to body.

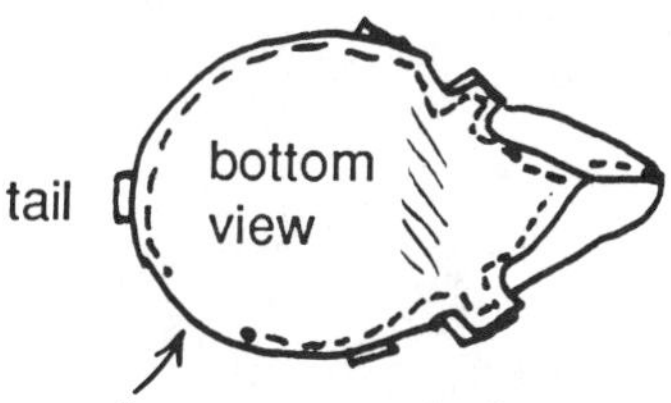

Leave open to turn.

Stuff, sew opening closed.

Sew bead eyes on, and pull thread between to indent eyes, sew nose, mouth, whiskers.

FEET: 1 1/2 by 2 inches tan felt
EYES: Two 3/8-inch black beads
THREAD: Black sewing thread
STUFFING: Small amount of fiberfill

Pattern Pieces

BODY (2), FRONT (1), EAR (2), TAIL (1), FEET (4)

Step 1: Cutting the Fabric

Cut out all the pieces. The felt TAIL, FEET, and EARS need no seam allowances.

Step 2: Making the Vole

A. Fold the EAR and insert it in the EAR SLOT with the fold toward the top, raw edges aligned. Sew the SLOT closed over the EAR.
B. Match BODY pieces face to face aligning the HEAD darts. Insert the TAIL at the base. Sew the BACK SEAM from the TAIL to the CHIN.
C. Align the FRONT with the BODY CHIN seam face to face and sew to the top of the ARM. Insert the folded PAW, raw edges aligned, and stitch across the ARM.
D. Continue to stitch this seam to the BODY lower corner. Insert the folded FOOT. Stitch around the corner to the TAIL.
E. Begin at the other side of the CHIN and stitch the opposite FRONT/BODY seam in the same manner, inserting the PAW and FOOT. Leave 1 inch open for turning and stuffing on the bottom.
F. Stuff firmly, poking small wads in the NOSE and ARMS to shape. Sew the opening closed.
G. Sew a BEAD EYE on one side of the HEAD. Push the needle through to the other EYE and pull to indent the EYES. Sew the second EYE bead in place.
H. Sew the NOSE with satin-stitch embroidery. Continue downward to stitch the MOUTH. Pull the MOUTH threads tightly to shape the MUZZLE. To sew a WHISKER, knot the thread 1 inch from the end and insert into the muzzle. Sew to the opposite side and knot the thread. Clip off WHISKER 1 inch from knot. Repeat for all WHISKERS.

WALRUSES are comical-looking mammals with enormous, apparently shapeless bodies that can weigh as much as 3000 pounds full grown. Even so they are admirably suited to the lives they live. Their short flippers can propel them through the water like fish, or maneuver safely around rocky shores like eels. The males with their super-sized canine teeth use these tusks to rake the mud on the ocean floor, and strain it for edible shell fish through their soup-strainer moustaches. Walruses like to live in crowds, flopping lazily on the shore like overweight sun bathers, turning from brownish gray to a bright brownish pink when the sun comes out. Walruses move slowly and clumsily on land, like someone tied in a bag. If one is hurt, another goes to its aid. Sadly, this group loyalty and limited mobility has made them easy to hunt, and their numbers have diminished steadily even though the males bravely defend their harems.

NOTE: Dried lentils provide a heavy shifting stuffing for this walrus toy to portray his floppy weight. For a bean-bag chair, increase the size of the walrus pattern 4 to 6 times, use a textured gray-plastic upholstery fabric, and stuff the enlarged walrus with styrene pellets.

Materials

BODY and FLIPPERS: 18 by 24 inches gray suede cloth, velveteen, or similar fabric

PATTERN

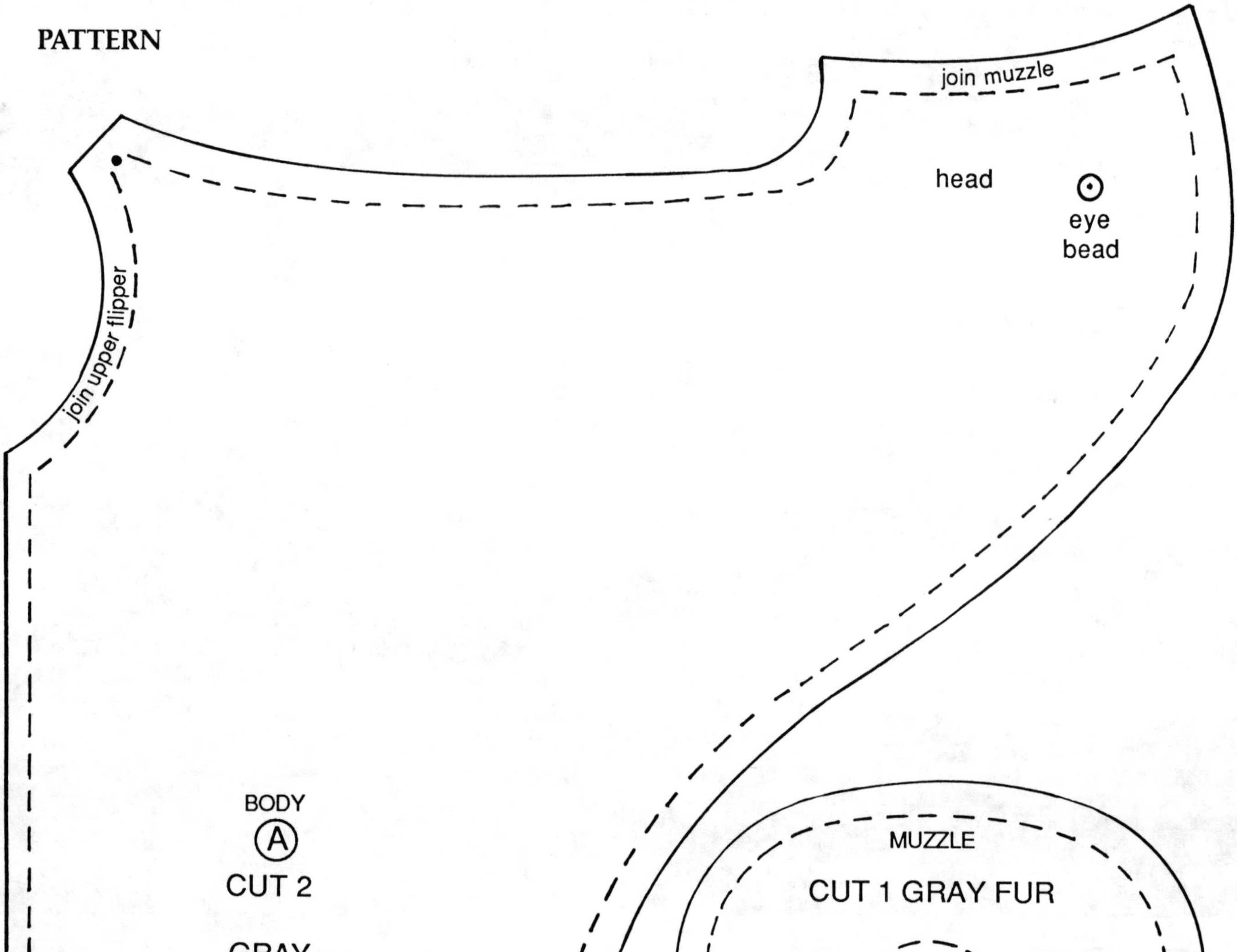

join muzzle
head
eye
bead
join upper flipper
BODY
A
CUT 2
GRAY
leave open to turn and stuff
join to body B
D
MUZZLE
CUT 1 GRAY FUR
join tusk
join tusk
clip seam allowances
fold
back flipper
BODY
B
C
join to body A
C

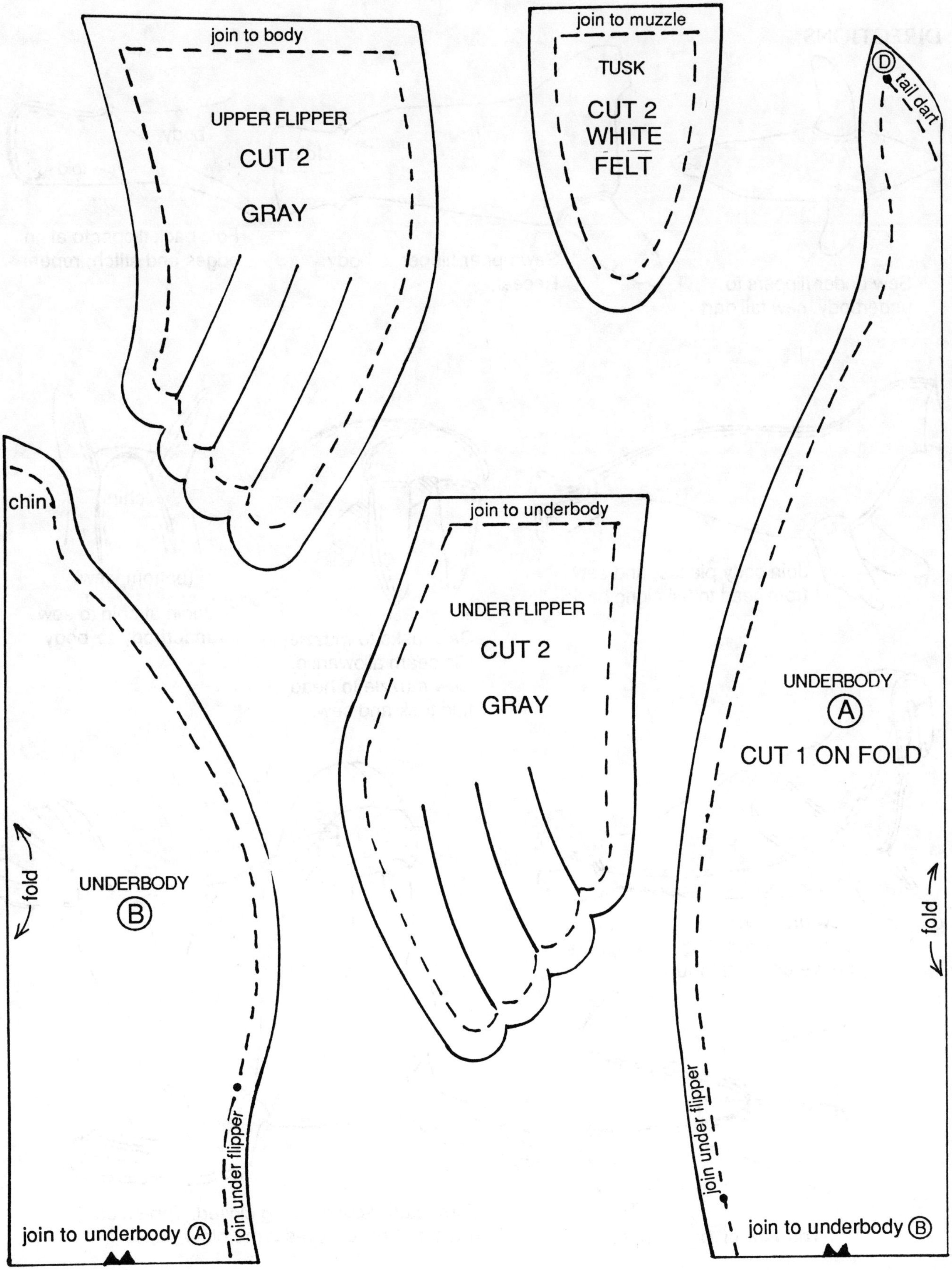

join to body
UPPER FLIPPER
CUT 2
GRAY
join to muzzle
TUSK
CUT 2
WHITE
FELT
D
tail dart
chin
join to underbody
UNDER FLIPPER
CUT 2
GRAY
UNDERBODY
A
CUT 1 ON FOLD
fold
UNDERBODY
B
fold
join under flipper
join to underbody A
join under flipper
join to underbody B

DIRECTIONS

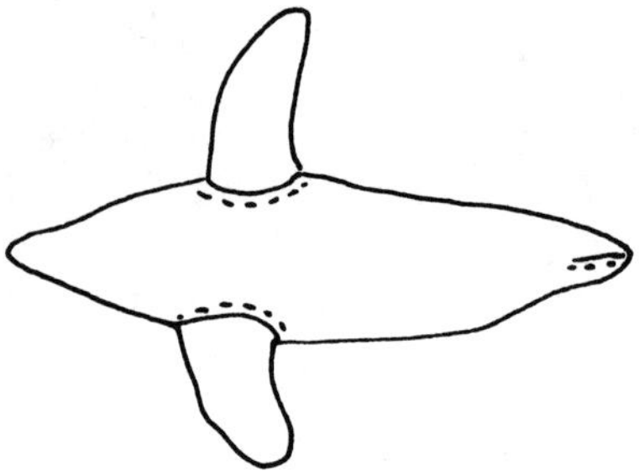

Sew under flippers to underbody, sew tail dart.

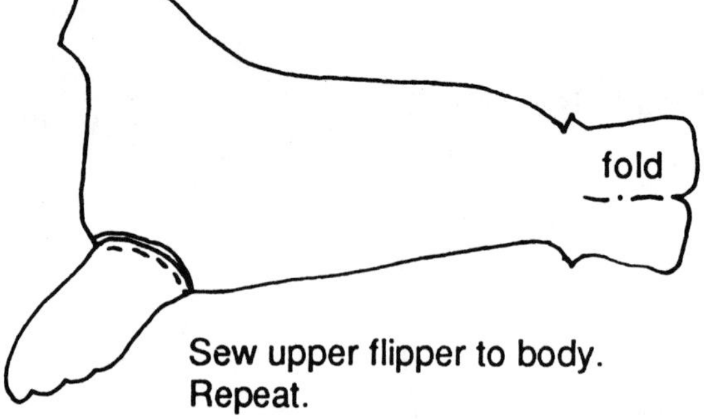

Sew upper flipper to body. Repeat.

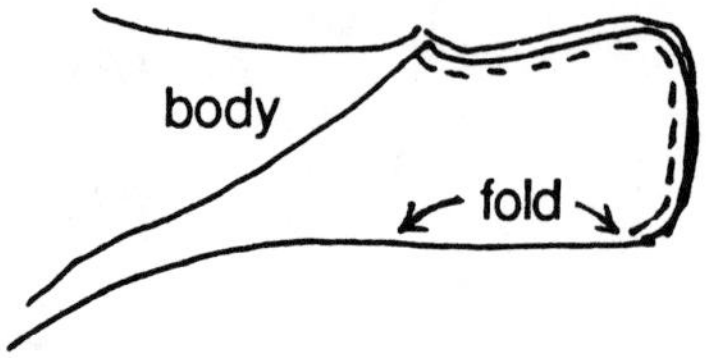

Fold back flipper to align edges and stitch; repeat.

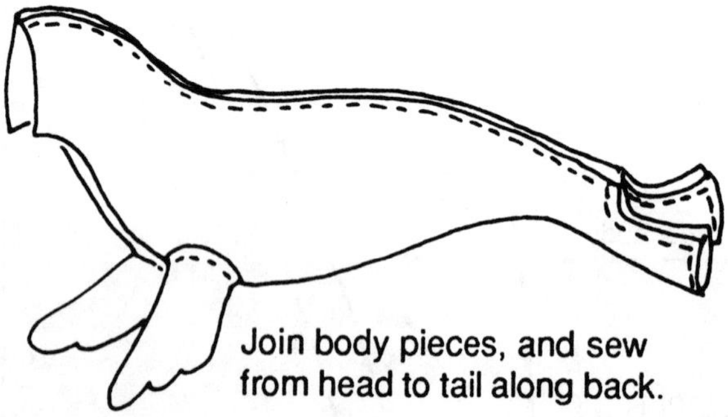

Join body pieces, and sew from head to tail along back.

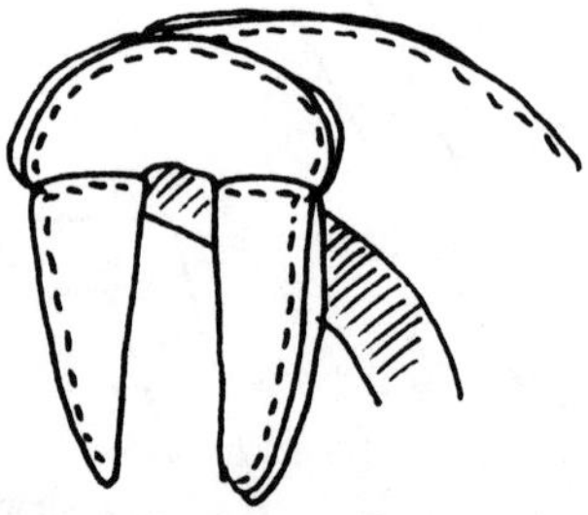

Sew tusks to muzzle, clip seam allowance. Sew muzzle to head, fold tusk and sew.

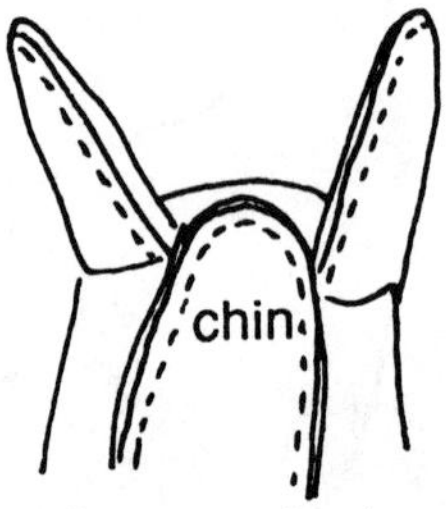

(bottom view)

Begin at chin to sew underbody to body.

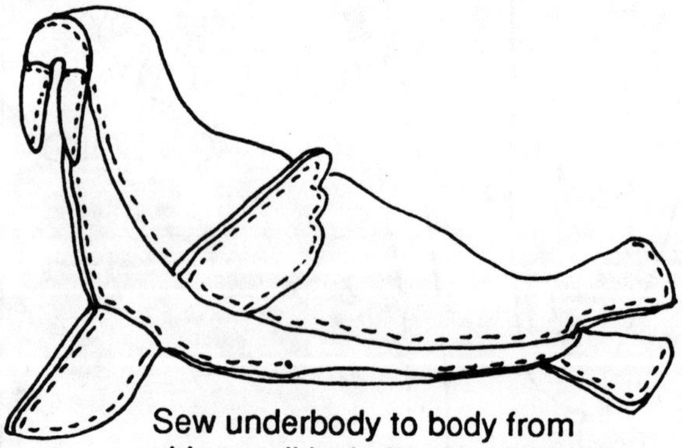

Sew underbody to body from chin to tail including front flippers. Leave opening to turn

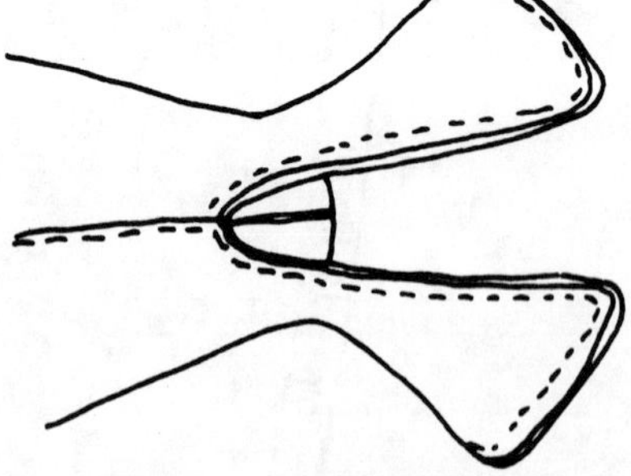

Top view of back flippers.

Turn, stuff, sew opening closed. Top-stitch flippers. Sew on eyes, embroider nose.

MUZZLE: 2 by 3 inches matching gray fur fabric, 1/4-inch pile
TUSKS: 2 by 3 inches white felt
EYES: Two black beads, 1/8-inch diameter
NOSE: Black embroidery floss
STUFFING: Small amount of fiberfill for head and flippers, 1 1/2 pounds of dried lentils, beans, popcorn, or similar shifting material for body

Tools:

Long narrow stuffing and turning tool

Pattern Pieces

BODY A and B (given in two pieces) (2), MUZZLE (1), UNDERBODY A and B (1), UPPER FLIPPER (2), UNDER FLIPPER (2), TUSK (2)

Step 1: Cutting the Fabric

Cut out all the pieces.

Step 2: Sewing the Walrus

A. Sew the UNDER FLIPPER to the UNDERBODY as marked. Repeat for the other side. Fold the TAIL DART and stitch.
B. Align the UPPER FLIPPER with the BODY and stitch. Fold the BACK FLIPPER (part of the BODY) to align the edges C and C, and stitch to C. Slash FLIPPER seam allowances to the seam line on the curve to avoid pulls when turned. Repeat for the other side.
C. Stitch the TUSKS to the MUZZLE. Fold the TUSK flat and stitch from the TUSK TIP to the MUZZLE. Repeat for the other TUSK. Clip the MUZZLE seam allowances as marked to free the seam allowance for later stitching.
D. Stitch the MUZZLE to the HEAD.
E. Align the UNDERBODY with the BODY, matching the UPPER AND UNDER FLIPPERS. Beginning at the CHIN sew the UNDERBODY to the BODY, including the FLIPPERS in the seam and ending at D. Pivot the needle in the fabric and stitch for 1 inch, leave a 3-inch opening on the BODY for turning and stuffing, and continue to stitch to the CHIN.
F. Trim and clip any seam allowances that might pull when turned.

Step 3: Finishing the Walrus

A. Begin to turn at the HEAD, and turn the TUSKS with a narrow tool such as a knitting needle with a blunt point. Be careful not to pierce the TUSK fabric. Use the same tool to push small wads of fiberfill into the TUSKS to stuff. Turn the HEAD and stuff the MUZZLE with fiberfill. Roll a tight ball of fiberfill for the HEAD. Stitch the HEAD stuffing ball to the seam allowances to hold it in place. Continue to turn the rest of the walrus.
B. Fill the FRONT and BACK FLIPPERS with fiberfill so they are firm but only 1/4 inch thick. Machine top-stitch (quilt) the FLIPPER LINES as marked on the pattern.
C. Arrange the walrus with the opening upward, and pour the lentils (or other shifting stuffing) into the opening until nearly full. Sew the opening closed, using a strong thread.
D. Hand sew one EYE BEAD in place. Insert the needle through the HEAD under the stuffing ball and come out at the opposite EYE BEAD MARKING. Sew the second EYE in place.
E. Embroider the NOSE with black embroidery floss.

XIPHOSURA,

XIPHOSURA, commonly called the Horseshoe Crab, is a large sea animal with a shell shaped like a horse's hoof. It is also known as the King Crab even though zoologists class it as an arthropod, not a crustacean like the Alaska King Crab. The Xiphosura is more closely related to scorpions and the extinct trilobites, now found only as fossils in stone. These hard-shelled sea creatures live in coastal waters, plowing through the mud in search of food. Their body is divided into two main parts, with the head and the thorax (chest with legs attached) at the front and the hinged abdomen at the rear. They grow to about 2 feet long, including the spiny tail used for defense.

No one has found a commercial use for Xiphosura, except perhaps to be ground up for fertilizer, so they are able to live fairly undisturbed lives.

NOTE: This soft, stuffed Xiphosura measures 7 by 11 by 1½ inches completed. The legs are not made separately, but are machine-stitch outlined on double fabric, then trapunto-stuffed with yarn sewn into the channels for dimension. Additionally, the legs and other areas are highlighted with glass beads. The only difficult part is turning the skinny tail. Make it fatter if you get too frustrated.

Materials

BODY: 11 by 16 inches gray-brown satin (as shown), or a more firmly woven fabric

UNDERSHELL LINING: 8 by 8 inches light-weight cotton fabric

THREAD: Black or contrasting machine-embroidery or regular sewing thread, matching sewing thread for beads

TRIM: A few strands of small glass beads

STUFFING: 4 ounces fiberfill, a few ounces 4-ply yarn

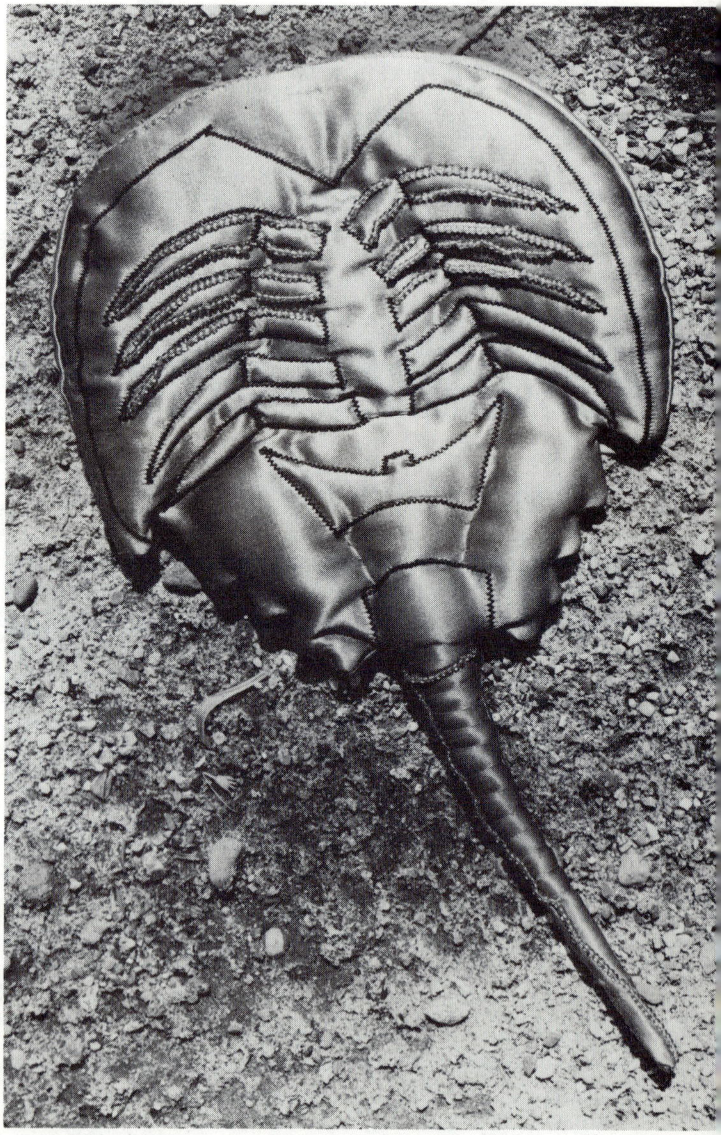

PATTERN

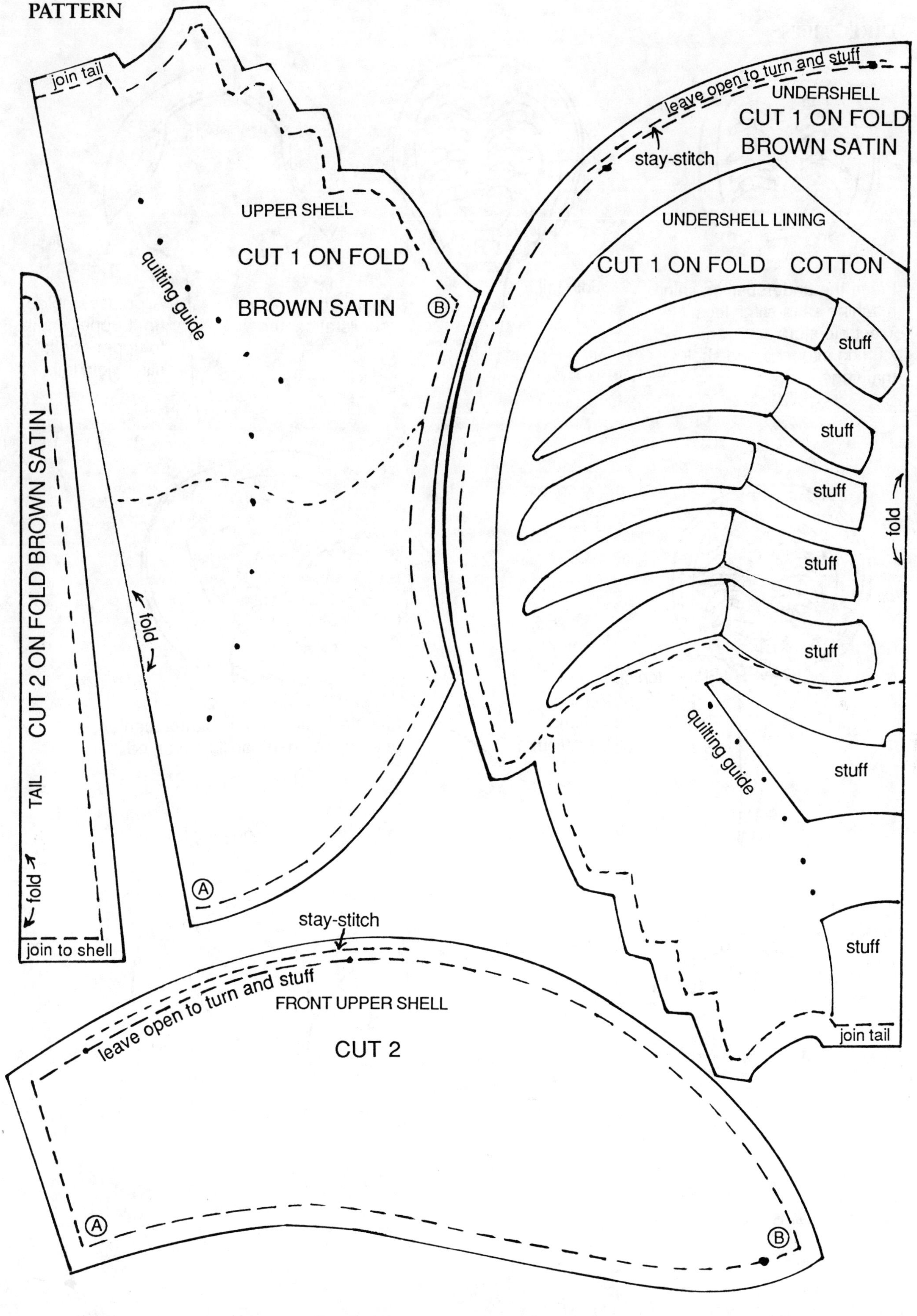
join tail
UPPER SHELL
CUT 1 ON FOLD
BROWN SATIN
quilting guide
fold
CUT 2 ON FOLD BROWN SATIN
TAIL
fold
join to shell
leave open to turn and stuff
UNDERSHELL
CUT 1 ON FOLD
BROWN SATIN
stay-stitch
UNDERSHELL LINING
CUT 1 ON FOLD COTTON
stuff
stuff
stuff
stuff
stuff
fold
quilting guide
stuff
stuff
join tail
stay-stitch
leave open to turn and stuff
FRONT UPPER SHELL
CUT 2

DIRECTIONS

Place the undershell on lining, machine satin-stitch legs. Trapunto stuff: sew yarn stuffing into legs and shell markings.

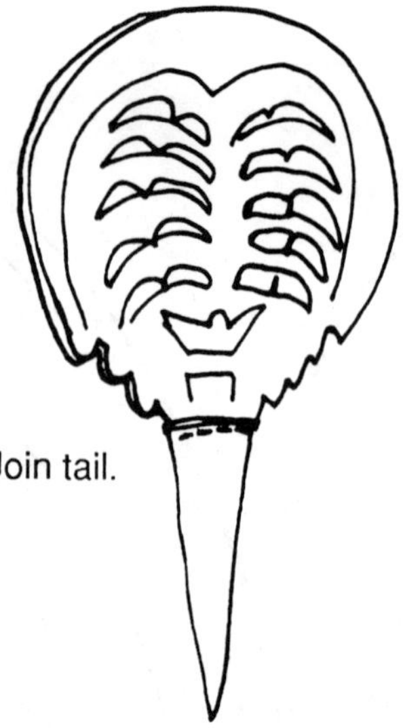

Join tail.

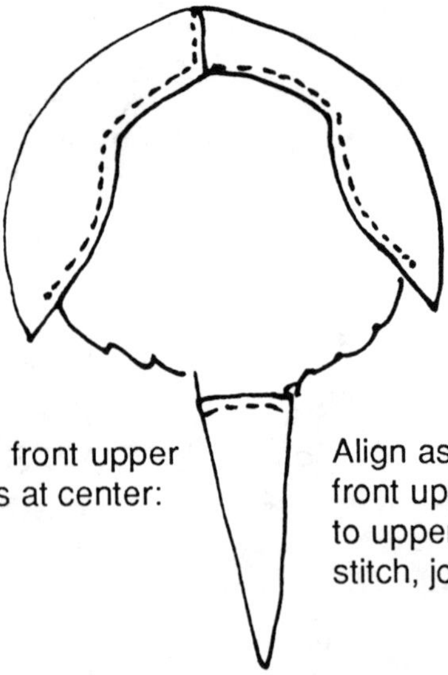

Align front upper shells at center: sew

Align assembled front upper shell to upper shell; stitch, join tail.

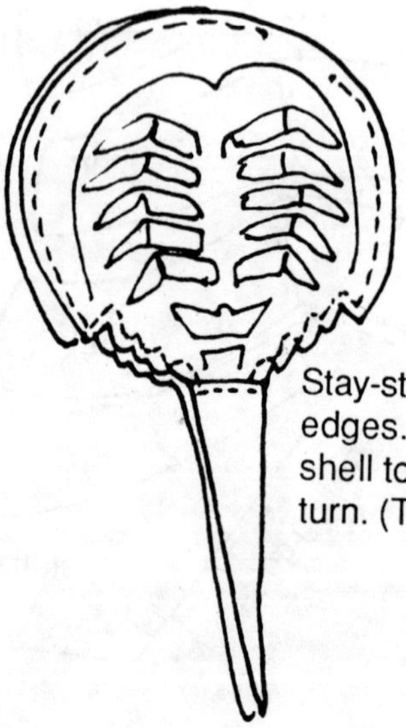

Stay-stitch opening edges. Join upper shell to lower; stitch, turn. (Tail will be difficult.)

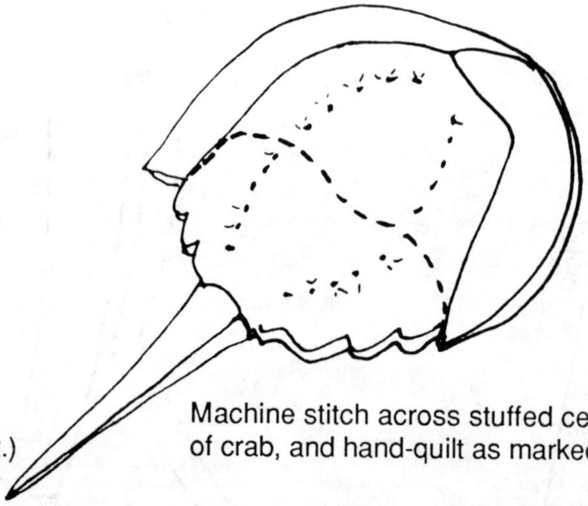

Machine stitch across stuffed center of crab, and hand-quilt as marked.

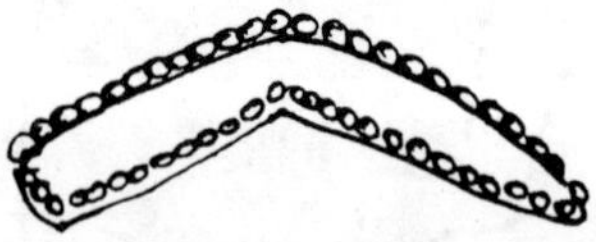

Optional: Decorate legs and tail with beads.

Tools:

Long narrow turning and stuffing tool, blunt tapestry needle, small beading needle

Pattern Pieces

UPPER SHELL (1), UNDERSHELL (1), UNDERSHELL LINING (1), FRONT UPPER SHELL (2), TAIL (2)

Step 1: Cutting the Fabric

Cut out all pieces.

Step 2: Sewing the Body

A. Pin the UNDERSHELL face up to the UNDERSHELL LINING. Machine satin-stitch the undershell markings, using a narrow zigzag setting.

B. To trapunto-stuff the legs and undershell features, sew yarn into the channels formed by the satin-stitching. To do this, thread the blunt tapestry with a double strand of yarn. From the back side, insert the needle into the lining and guide it between the lining and the face fabric. Sew the length of the leg, emerging at the satin stitching. Pull the yarn stuffing into the leg channel, smooth the fabric, and clip off the yarn where it emerged. Continue to stuff in this manner until the legs and markings are fully stuffed and puffy on the face side.

C. Join the TAIL to the UNDERSHELL.

D. Align the FRONT UPPER SHELL pieces at the center seam and stitch.

E. Pin and stitch the FRONT UPPER SHELL to the UPPER SHELL from A to B. Join the TAIL to the UPPER SHELL.

F. Stay-stitch the seam allowance outside the seam line on both shell pieces at the opening to secure the edges from fraying. Match the UPPER SHELL to the UNDERSHELL, and stitch around the perimeter, leaving the opening for turning.

Step 3: Finishing the Shell

A. Push the TAIL into itself with the long narrow turning tool to begin turning. Next turn the body. Complete turning the TAIL pushing it carefully through itself. Lighterweight fabric will turn more easily than the coat lining with furry backing I used. You may need to use a narrower tool such as a knitting needle, but be careful not to poke through the fabric since this will ruin the TAIL. Roll the TAIL between your hands as you work to loosen the lumps.

B. Stuff the ABDOMEN (back) portion of the crab. Machine top-stitch across the BODY at the bottom of the LEGS as marked to divide the shell parts.

C. Stuff the HEAD AND THORAX section fully and hand-sew the opening closed with hidden stitching.

D. To shape the BODY by quilting, thread a sewing needle with matching thread. Sew a hidden knot at the first QUILTING GUIDE MARK near the TAIL on the UNDERSHELL. Stitch through to the UPPERSHELL and pull the needle out. Insert the needle 1/8 inch away and emerge at the second QUILTING GUIDE MARK. Pull the thread to achieve the indented shape you want, and continue in this manner for the entire BODY to sculpture the shape as you sew.

E. Select the areas you plan to embellish with beads. Using the small beading needle and matching thread, sew the beads in lines on the LEGS and TAIL as shown in the photograph.

YAKS live in the high mountains of Southeast Asia. This hardy mountain variety is never seen in zoos since most climates are too warm for it. Wild yaks grow about 6 feet tall, weigh about 1200 pounds, and have brown hair so long it may drag on the ground. Domestic yaks, like the one shown, have shorter, shaggy hair, shorter or no horns, and are smaller than the wild yaks. They are prized by the Himalayan people for their many useful qualities. Yaks can carry 300 pounds of weight, or a saddle and rider up a steep mountain pass. Yaks pull the plows to till the rocky mountain fields. They provide milk, furs, and meat.

The yak, with its massive shoulder hump, horns, cloven hooves, thick fur and low-carried head, looks like its relative the buffalo, and is the largest of all the oxen family. Another close relative is the shaggy musk ox with its large swooping horns and long shaggy coat slung like a blanket over its back.

NOTE: To make this animal, be sure to brush the long fur out of the seams while stitching. For easier sewing increase the size of the yak. The larger yak will probably need dowel stick supports in the legs to carry the added weight.

Materials

BODY, REAR, and UNDERBODY: 10 by 16 inches dark brown or variegated shaggy fur, 1- to 2-inch pile

PATTERN

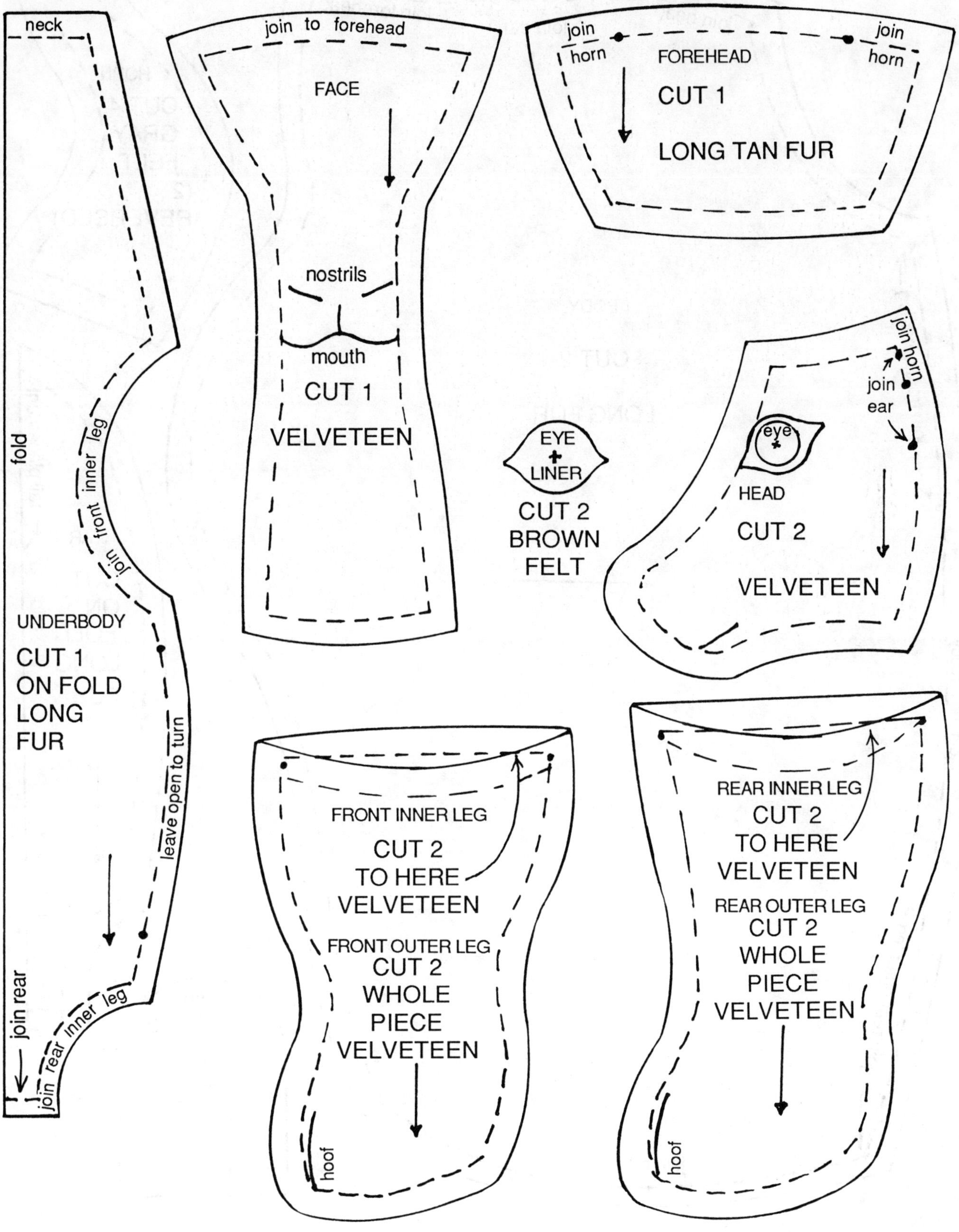

neck
fold
join front inner leg
UNDERBODY
CUT 1
ON FOLD
LONG
FUR
leave open to turn
join rear
join rear inner leg
join to forehead
FACE
nostrils
mouth
CUT 1
VELVETEEN
join
horn
FOREHEAD
join
horn
CUT 1
LONG TAN FUR
EYE
LINER
CUT 2
BROWN
FELT
join horn
join
ear
eye
HEAD
CUT 2
VELVETEEN
FRONT INNER LEG
CUT 2
TO HERE
VELVETEEN
FRONT OUTER LEG
CUT 2
WHOLE
PIECE
VELVETEEN
hoof
REAR INNER LEG
CUT 2
TO HERE
VELVETEEN
REAR OUTER LEG
CUT 2
WHOLE
PIECE
VELVETEEN
hoof

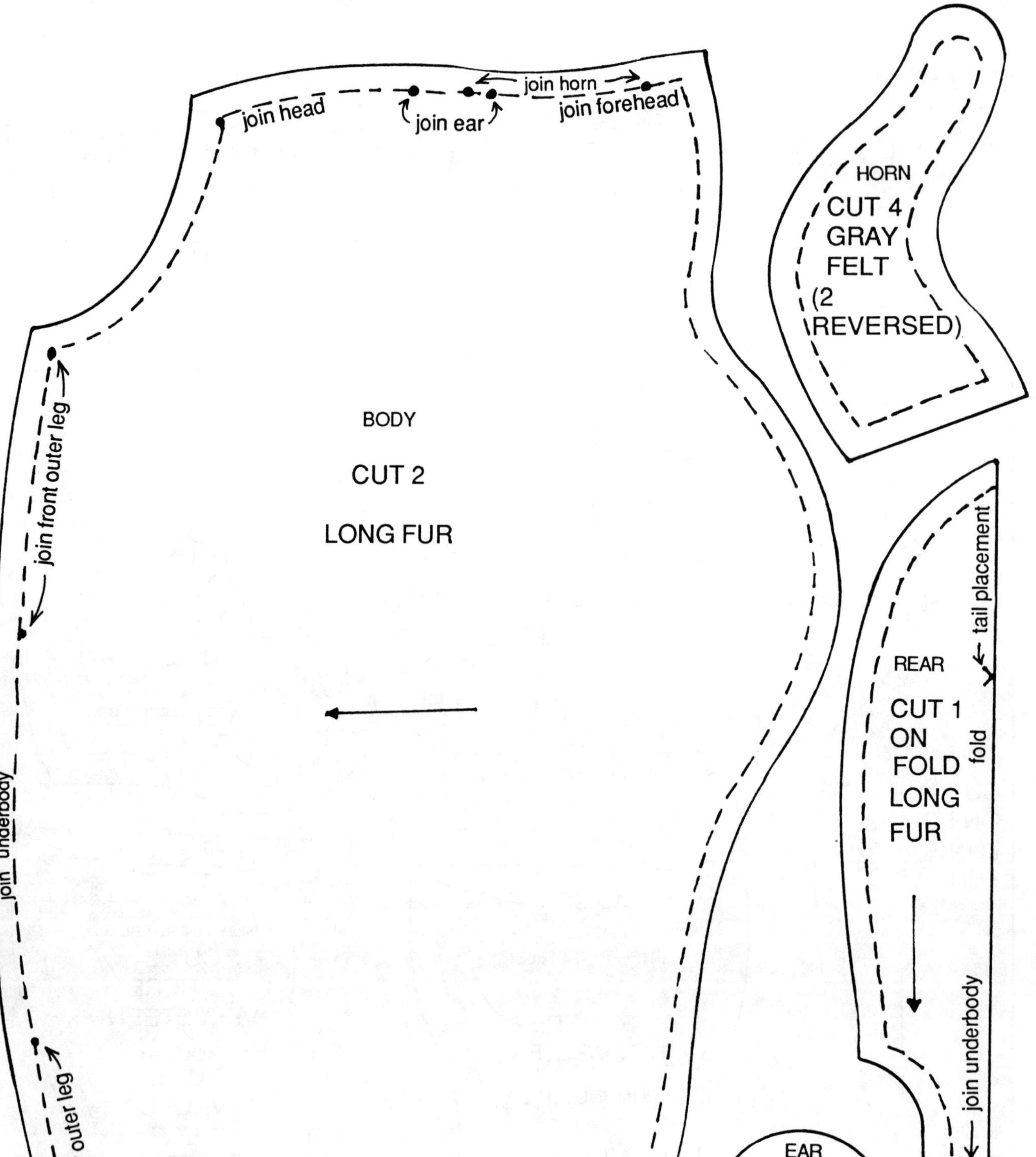
join head
join ear
join horn
join forehead
BODY
CUT 2
LONG FUR
join front outer leg
join underbody
join rear outer leg
join rear
HORN
CUT 4
GRAY
FELT
(2
REVERSED)
tail placement
REAR
CUT 1
ON
FOLD
LONG
FUR
fold
join underbody
EAR
CUT 2
BROWN
FELT
fold

DIRECTIONS

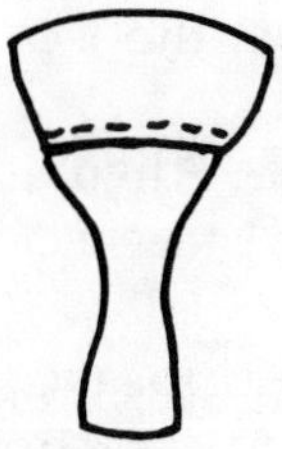

Sew forehead to face.

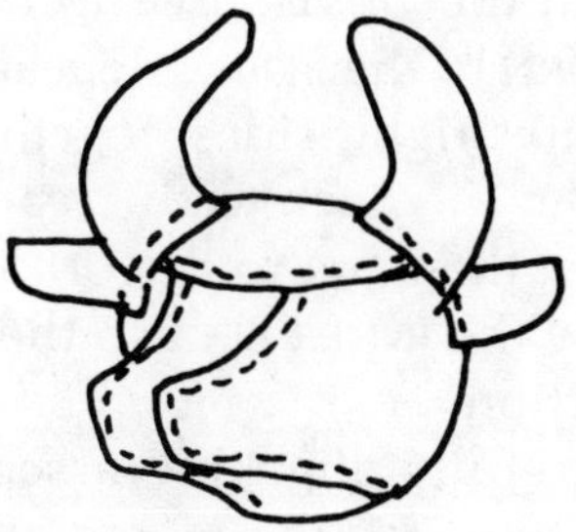

Sew head to forehead/ face; repeat. Insert eyes through eye liner into head. Baste ears to head, then horns. (Back view, horns overlap ears)

Assembled head (right side view): ears go on before horns.

Join outer legs to body. Join bodies at back seam. Sew body from neck to rear.

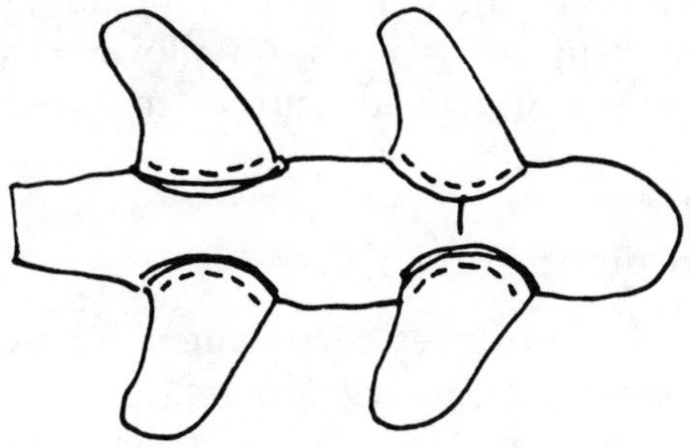

Join rear to underbody, join inner legs.

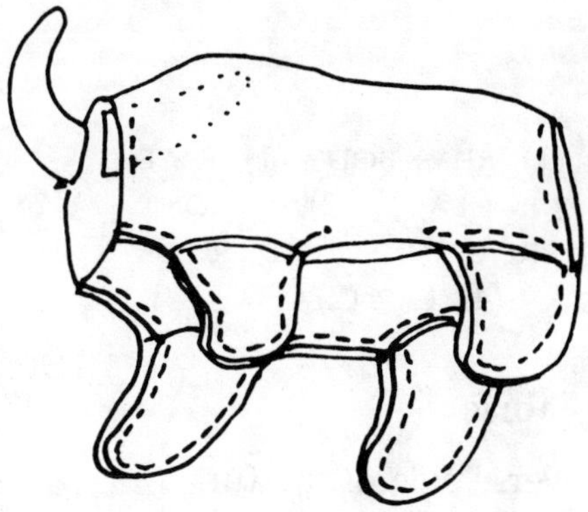

Align underbody/rear/legs to body/legs and stitch. Leave opening to turn. Baste horns to body, aligned with head horns.

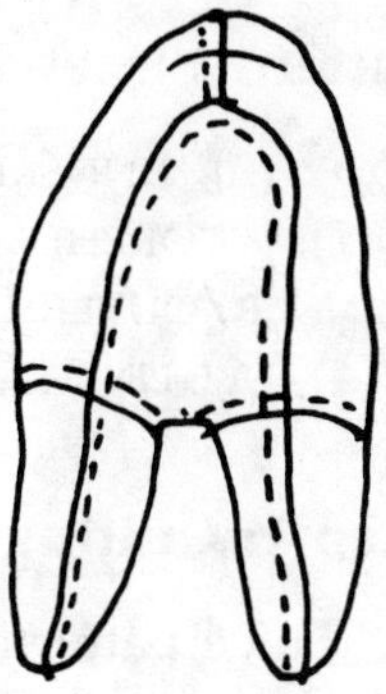

Rear view

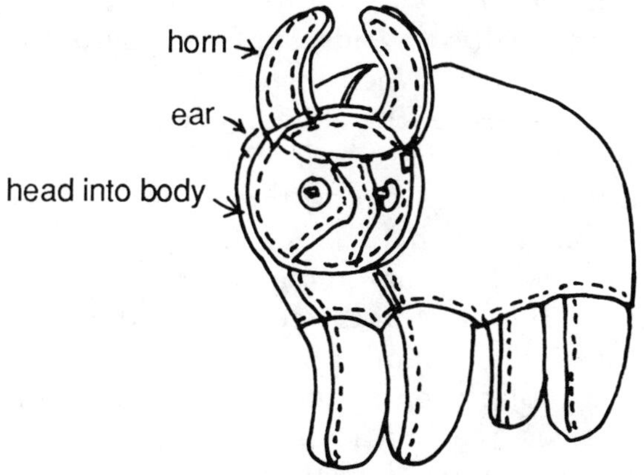

Insert head right side out into body, align horns, and sew. Clip seam allowances.

Turn. Stuff, sew opening closed. Embroider nose, mouth, hooves; sew on yarn tail.

FACE, HEAD, ALL LEGS, 8 by 10 inches brown velveteen

FOREHEAD: 1½ by 3 inches shaggy or curly 1-inch fur fabric, brown or tan

HORNS: 3 by 5 inches gray felt

EARS and EYE LINERS: 2 by 2 inches dark brown felt

TAIL: 64 inches loosely spun dark brown yarn

STUFFING: 4 ounces

EYES: ⅜-inch amber post-and-washer eyes

TRIM: black embroidery floss

Tools

¼-inch dowel or chopstick for turning and stuffing

Pattern Pieces

BODY (2), UNDERBODY (1), REAR BODY (1), FACE (1), FOREHEAD (1), HEAD (2), FRONT INNER/OUTER LEG (4), REAR INNER/OUTER LEG (4), EYE LINER (2), HORN (4), EAR (2)

Step 1: Cutting the Fabric

A. Trace pattern on reverse side of the fur.

B. Cut out all pieces.

C. Mark the EYE placements.

Step 2: Assembling the Yak

A. With right sides together, join FOREHEAD to FACE.

B. With right sides together, join HEAD to the FOREHEAD/FACE piece. Since the curve of the nose is a sharp corner and the pieces are small it's best to sew with the HEAD piece upward for best control, and maintain even seam allowances. Baste first if necessary.

C. Clip a small hole in the HEAD for the EYE. Insert the EYE POST through the EYE LINER, through the HEAD, and into the EYE WASHER. Affix the washer firmly to the back.

D. Fold the top of the EAR forward as marked and baste to the HEAD. Baste the HORNS to the FOREHEAD. The HORN will overlap the EAR slightly on the seam allowance, so be sure to baste the EAR on first.

E. Join the OUTER LEGS to the BODY. Baste the HORN to the BODY. Repeat for the other side.

F. With right sides together sew the BODY from the neck to the rear.

G. Join the REAR to the UNDERBODY. Align and sew the INNER LEGS to the REAR/UNDERBODY section.

H. Carefully align the assembled UNDERBODY section to the assembled BODY section, matching all the legs. Sew all around from the neck to the back seam, leaving a 3-inch opening for turning on the belly. Pivot the fabric on the needle to turn corners for the legs.

I. Turn the HEAD right side out and insert into the BODY. The EARS are tucked inward with only the ends sewn into the seam. Align the HORNS pointing upward and pin. Align the neck seams, and stitch all around including the HORNS. Clip the HORN seam allowances at the corners and inside curves to avoid pulls.

Step 3: Completing the Yak

A. Clip seam allowances that might cause pulls, especially at the leg corners.

B. Begin to turn at the HORNS. Insert the dowel, sharpened but blunted, into the HORN and carefully push it right side out. This may be quite difficult, but persist. Stuff the tips of the HORNS. Next turn the LEGS in the same manner. Finally turn the entire BODY.

C. Using small soft wads, stuff the HORNS and the LEGS first. When they are firmly filled, stuff the rest of the animal, making sure to fill the top of the LEGS firmly. Sew the BODY closed, using a strong thread and hidden stitching. Brush the long hair out of the seams with a dog-grooming brush, or rub across the hairs in the seam with the point of a needle to remove them.

D. Using black embroidery floss, sew the NOSE, MOUTH and HOOF cleft lines.

E. Double the yarn four times to make sixteen 4-inch strands. Tie thread around one end and sew the TAIL firmly to the REAR. Clip the loops at the lower end of the TAIL.

ZEBRAS belong to the horse family, but they are much harder to train since they are extremely wild and savage fighters and very stubborn. Their dramatic, wide black-and-white stripes dazzle in the full sunlight of the African plains, making them highly visible to predators, so they are far more nervous and active than, for example, dun-colored wildebeests. But at dusk when the lions hunt, zebras' stripes make them almost invisible against the tall grass and shadows, a good camouflage. By contrast to the wide-striped common plains zebra, the northern bush zebra has finer stripes and appears gray from a distance.

Zebras spend their day grazing, and travel continuously in small bands to find grass. Until

PATTERN

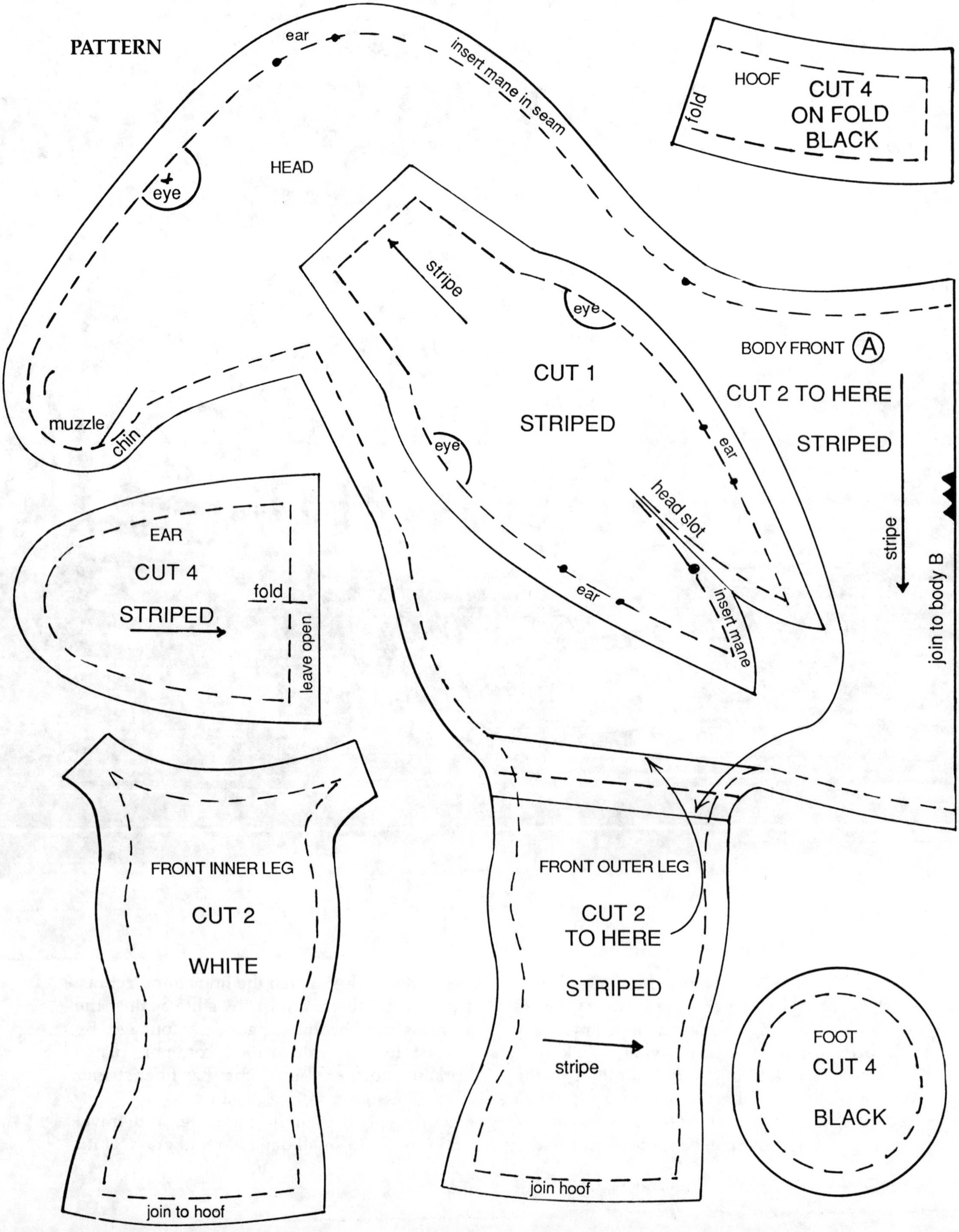
ear
insert mane in seam
HEAD
eye
muzzle
chin
HOOF
CUT 4
ON FOLD
BLACK
fold
stripe
eye
CUT 1
STRIPED
eye
ear
head slot
ear
insert mane
BODY FRONT A
CUT 2 TO HERE
STRIPED
stripe
join to body B
EAR
CUT 4
STRIPED
fold
leave open
FRONT INNER LEG
CUT 2
WHITE
join to hoof
FRONT OUTER LEG
CUT 2
TO HERE
STRIPED
stripe
join hoof
FOOT
CUT 4
BLACK

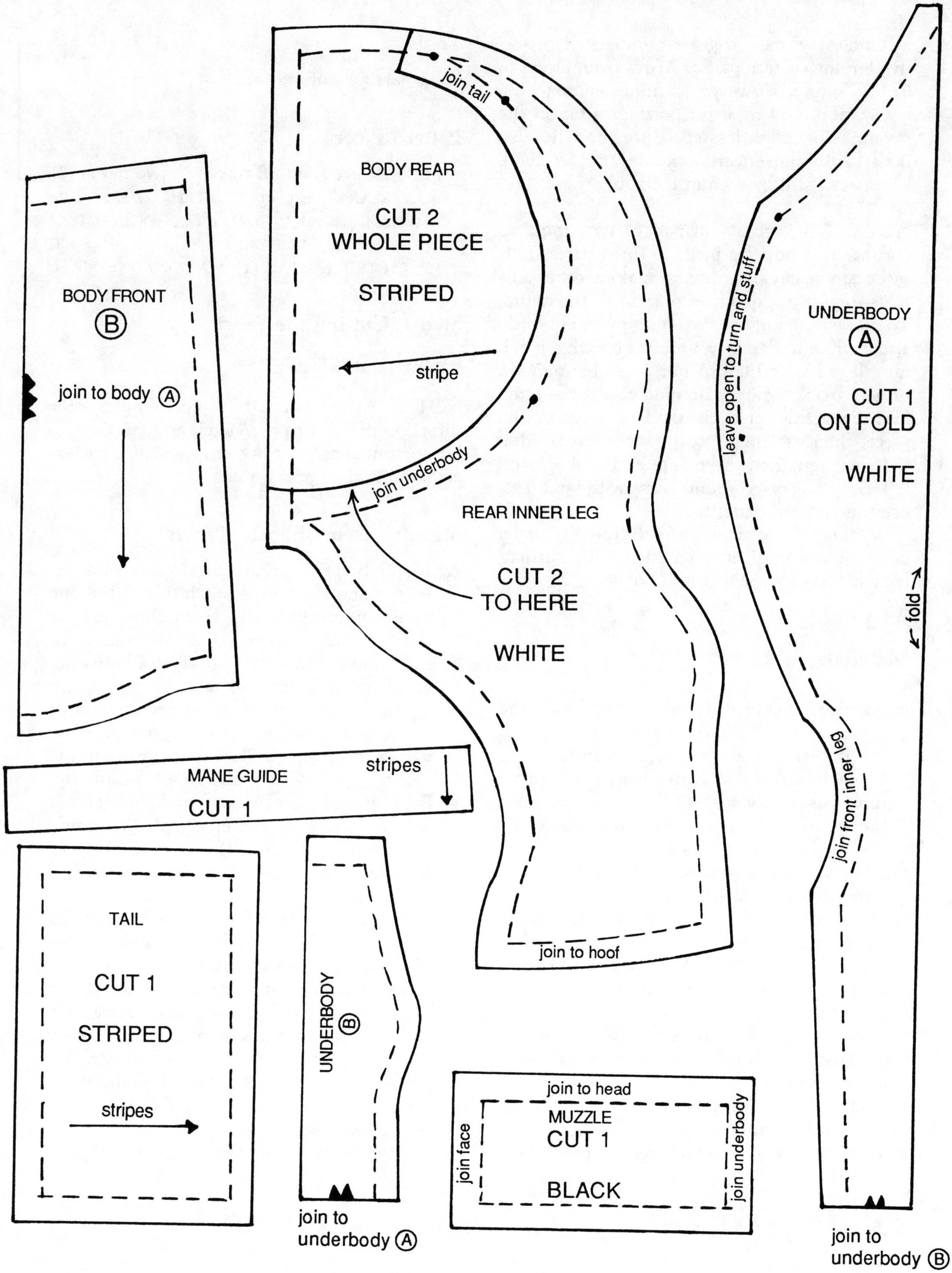
BODY REAR
CUT 2
WHOLE PIECE
STRIPED
stripe
join tail
join underbody
REAR INNER LEG
CUT 2
TO HERE
WHITE
join to hoof
BODY FRONT
B
join to body A
UNDERBODY
A
CUT 1
ON FOLD
WHITE
leave open to turn and stuff
fold
join front inner leg
join to underbody B
MANE GUIDE
CUT 1
stripes
TAIL
CUT 1
STRIPED
stripes
UNDERBODY
B
join to underbody A
join to head
MUZZLE
CUT 1
BLACK
join face
join underbody

a hundred years ago great numbers of zebras lived in the eastern part of Africa from Egypt to Cape Colony. However, hunting, encroaching civilization, and tribes of grazing cattle on the savannas have left less space for the wild animals. Although nearly extinct in the wild, zebras can still be seen in the zoo.

NOTE: The zebra's striped pattern requires cutting the body/leg piece in three parts. This piece can be cut all in one for making other animals, or for applying decoration to the zebra. To make a donkey, make a one-piece tan body and a white underbody, and finish with a black muzzle, ears, and tail. A horse can be made in brown, black, white, palomino gold, or spotted fabric. For the horse, cut the body/legs in one piece, then use the unicorn pattern to shorten the ears, lengthen the mane, and make a full tail. For a merry-go-round horse with bent legs, use the unicorn pattern.

Because of the small parts, follow the order of construction given for best results, particularly in making the legs and hooves.

Materials

BODY FRONT, BODY REAR, OUTER LEGS, FACE, and EARS: 10 by 24 inches of firmly woven cotton/polyester black and white striped fabric (3/16-inch stripes shown). For a scaled-up zebra use a wider stripe. Other possible choices are polyester, velveteen, suede cloth, felt, or decorative fabrics

UNDERBODY and INNER LEGS: 10 by 15 inches firmly woven white fabric

MUZZLE, HOOVES, and FEET: 4 by 8 inches firmly woven black fabric

MANE and TAIL: 10 feet of black and 10 feet of white 4-ply yarn, double the amount for 2-ply yarn

EYE DISKS: 1½ by 3 inches white felt

EYES: Two ½-inch (12.5 mm) post-and-washer brown eyes

THREAD: White sewing thread

STUFFING: ½ pound fiberfill

ARMATURES: Two 3/8-inch dowels, 6 inches long

Tools

Long narrow stuffing tool

Pattern Pieces

BODY FRONT A and B (given in two parts) (2), BODY REAR (2), FRONT OUTER LEG (2), FRONT INNER LEG (2), BACK INNER LEG (2), HOOF (4), FACE (1) MUZZLE (1), UNDERBODY (1), EAR (4), FOOT (4), EYE DISK (2), TAIL (1), MANE GUIDE STRIP (1)

Step 1: Cutting the Fabric

Cut out all pattern pieces.

NOTE: Arrows on pattern pieces indicate the direction of the stripes. Match and cut the two body front pieces so the stripes will meet exactly along the back seam.

Step 2: Assembling the Pieces

A. Match two EARS, right sides facing, and sew with a short machine stitch. Leave the end open for turning. Clip seam allowances at the tip, and press flat. Fold the EAR vertically, pin to the HEAD with the fold forward, and baste in place. Repeat.

B. To make the TAIL, measure ten strands of black yarn 7 inches long and ten of white yarn 7 inches long. Place the strands on the TAIL with 3 inches protruding from the tip. Fold the TAIL over the yarn and stitch across the TAIL TIP. Tuck the enclosed yarn inside the seam, and stitch the TAIL lengthwise, leaving the top open. Pull the short end of yarn to turn and stuff the TAIL.

C. To make the MANE, cut twenty-four (as needed) 3-inch pieces of white and twenty-four 3-inch pieces of black yarn. Loop each piece of yarn. Match the yarn color to the MANE GUIDE STRIP colors, alternating two white with two black yarn loops, and sew the yarn tips to the MANE STRIP for the entire length. Press the GUIDE STRIP folded toward the base of the MANE (to keep the strip out of the final seam.

D. Pin the BODY FRONT to the BODY REAR and

DIRECTIONS

Sew ears, turn,
fold, baste to head.

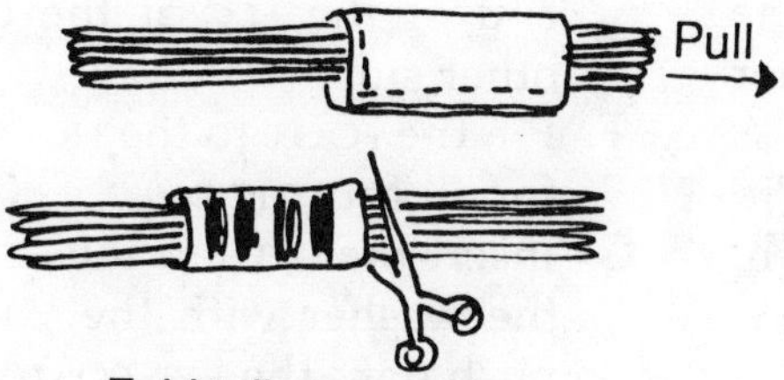

Fold tail over yarns,
sew tail across yarn,
pivot and sew length.
Pull yarn to turn and stuff.
Trim off extra yarn.

Sew yarn
to mane
strip.

Assemble body pieces:
front, leg, rear; repeat.

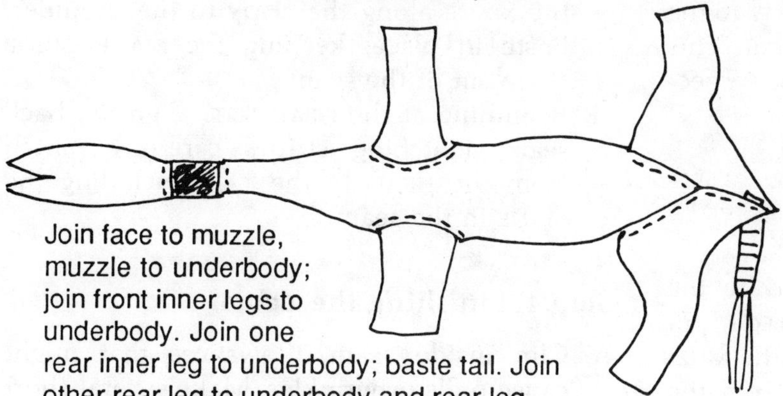

Join face to muzzle,
muzzle to underbody;
join front inner legs to
underbody. Join one
rear inner leg to underbody; baste tail. Join
other rear leg to underbody and rear leg.

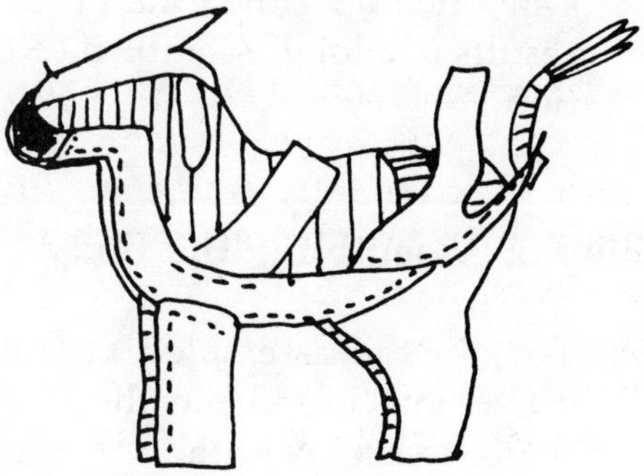

Join body to underbody from face
to front leg base; repeat.

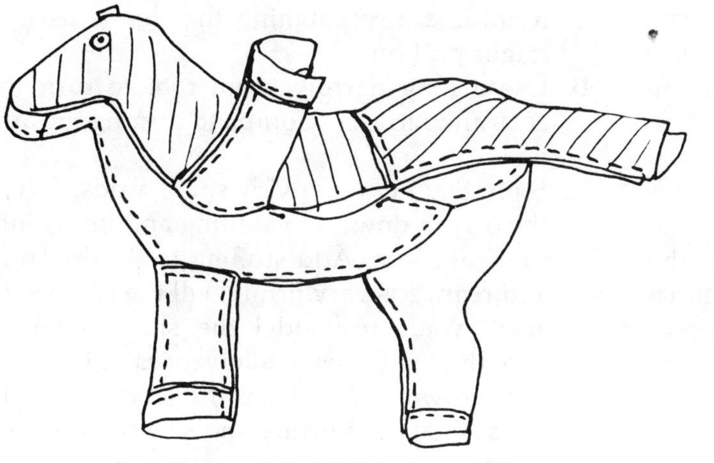

Insert eyes, join hoof to leg,
sew from hoof to base of
rear leg, join foot; repeat.

Baste mane to neck/face, sew back
seam of rear leg to tail, repeat. Sew
back seam from head to tail.

Detail:
join foot to hoof
on all 4 legs.

Turn, stuff.

For horse make longer mane and
tail, and shorter ears. Cut body in
one piece.

stitch. Align the FRONT OUTER LEG with the BODY FRONT and stitch. Repeat for the other side.

E. Pin the FACE to the MUZZLE and stitch. Pin the MUZZLE to the UNDERBODY and stitch.

F. Join the FRONT INNER LEG to the UNDERBODY. Repeat for the other FRONT INNER LEG.

G. Pin the REAR INNER LEG to the UNDERBODY. Baste the TAIL to the REAR INNER LEG. Align the other REAR INNER LEG with the joined REAR INNER LEG and the UNDERBODY, and stitch the crotch from the UNDERBODY to the TAIL, including the TAIL in this seam. This results in a long assembled UNDERBODY section.

Step 3: Assembling the Body

A. To join the assembled UNDERBODY to the BODY, match and pin the FRONT LEGS, pin the UNDERBODY to the NECK, align the MUZZLE to the nose on the HEAD, and pin the FACE to the HEAD, including the basted EARS in this seam. Stitch from the front of the LEG to the end of the FACE. Repeat for the other side, being careful to align one side with the other especially at the MUZZLE.

B. Open the FRONT LEG flat, and join the HOOF right sides facing. Repeat for the other FRONT LEG and HOOF.

C. Fold the FRONT LEG AND HOOF to align the matching back edges of the LEG, and stitch from the HOOF to the REAR LEG HOOF. Repeat for the other side, but leave an opening on the BODY for turning and stuffing.

D. Join the HOOF to the REAR LEG. Repeat for the other REAR LEG.

E. Fold the REAR LEG AND HOOF to match the back seams, and stitch from the HOOF to the end of the LEG at the tail. Repeat for the other side.

F. Pin the FOOT to the HOOF and stitch. Repeat for all four HOOVES.

G. Insert the EYES in the HEAD as marked. Pad the washer with the WHITE FELT DISK, and push onto the EYE POST. (The slightly larger EYE WASHER creates the bony eye socket ridge).

H. Pin the MANE GUIDE STRIP to the FACE, ½ inch above the EAR, and continue pinning the MANE along the BODY to the shoulder. Baste in place, keeping the MANE GUIDE STRIP out of the seam.

I. Beginning at the HEAD SLIT, align the back seam, matching stripes carefully. Stitch from the HEAD to the TAIL, including the MANE in the seam.

Step 4: Finishing the Zebra

A. Clip inside seam allowances that might cause pulls or wrinkles. Make several short clips to the seam line on inside corners. Reinforce any stitching that looks as if it might pull out.

B. Use a long narrow blunt tool to turn the LEGS and MUZZLE. Complete turning the animal.

C. Stuff the HOOVES with small wads. Wrap the 6-inch dowels in stuffing and insert into the front legs. Add stuffing to fill the front and rear LEGS very firmly. Fill the HEAD with small wads to model the shape, making sure the inside seam allowances of the EARS face downward to keep the EARS erect. Fill the animal very firmly and sew the opening closed.

D. To finish, trim the MANE evenly to about ¾ inches long, and trim the TAIL evenly.

Index